Wellington

Portrait of Wellington by Goya,
reproduced by courtesy of the Mansell Collection

Wellington

STUDIES IN THE MILITARY
AND POLITICAL CAREER OF
THE FIRST DUKE OF WELLINGTON

edited by
Norman Gash

MANCHESTER UNIVERSITY PRESS
in association with the University of Southampton

Manchester and New York
Distributed exclusively in the USA and Canada by St. Martin's Press

Copyright © Manchester University Press 1990

Published by Manchester University Press
Oxford Road, Manchester M13 9PL, UK
and Room 400, 175 Fifth Avenue,
New York, NY 10010, USA

Distributed exclusively in the USA and Canada
by St. Martin's Press, Inc.,
175 Fifth Avenue, New York, NY 10010, USA

British Library cataloguing in publication data
Wellington: studies in the military and political
  career of the first duke of Wellington.
  1. Great Britain. Wellington, Arthur Wellesley, Duke
  of
  I. Gash, Norman   II. University of Southampton
  941.07′092′4

Library of Congress cataloging in publication data
Wellington : studies in the military and political career of the first
  duke of Wellington / edited by Norman Gash.
    p.   cm.
  ISBN 0–7190–2974–0
  1. Wellington, Arthur Wellesley, Duke of, 1769–1852. 2. Generals—
Great Britain—Biography. 3. Great Britain. Army—Biography.
4. Statesmen—Great Britain—Biography. 5. Great Britain—History,
Military—1789–1820. 6. Great Britain—Politics and
government—1800–1837. I. Gash, Norman.
DA68.12.W4W55   1990
941.07′092—dc20
  [R]

ISBN 0 7190 2974 0 *hardback*

Phototypeset in Linotron Sabon
by Northern Phototypesetting Company, Bolton.

Printed in Great Britain
by Biddles Ltd, Guildford and King's Lynn.

Contents

Abbreviations

The following standard abbreviations have been used in the bibliographical references.

WD   *Despatches of the Duke of Wellington, 1799–1818*, (compiled by Lt Col. Gurwood) 13 vols, London, 1834–9.

WMSS.   Wellington Papers (uncatalogued) held at Apsley House up to 1983.

WND   *Despatches, Correspondence and Memoranda of the Duke of Wellington, 1818–1832*, (ed. by his son), 8 vols, London, 1867–80.

WP   Wellington Papers, Southampton University Library.

WPC   Wellington, *Political Correspondence*, vol. 1, 1833–1834; vol. II, 1834–1835, *Prime Ministers Papers Series* (Historical Manuscripts Commission), London HMSO, 1975, 1986.

WSD   *Supplementary Despatches, Correspondence and Memoranda of the Duke of Wellington* (ed. by his son), 14 vols, London, 1858–1872.

The place of publication of printed sources is London unless otherwise stated.

Preface

The purpose of these essays is, firstly, to pay a collective tribute to one of the best-known figures in modern British history; and, secondly, to commemorate the transfer of his papers to the custody of Southampton University.

The Wellington Papers, an archive of some 100,000 pieces of correspondence comprising the official, military, and diplomatic papers of Arthur Wellesley, first duke of Wellington, were accepted for the nation in lieu of duty on the estate of the seventh duke of Wellington in 1978. In 1983 the Secretary of State for Education and Science allocated the collection under the national heritage legislation to the University of Southampton and the collection was transferred to special accommodation in the University's library. There have always been close links between the University and the dukes of Wellington. The fourth duke was prominent in the campaign for a university for Wessex and became in 1902 President of the new University College of Southampton. In 1952 the seventh duke, who from 1949 had been President of the University College, became the first Chancellor of the new University of Southampton. At Southampton the manuscripts rejoined extensive printed collections belonging to the first duke, his parliamentary papers and a large pamphlet collection.

The archives arrived at Southampton uncatalogued. The library has produced a summary list to make the papers accessible for research but a collection of this size and importance, covering such a wide range of subject-material, needed detailed cataloguing. To make such a project practicable, the library developed a computerised cataloguing system. Automatic indexing of catalogue descriptions allows searching on any topic or date-range and it is the intention to make the catalogue database available as widely as possible. At present it is mounted on one of the University's mainframe computers, accessible by way of the Joint Academic Network and the public switched-telephone system and it is hoped to publish it in a portable electronic form. The detailed catalogue covers the papers for 1819–32 and work is in progress on the Peninsular War material. Other parts of the collection, to which there are some indexes, will be fully catalogued subsequently. The library has also been active in conserving the archive. As early as 1814 part of the collection was damaged during a shipwreck in the Tagus. In addition some 10 per cent of the papers, including important sequences for 1811, 1822, 1829 and 1832, have suffered badly from water and mould damage. While the whole collection is receiving routine conservation treatment to ensure its long-term preservation, considerable progress has also been made with work on the more fragmentary material, notably that for 1829.

Even before the arrival of the papers at Southampton an advisory committee, including several outside independent members, was established at the University under the chairmanship of the Vice-Chancellor to supervise the management of the collection and deal with matters of general policy. To mark the start of what was clearly going to be a new era in the history of Wellington studies the committee later came to two decisions. The first was to hold an international conference on the life and times of the first duke. Under the title of the 'Wellington Congress' and organised by Professor Donald Horward of Florida State University and Dr Charles Esdaile, the first Wellington Research Fellow at Southampton University, this was held at Southampton in July 1987, when over forty papers were discussed by some hundred and forty delegates from eight different countries. The second decision was to provide a more permanent literary memorial by commissioning a special volume of Wellington essays. Though planned separately the two projects were naturally linked. Many of the essays here are extended versions of, or incorporate material from, Congress papers; the three shorter essays are substantially the same as papers read on that occasion.

The actual choice of topics and authors has, however, been governed by the particular design of the book. A collection of pieces by different authors cannot pretend to be a substitute for a biography. Yet, by exploring aspects of the duke's career that previous biographers had not the time, inclination or facilities to examine in detail, these essays may serve to enlarge our knowledge and understanding of that remarkable man. Though not a biography, they have a biographical purpose. For this reason topics have been selected to illustrate the whole range of Wellington's long and varied career and they have been placed in chronological order rather than on a subject basis. The significant period of his military life lasted about twenty-five years. When his active soldiering came to an end in 1818, there were another thirty-four years in which he remained one of the great public figures of his day. That circumstance, together with the greater concentration of previous historians on his purely military career, will explain the balance of the present essays. Their more specialised nature, and the larger number of authors involved, also differentiate this collection of essays from the brief but elegant *Wellington Studies* written thirty years ago to celebrate the centenary of Wellington College under the editorship of Sir Michael Howard, later a distinguished foundation member of the Southampton University Wellington Committee. It is a mark of the wide appeal of Wellington studies in the English-speaking world that nearly half the present contributions have come from the other side of the Atlantic – two from Canada and three from the United States. Of the British authors four are from Southampton University itself, and include two young research graduates who were among the first to work on the Wellington archives in their new home.

I take this opportunity of expressing my thanks, first to two successive Vice-Chancellors of Southampton University, Dr J. M. Roberts and Dr G. R. Higginson, together with the other members of the Wellington Committee who honoured me with the invitation to become editor; then, to my editorial committee colleagues, Professor Paul Smith, Emeritus Professor F. C. Mather, Dr Esdaile, and Dr C. M. Woolgar, the university archivist, who contributed the second and third paragraphs of this preface.

Langport, Somerset   Norman Gash
March 1989.

Neville Thompson

1

The uses of adversity

The duke of Wellington, although never one of those calling for reform on all subjects in season and out of season, was always ready with practical advice for the improvement of the world. In this helpful spirit he pronounced that the duty of the historian was:

> to seek with diligence for the most authentic details of the subject on which he writes, to peruse with care and attention all that has been published; to prefer that which has been officially recorded and published by public responsible authorities; next, to attend to that which proceeds from Official Authority, although not contemporaneously published, and to pay least attention to the statements of Private Individuals, whether communicating in writing or verbally; particularly the latter, if at a period distant from the date of the operation itself; and, above all, such statements as relate to the conduct of the Individual himself communicating or making the statement.[1]

It is true that the duke was addressing the tendency to speculation among military historians, particularly historians of Waterloo, but he intended his observation to be of general application. Adhering strictly to this standard of evidence would have prevented any writing about his early life while he was alive and made it almost impossible thereafter, which would certainly not have displeased him. He did his best to draw a veil over his first quarter-century and would not have been amused by the attempt to fit the bits and pieces of evidence that can be recovered into a pattern related to the mature hero. He never considered writing an autobiography or authorising a biography; and the military despatches he allowed Colonel John Gurwood to publish rigorously excluded all personal material. He did not have any friends from his youth with whom he talked over his early days. And when he was questioned by those who were secretly violating his obsession with privacy by keeping journals of his conversations, his memory, otherwise so remarkable to the end of his days, would fail him and he would have to confess that he could not remember. This was perhaps no more than the truth, for he had no desire to remember and every reason to suppress the recollection; though even he could not prevent it from rising to haunt him when he thought he saw in his two sons what he had been but without his motive and strength of purpose to change.

For a military genius in an age of war the duke made a very late and uncertain start. Until his mid-twenties, when his exact contemporary Napoleon Bonaparte, having dispersed the opponents of the Directory with a whiff of grapeshot, was proceeding to the conquest of Italy, no one, not even Wellington himself, could have said that he would take the army seriously as a profession. Even then he was forty before it was clear, following the battle of Talavera, that he was an outstanding general and forty-four before the battle of Vitoria made him a national hero. In the next two years this reputation was swiftly consolidated and extended and by the morrow of Waterloo he was one of the greatest figures of his age and of all time.

One at least of Wellington's early biographers did not consider that there was anything which called for explanation in this start to his brilliant career. In envious tones he pointed out that the duke began life 'under circumstances of peculiar advantage'. 'Nobly born, carefully educated, and connected with people enjoying political influence, he was subjected to no early wrestling with fate. He was launched upon the stream of life under the most favourable auspices, tasting neither the bitterness of poverty nor the humiliation of obscurity.'[2] So it must afterwards have seemed to many people, and Wellington certainly did nothing to disabuse them of the idea. But apart from the practically necessary advantage of being born into the aristocracy, he had to overcome enormous personal, social and political obstacles in order to become a great soldier and a great man. Although he did not talk about them, it was these struggles which defined the character and even the achievements of the duke of Wellington. If there is not much material on his youth, because unlike his eldest brother, Lord Wellesley, no one considered him very remarkable, what there is falls into a pattern that Leon Edel calls 'the figure under the carpet, the evidence in the reverse of the tapestry, the life myth of a given mask'.[3]

He was born into the closely-knit, defensive Anglo-Irish aristocracy on or about 1 May 1769 and grew up with an instinctive conviction of the inferior capacities and motives of ordinary people which later events did nothing to shake. On his sixty-second birthday, at the time of the parliamentary reform bill, he reminded his confidante Mrs Arbuthnot that he had told her years ago that:

> the people are rotten to the Core. . . . They are not bloodthirsty, but they are desirous of Plunder. They will plunder, destroy and annihilate all Property in the Country. The majority of them will then starve; and we shall witness scenes such as have never yet occurred in any part of the World.[4]

A year before his death he was convinced that the Crystal Palace Exhibition would provide the signal for a general insurrection. The precariousness of the Ascendency's position in the late eighteenth century as Catholic and Presbyterian resentment of its monopoly of power, privilege and place became more strident and even revolutionary also imbued him with a strong, even exaggerated respect for established institutions as bastions of aristocracy, monarchy and civil peace. Although he was often persuaded to act otherwise, beginning in 1793 when as a member of the Irish House of Commons he voted for giving the franchise to Catholics in that country, he believed to the end of his life that a united defence of all privileged institutions was the best guarantee of the social order. Like other members of the Irish aristocracy, perhaps more than most, Wellington and his family had to beg for favours from the Lord Lieutenant and the British government on which they were dependent. But his sensitive nature revolted against this demeaning necessity and he developed a higher sense of aristocracy than the practice he saw in Ireland, or in England for that matter. Once he had succeeded in the world he was stung by any imputation that he was seeking special advantage and was contemptuous of aristocratic concern with honours, places, pensions and ease over the proper performance of exemplary duty in society, parliament, local government and the army. The duke never expressed any nostalgia for Ireland after he was securely established in England. He never went back after 1809. And in his will of 1807 he particularly desired that his children 'may not be allowed to live in Ireland or even to go there or to have any connection with that country'.[5] But much as he might struggle to free himself from it, Ireland had set his feet on the path to becoming the most aristocratic of the aristocrats, the example and reproach to the rest of his order.

In old age Lord Wellesley recalled their parents as 'alas! frivolous and careless personages like most of the Irish nobility at the time'.[6] The father, Lord Mornington, was a notable composer and professor of music (his settings were used for two of the psalms at the duke's funeral) but he neglected his estates and political opportunities. When he died in 1781 at the age of forty-five in London, to which he had moved his family some years before, he left large debts and six children (two had died in infancy) ranging in age from twenty to eight. His widow, who was thirty-eight, had devoted her life to child-bearing and fashionable society since her marriage at sixteen, and although she was a woman of strong views, the task of ensuring the family's survival, much less prosperity, was too much for her.

Most of the burden fell on her eldest son, the new Lord Mornington, who was able, ambitious and resentful of this doubly encumbered inheritance. Abandoning his studies at Christ Church, Oxford, where he had made a name for himself as a brilliant classical scholar and where by good fortune one of his closest friends was William Wyndham Grenville, whose cousin William Pitt soon became prime minister, he threw himself into advancing his own and his family's fortunes as a member of the Irish House of Lords and the British House of Commons. Fortunately his sister and all the brothers but one showed evidence of useful talent. Anne with proper tutoring made two good marriages. The second brother, William, was well provided for later in the year of their father's death when he inherited the estates of a relative; he changed his name to Wellesley-Pole and embarked on a career first in Irish and then in British politics, becoming Lord Maryborough in 1821. The two youngest brothers, although only eleven and eight, seemed responsive to the encouragement of their brother and mother. Gerald duly became a clergyman; Henry a diplomat and in 1827 Lord Cowley.

The problem lay with the fourth child and third son, Arthur, who was twelve at his father's death. Apparently listless, dull and idle, but sufficiently musical to alarm his father's impoverished heir and widow, it is more likely that he was shy, introspective, thoughtful, even intellectual in his own way, and sensitive to the low regard in which he was held by his family. But he was certainly no classical scholar and in 1784 he was removed from Eton after three years to concentrate the straitened resources more effectively on Gerald and

Henry. He spent some time with a tutor in Brighton and then, to economise, joined his mother for a year in Brussels where she was living. This did nothing to raise him in her estimation or cement their mutual affection. The dowager Lady Mornington survived her husband by half a century, living to glory in the success of all her children; but she was despised and neglected by them all, and by none more than the duke whose avoidance of her was a matter of considerable comment. When his mother went back to London he was sent for a year to the Royal Academy of Equitation at Angers, an aristocratic finishing school, which in addition to riding taught fencing, 'dancing' (a stylised form of exercise), as well as some mathematics and literature. But apart from perfecting his courtly French he seems to have learned little at Angers. His English governor, who accompanied him, later recalled that he had been sickly and spent most of his time on a sofa playing with a white terrier.[7]

The sojourn at Angers pointed to the conventional refuge of younger sons, a place in the army, but when he returned to England at the end of 1786 he was totally dependent for this or anything else on his eldest brother. Lord Mornington, now a junior Lord of the Treasury, reminded the Lord Lieutenant of Ireland that he had promised to consider his brother for a commission. 'He is here at the moment,' Mornington added, 'and perfectly idle. It is a matter of indifference to me what commission he gets, provided he gets it soon.'[8] By March 1787 his brother had purchased Wellington his first commission in the 73rd Highland Regiment, then stationed in Ireland, and later in the same year he was appointed aide-de-camp to the Viceroy. He spent the better part of the next decade in Dublin, doing a little regimental duty; keeping an eye on the diminishing family estates; attending the Lord Lieutenant; voting at the government's call as MP for the family seat of Trim when Wellesley-Pole transferred to the British House of Commons; reading, playing his violin, gambling and running up considerable debts. His brother continued to raise money for his successive promotions in the army and other uses through loans and mortgages; and by 1797 the amount owing was about £3,300.

In the midst of this fashionable and undemanding round the event occurred which totally transformed Wellington's life. He fell in love and in 1792 proposed marriage to Catherine Pakenham. The attraction was undoubtedly sincere on both sides. Kitty, as she was generally called, was pretty and intellectual and as the second daughter of Lord Longford no great prospect for a fortune hunter. But she was far too good for the penniless, idle and seemingly unambitious younger son of a declining family. Lord Longford rejected the proposal and sharpened his refusal with a lecture on how the suitor might correct his many faults and apply himself to a useful career in order to rise in the world.[9] The final rejection came two years later from Kitty's brother, who became the head of the family later in 1792 at the age of eighteen, and who felt at least as strongly as his late father about the kind of husband who would be appropriate for his sister. The only consolation was a vague understanding that he might reapply if his prospects happened to improve before Kitty had a better offer.

The first refusal was a terrible and humiliating blow. But it galvanised the sensitive and proud young man into a level of activity and concentration that he sustained to his death almost sixty years later. He began to speak up in the Irish House of Commons. With his brother's indispensable help he purchased his way from captain to lieutenant-colonel by the end of 1793. In the summer, autumn and winter of 1794–5 he went on his first military campaign and acquitted himself well as an infantry commander in the ill-starred expedition to the Netherlands. But by June 1795 he was determined to sell his army commission if he could secure a good civil appointment and begged the Lord Lieutenant for the next vacancy at the Revenue or Treasury Board: 'I hope I shall not be supposed to place myself too high in desiring to be taken into consideration upon the first vacancy at either of them' he diffidently wrote. 'You will perhaps be surprized at my desiring a civil instead of a military Office: It certainly is a departure from the line which I prefer; but I see the manner in which the military Offices are filled, & don't wish to ask you for that which I know you can't give me.'[10] A snug berth in the Revenue or the Treasury might have been sufficient to claim Kitty Pakenham but in the struggle for place it was beyond his or his brother's claims on the Viceroy. Lacking the influence for a better military posting, he sailed for India with a heavy heart in June 1796 without even an Irish sinecure which would have helped with his debts.[11]

It was in India during the next eight years that Wellington really learned his military trade by unrelenting application. He gave up his violin, his health became robust and, like Winston Churchill a century later, he educated himself from the library he brought from England. It was to India too, by a crucial turn of events, that Lord Mornington came in glory as Governor-General in 1798. Here the marquess Wellesley (as Mornington became in 1799) could give free rein to his naturally autocratic and imperial temperament. But for the first time in their lives the soldier was now as important to the administrator as the ruler to the field commander. Wellesley was Wellington's father figure, his patron and protector and his model of a great man. In many ways Wellesley was a great man; certainly, like Lord Curzon a century later, he always looked, acted and sounded like a very great man. But in India Wellington saw the emotionalism, unreliability, deviousness, idleness and raffishness that were the dark side of his brother's undoubted abilities and began shaping himself more in reaction than in imitation. Wellesley's continued patronising, now so much less necessary and justifiable, became a great source of irritation. When Wellington tried to escape from his brother's shadow and assert his independence by repaying his debts, Wellesley loftily waved him away: 'I am in no want of money, and probably never shall be; when I am it will be time enough to call upon you.'[12] By the time the profligate Wellesley did need money, after Waterloo, Wellington was the dominant brother and, apart from buying Apsley House at a generous price, refused to help unless Wellesley submitted to humiliating conditions to reform his ways.

When the two returned to England in 1805 Wellington was a major-general, a Knight of the Bath (a notable honour when the order was limited to twenty-four) and had a considerable fortune in prize money. His military engagements in India may not have been fully understood or appreciated at home but his reputation was sufficient for him to be accepted into the high political circle in which his brother had moved before leaving. As the best way of advancing his career he entered the House of Commons, in the first place to defend Wellesley against charges of corruption and misusing the East India Company funds in conquests, and then stayed to become, appropriately it seemed, Chief Secretary for Ireland in the Duke of Portland's ministry from 1807 to 1809. It was this political position and the still undiscredited reputation of Lord Wellesley, whom the government was hoping to attract into some position below that of prime minister, that secured Wellington a place in the Copenhagen expedition of 1807; the expedition to Portugal in 1808; and, despite the Convention of Cintra, the command of the British forces in the Peninsula in 1809. Here at last his military talents were displayed in an arena in which every move was followed with close attention at home.

On his return from India too, Wellington was a worthy match for the still unmarried second sister of an Irish earl. He and Kitty had kept in touch over the years through intermediaries and from London he renewed his suit by correspondence. Dismissing her prudent suggestion that they should meet before the final decision he went to Dublin with his clerical brother Gerald in April 1806 to claim his bride.[13] This seems an uncharacteristic act of impulsive and romantic folly. He afterwards claimed that he had been tricked into the marriage by appeals to his sense of honour and duty. As he told Mrs Arbuthnot in 1822: 'I was not the least in love with her. I married her because they asked me to do it & I did not know myself. I thought I should never care for anybody again, & that I shd be with the army &, in short, I was a fool.[14] He certainly did not marry for love; but the real reason was vindication. At last he had managed to expunge the greatest humiliation of his life. With this as its foundation it is not surprising that the marriage was no source of happiness and consolation for the reverses of youth. Only a small part of its failure lay in the duchess's inability or disinclination to play the role of a great man's consort that the duke expected. After the first couple of years, during which their two sons were born, they practically lived apart. Not the least of the attractions of the Peninsular War must have been that it took him far away from his wife. Duty was not the only reason that Wellington never came home until 1814 and never expressed any interest in his wife's going to Portugal or Spain.

What would have been a private tragedy in an ordinary individual had public consequences in the duke of Wellington. By reinforcing the rigid, private and self-sufficient personality he had developed in reaction to the rejection of his first proposals, the domination of his eldest brother and the long, lonely years of self-discipline and self-reliance to establish himself in India, his unhappy marriage contributed to making him the very embodiment of the austere and detached classical hero by the time he became a great military figure. In the later stages of the Peninsular War, even more after Waterloo, and most of all after his return to England at the end of 1818, the duke lived in the public eye. As the *Quarterly Review* said after his death: 'like a city built on a hill, or his own colossal statue on the arch, he could not be hid. He was the observed of all observers, and the object of universal, royal-like homage, which he neither courted nor shunned'.[15] Rarely has anyone lived up better to public expectations of what a great man should be. Spare of frame, laconic of speech, ascetic in habits, modest, dedicated to the public good as he saw it and untainted by any hint of corruption or personal scandal, he inspired respect, admiration and above all confidence in the army and in politics. His customary saying, 'I am the Duke of Wellington and must do as the Duke of Wellington doth', which contemporaries took as wry humour, revealed an important truth.

His private personality was more complex than his public one, but close enough that, apart from giving up physical relations with women which he apparently did after 1820, living up to his reputation involved no great renunciation or strain. The man had became the mask and the mask became the man. The few strange romances in which he engaged in his last twenty years were known to very few and the occasional public outburst of anger did him no more harm than the deafness and arthritis that made him seem even more monumental. He generally found ample outlet for his sensitivity and sentimentality in music, even when deafness robbed him of much of its pleasure; playing with children other than his own; and above all in the company of beautiful, accomplished and safely-married women. He was the able defender of his reputation in the endless correspondence with those impertinent enough to suggest that his views and conduct fell short of the ideal and his main fear was that he would be disgraced by some act of foolishness by his wife or sons. Neither was in fact likely to become reality. The duchess lived her unhappy life outside the public arena until her death in 1831; but the anxiety that he might not be so fortunate next time was a powerful motive in preventing the duke from remarrying. His sons, in whom only he detected too much of their mother, discharged their conventional duties in the army and parliament in unremarkable ways. The elder, Lord Douro, provided a wife whose company his father loved, while the younger, Lord Charles Wellesley, contributed grandchildren for him to indulge.

The duke of Wellington was not a common man and, unlike what Walter Bagehot said of Lord Palmerston, a common man might not have been cut out of him. He was, as Charles Greville who knew him well and who had written so many hard as well as perceptive things about him for thirty years, said after his death: 'In spite of some foibles and faults . . . beyond all doubt, a very great man – the only great man of the present time – and comparable, in point of greatness, to the most eminent of those who have lived before.'[16] But this does not mean that he cannot be understood and his achievements explained in human terms. The uses of adversity may not have been sweet but they created a figure to which his own generation and generations since have looked as the very symbol of aristocratic honour and duty.

Notes

1 Earl of Ellesmere, *Personal Reminiscences of the Duke of Wellington* (1903), p. 192.

2 J. H. Stacqueler, *Life of Field Marshal the Duke of Wellington,* i (New York, 1853), pp. 1–2.

3 Leon Edel, 'The figure under the carpet' in *Telling Lives: The Biographer's Art,* ed. Marc Pachtet (Washington, 1979), pp. 24–5.

4 Wellington to Mrs. Arbuthnot, 1 May 1831. *Wellington and His Friends,* ed. 7th duke of Wellington (1965), p. 95.

5 Joan Wilson, *Wellington's Marriage: A Soldier's Wife* (1987), p. 101.

6 Marquess Wellesley to Sir John Newport, 28 February 1840. Iris Butler, *The Eldest Brother: The Marquess Wellesley* (1973), p. 27.

7 Sir Alexander Mackenzie to Lord Ellesmere, 6 October 1853. Ellesmere, *Personal Reminiscences,* p. 102n.

8 Mornington to Duke of Rutland December 1786. Sir Herbert Maxwell, *The Life of Wellington,* i (1899), pp. 5–6.

9 Wilson, Wellington's *Marriage: A Soldier's Wife,* p. 11.

10 Arthur Wesley, Trim, to Lord Camden, 25 June 1795. Camden Papers U840 C266. Kent Archives Office, Maidstone. A summary transcription of the letter is printed in Maxwell, *Wellington,* i, p. 16.

11 Same to same, 28 May and 14 June 1796. Camden Papers U840 C266 and 266/5.

12 Mornington to Arthur Wellesley, 19 June 1799, WSD, i, 246.

13 Wilson, *Wellington's Marriage,* chs 5–9.

14 Francis Bamford and the Duke of Wellington eds, *The Journal of Mrs Arbuthnot, 1820–1832,* i (1950), p. 169, (27 June 1822).

15 'Apsley House', *Quarterly Review,* March 1853, p. 447.

16 Lytton Strachey and Roger Fulford eds, *The Greville Memoirs 1814–1860,* vi (1938), p. 360 (18 September 1852).

Edward Ingram

2

Wellington and India

The tide of imperial history has recently changed direction. Instead of asking how far European empire-builders controlled the lives of the inhabitants of colonies they ruled but perhaps did not govern, historians are trying to discover how far the colonies governed life in the metropolis. That colonies governed English life in the twentieth century is taken for granted: the post-war burden of the Englishman's fatal fondness for empire has become an historical cliché. Earlier, however, one is not so sure. P. J. Marshall, asking who in England valued India in the early nineteenth century, and M. E. Yapp, arguing that British strategy in the Middle East was determined by European rather than Indian interests,[1] seem to suppose that returning Nabobs, having made, if they were lucky, the fortune they had gone abroad to seek, disappeared into the countryside leaving no trace. One Nabob, however, won the battle of Waterloo and faded into obscurity as prime minister and commander-in-chief. Of the many historical roles played by the duke of Wellington, one was that of the conduit by which recognition of the value of India to Great Britain as a great power flowed into the heart of the British political establishment.

The eight years Wellington spent in India from February 1797 to March 1805 seem to exemplify the late-Victorian utility of colonies as a repository, or in this instance forcing ground, for difficult younger sons. Having gone out an impecunious junior colonel of no particular note, whose promotion had been purchased for him in aristocratic fashion and with aristocratic speed, he came back a major-general, with the order of the Bath and financial independence from prize money worth £30,000. He had been fortunate, of course. His eldest brother Richard, Marquess Wellesley, had followed him to India to be governor-general and with the 'taste for conquest and aggrandize-ment'[2] that gave Wellington opportunities in the Fourth Mysore War and Second Maratha War to experience various types of warfare and military command. What William Springer calls Wellington's military apprenticeship[3] gave no indication, however, of the ruthlessness and ability he would show in the Peninsula, where the Portuguese would pay the price of the mistakes he had made in the Deccan.

Technically, Wellington may not be called a Nabob, for he went to India in the service of the Crown not the East India Company, as did his brother Wellesley, who took with him a third brother, Henry, as his private-secretary, later appointing him lieutenant-governor of the territory annexed from Oudh. Yet they went for the reason others went, making themselves the exception proving the rule that success in high office in India came from not attracting notice in England. The bog-Irish Wellesleys used India to take a giant stride from the furthest fringe of the British oligarchy to the centre of it. Wellesley himself, who had marked time in minor posts throughout the 1790s, returned to London – despite recall from Calcutta in virtual disgrace – to the offer of high office from friends of both William Pitt and Lord Grenville, and despite then squandering fortune and reputation, was able while at the foreign office from 1810 to 1812 to sustain in the Peninsula the career he had helped to launch in India. Arthur owed everything to Richard, and both owed to India their chance in life.

This essay will show how the Wellesleys took their chance in India, and how Arthur in later life paid their debt by treating India as necessary for Britain's greatness, just as it had been necessary for his own. In the Peninsula he foisted an Indian subsidiary alliance on Portugal; in the 1820s he acted as unofficial secretary of state for India in the earl of Liverpool's administration; as prime minister he began with his president of the Board of Control for India, Lord Ellenborough, the series of policy initiatives in the Middle East known as the Great Game in Asia; and as former and would-be commander-in-chief he expressed opinions on Indian strategy in the First Afghan War that provided the foundation for the Punjab School of Indian defence. India cast a long shadow over the career of the duke of Wellington and through him over the history of Great Britain as a great power.

The decisive moment in Arthur Wellesley's early career occurred upon the arrival of his brother Richard at Calcutta in May 1798, one year after his own arrival there. Although Arthur would mock Richard's grandiose dream of an Anglo-Indian empire stretching from Cape Comorin to the river Sutledge, if not beyond it, and criticise the subsidiary alliances by which Richard hoped to control the Indian states, he was happy enough to be offered appointments for which he was too junior, either as a favour to Richard, or by Richard himself on the ground that for Indians he would personify the governor-general, just as the governor-general personified the Crown. Neither brother saw himself as personifying the East India Company.

Arthur began playing his role as brake upon his more headstrong brother six weeks after Wellesley's arrival. The opportunity Wellesley thought he had spotted in June to force war on Mysore was denied him by Arthur's explanation of the facts of Indian geography, in particular the effects of monsoons on campaigning. What was prohibited by the monsoon in the summer might be tried the following winter, however, so in the autumn of 1798 Wellesley sent Arthur to Madras to ginger the government, this 'parcel of blockheads . . . who know nothing',[4] into preparing for a war both they and Arthur expected to be far more difficult to win than it turned out to be. Many of Wellesley's problems in India – and Arthur's opportunities to prove himself in the field – followed from the ease with which the British defeated Tipu Sultan of Mysore in the spring of 1799.

The Fourth Mysore War offered Arthur the chance to show his worth as a staff officer, as an administrator, and as an independent commander in the field. Helping to get the Madras Army ready for war, gathering the thousands of teams of bullocks it depended on for transport, gave him an object lesson in the importance of well-organised supplies. When the campaign opened, he was made one of a council of four officers who were to advise the commander-in-chief at Madras on political issues and help to devise terms of peace; after the victory in May, though still only a colonel, he was given command at Seringapatam, Tipu's former capital, in preference to Major-General David Baird, who was entitled to it; and when one of Tipu's former vassals, Dhoondhia Vagh, began in 1800 to raid territory now ruled by British allies, Arthur was given command of a force of cavalry that chased him northwards into Maratha territory, pinning him down and destroying him early in September. This success was to lead Arthur perilously close to disaster three years later. He drew from it the false conclusion that Indian states relied principally on cavalry, whereas they had switched back to reliance on infantry and artillery.

The degree of Arthur's reliance on Wellesley for opportunities to make a name for himself was shown most clearly in the quarrel between them in 1800–1 over Wellesley's decision to give to Baird instead of Arthur the command of the expeditionary force the War Office had ordered the government of India to send to the Red Sea, to help defeat the French army of occupation in Egypt. Having refused earlier in the year Wellesley's offer of the command of troops being collected for an attack on Batavia, through unwillingness to serve under the overall command of the British naval commander-in-chief, Arthur had agreed to go to Ceylon, to prepare an expedition against Mauritius, despite thinking Wellesley's plan of attack 'the greatest nonsense'.[5] The diversion of his troops to the Red Sea so annoyed Arthur that he injured their chances of arriving in time to be of use by sending them to Bombay instead of straight to Mocha, on the ground that 'articles of provision are not to be trifled with or left to chance'.[6] Here, however, is not another early example of Arthur's sensible concern with supplies, for where could he have expected to find them on the way to Mauritius? All his younger brother Henry's tact was needed to dissuade him from resigning and going home to England in pique.

Owing to Arthur's quarrel with Wellesley over Baird, the relationship between them would never again be as amicable as it had been during their first two years together in India. After two more dull years at Seringapatam, however, Arthur would be rewarded by Wellesley with command of the army sent north from Mysore in 1803 to restore Peshwa Baji Rao II to the throne at Poona from which he had been driven by Jeshwant Rao Holkar.

The crisis at Poona in 1802, and the opportunity it gave Wellesley to try to turn himself into the arbiter between the most powerful Maratha princes, led eighteen months later to Arthur's baptism of fire as an army commander – he had been promoted to major-general in 1802 – at the battles of Assaye and Argaon. Wellesley had been determined since arriving in India to turn the Maratha princes into dependants of the government of India, either by tying them individually to the British, or, having foisted a subsidiary alliance upon the peshwa, by claiming this acknowledgment of British paramountcy bound all of them. For four years the Maratha princes, both individually and as a group, had resisted Wellesley's blandishments, denying the existence of the dangers from which he offered to protect them, until the overthrow of Baji Rao II by Jeshwant Rao Holkar in October 1802 seemed to leave him no alternative to accepting a subsidiary alliance, the standard device used by the government of India to deprive its allies of their independence while seemingly offering to protect them against their subjects as well as their enemies.

By 1802 Arthur had become as critical of Wellesley's political goals as he had become of the chances of reaching them, either by threatening force or by resorting to it. The Indian states could be expected to refuse the subsidiary alliances proffered them, and Wellesley's argument that such refusals were tantamount to a declaration of hostile intent, which ought to be forestalled, was absurd. 'One country has no right to commence a war upon another because . . . it refuses to draw closer the terms of its alliance with the country which proposes it.'[7] When Baji Rao II, as his reward for tying himself to the British, was duly restored in May 1803 to his throne without much opposition, Arthur doubted whether the other Maratha princes were likely to follow his example. They would certainly not accept that they were bound by his decision and were more likely to try to remove his British shackles, if only to replace them with shackles of their own.

The subsidiary alliance was the standard bargain made between the government of India and the ruler of an Indian state losing power, for the benefit of him, his chief notables, and Anglo-Indian soldiers and civil servants, at the expense of his subjects and the East India Company. The ruler permitted a British agent to reside at his capital, surrendered control over his foreign affairs to the British, and agreed to pay for the services of units of the Indian Army, who would be stationed in his territory. In return the political structure of his state was frozen and he was guaranteed his throne. After 1798 Wellesley changed the established practice by demanding territory rather than tribute in return for the troops he provided, and chose territory running along the frontier of the next state he wished to entrap. Indian Army officers put in command of the subsidiary troops and civil servants sent to administer the territory surrendered were delighted with the system because of the opportunities of promotion it brought them. The peasants who had to pay for their services were not so delighted. Nor were they to be in Portugal in 1809 when Arthur imposed on them an alliance identical to the subsidiary alliances of which he had been so critical in India.

Arthur criticised the alliance made with the peshwa by the treaty of

Bassein, because it tied the British to the fortunes of a prince too weak either to defend himself or to help the British to defend him. Instead of strengthening them, he would expect them to strengthen him by enforcing on his neighbours claims to suzerainty and demands for tribute he was incapable of enforcing for himself. When it became clear in the spring of 1803 that the two most powerful Maratha princes, Daulat Rao Sindhia and the Bhonsla Raja of Berar, might take up arms against the British rather than make similar bargains with them, Arthur soon learned that no support was to be expected from any of the other Maratha princes of the Deccan.

The Second Maratha War finally broke out in July 1803 when Sindhia and the raja of Berar refused to withdraw their armies from a position which Arthur declared to be threateningly close to the northern frontier of the territory of the government of India's most favoured ally, the nizam of Hyderabad. The commander-in-chief in India, General Lake, given the choice of field in which to take command, chose northern India, leaving Arthur in the Deccan with an army of 20,000 men, made up of British, British Indian, and Hyderabad troops. The Marathas' task, as Arthur conceived it, was to strike southwards into Hyderabad, where they could live off the land, forcing the British to follow them but refusing to give battle. Arthur's own task was to bar their way and to force on them the battle they would, or ought to, try to avoid. The success of both sides might depend on the state of the rivers, which Arthur supposed must give him the advantage, for he was proud of the use he made of pontoons to pass rivers otherwise impassable in the rainy season: 'I had Caesar's *Commentaries* with me in India and learnt much from them . . . I passed over the rivers as he did by means of baskets and boats of basket work; only I think I improved upon him.'[8]

Despite Arthur's claims, his superior generalship was not to determine the outcome of the war in the Deccan. After marching and counter-marching for three months and failing to compel Sindhia and Bhonsla to divide their forces, he blundered into their combined force at Assaye on 23 September, with half his own troops a day's march away. By following what became the British rule never to retire before an Indian army and by not waiting for his troops to come up with him, Arthur took the Marathas by surprise. Fortunately for him, as they had expected him to collect his whole force before attacking, some of the bullocks of their artillery train had been turned out to graze. As it was, the battle was extraordinarily bloody, cost the lives of a third of the British troops involved, and belied every assumption made about the Marathas. They wanted to fight; they were ready to fight; they were better equipped to fight than the British; and they lost owing to Wellesley's tactics in the months leading up to the battle, rather than to Arthur's tactics during the battle itself, admirably flexible though they were. Once again Arthur owed his success to his brother.

The battle itself showed the Maratha infantry to be the equal of the British and their artillery to be superior. Having manoeuvred to the Marathas' flank, Arthur was surprised to find them carrying out at speed and in battle conditions the complicated infantry manoeuvres needed to shift their front to the flank he had exposed to attack. The frontal attack he had then to carry out to escape the withering fire from the Maratha artillery succeeded only owing to the steadiness of the British regiments, the good sense of the British sepoys in using their knapsacks and, when necessary, lying down to protect themselves, and the early engagement of the British cavalry. The British won with the more primitive, rather than the more sophisticated tactics: their bayonets and sabres eventually making up at close quarters for the superiority of the Marathas' musket and artillery fire. 'The victory was nowhere near so complete as it might have been', however, as by the end of the day the British cavalry were too tired to pursue the retreating Marathas, who were left with an excellent opportunity to counter-attack.[9]

The Marathas had better weapons, as good training, but a poorer command structure than the British, owing to political conditions of which Wellesley had been quick to take advantage. The Marathas' infantry had proved remarkably steady, their officers and cavalry equally unpredictable. A fluid market had existed in eighteenth-century India for the sale of military skill, which limited the reliance any prince could reasonably place on troops he had hired for wages or the promise of spoils. Conversely, one of Arthur's advantages lay in his regular cavalry. His troopers, whose mounts were supplied to them, were more willing to take risks by pressing home an attack than were the Pindaris serving with the Marathas, who mounted themselves. Indian armies, unlike British ones, often tended to melt away at the first sign of determined opposition. The Maratha army at Assaye proved no exception, despite its tactical brilliance. Sindhia and Bhonsla left shortly after the battle began, and neither their cavalry nor the whole of their infantry were ever fully committed.

To make up for the lack of a politically reliable officer corps, the

Marathas had hired European mercenaries, mostly Frenchmen and Englishmen, who turned out to be no more reliable than the Indians they replaced. In India to make their fortunes, and spotting the British as the likely winners, they became increasingly anxious to find ways to extract themselves with profit from the crisis in Anglo-Maratha relations. Pierre Perron, the commander of Sindhia's armies in the north, for example, 'has a very considerable property in our funds, to enjoy which in security is his first object'.[10] Wellesley offered him and others like him the chance to sell themselves out, which explains the detachment shown by Perron's counterpart at Assaye, and may explain why Sindhia was unable to persuade the raja of Berar to counter-attack the British, when Arthur failed to follow up his victory.

The same lack of political commitment defeated the Marathas when the two armies clashed again at Argaon, the second of Arthur's Indian victories, in November 1803, this time with more serious consequences. Once again the Maratha artillery proved to be so superior to the British that the units at the head of the British column broke and fled. They were reformed only when Arthur, adopting the tactic he had witnessed at Assaye and would later employ against Napoleon at Waterloo, ordered the sepoys to lie down. Once again, too, the Maratha army was defeated partly because Sindhia failed to commit his troops, leaving the raja of Berar without support and unable to take advantage of their superiority in numbers. Although less bloody than Assaye, the Marathas' defeat at Argaon gave Arthur the strategic initiative. He was now able to divide the forces of Sindhia and the raja of Berar by striking eastwards into Cuttack, the raja's territory lying along the east coast of India and coveted by Wellesley as the bridge between Bengal and Madras.

By the end of the year the Marathas had agreed to make peace on the terms offered by the British, earning Arthur a knighthood and setting up another disagreement with Wellesley in 1804. Arthur had succeeded in dividing the Marathas by offering an armistice to Daulat Rao Sinhia while continuing the campaign against the raja of Berar, and, like Sindhia, assumed that conciliatory treatment from Wellesley would be the reward of submission, as it had been for the nizam of Hyderabad. The terms of the subsidiary alliance imposed on Sindhia were so harsh, in Arthur's opinion, that no reliance could be placed upon his help in extending British paramountcy over his rival, Jeshwant Rao Holkar.[11] The family, as well as the East India Company, would benefit from stabilising relations with the Marathas, because Arthur realised, as his brother seemed never to do, that their success had depended on keeping one step ahead of the arrival in England of the news of the war. By 1804 it was clear that the outbreak of more fighting would undermine their claim that beyond victory lay stability for Bengal and Madras and prosperity for the East India Company.

Arthur's relations with Wellesley had deteriorated and, according to Arthur, Wellesley's chances of risking rather than consolidating his reputation had increased, after the return of their brother Henry to England in 1803. Throughout his term in India, Wellesley preferred to surround himself with a group of bright younger men, using Arthur as his pipeline into and manager of the army, and Henry to perform the same role with the civil service. With Henry in England and Arthur in the Deccan, 'we want at Calcutta some person who will speak his mind to the governor-general . . . who has nerves . . . to oppose his senti-ments when he is wrong'.[12] Arthur left India somewhat bitter that Wellesley, by mishandling relations with Sindhia, and Lake and Arthur's own subordinates by mishandling the campaign against Holkar in 1804, had squandered the family's success. Instead of returning to applause, Arthur, back in London, found himself obliged to defend Wellesley's record.

Such disagreements and even disappointments with one another do not detract from the achievement of the brothers in transforming the British territories in India into an Indian Empire for which they provided the ideological foundation. Unlike their predecessors, the Wellesleys emphasised the power and dignity of the British state in India, the morality of British conquests, and the superiority of the British race and European culture. Englishmen serving in India were expected to follow Burke's directive to behave as they would at home. War against Indian princes was always declared to have been forced on the British and the conquest of territory justified as providing the military shield behind which legitimate rulers might be restored to thrones from which they had been driven by tyrannical usurpers like Hyder Ali and Tipu Sultan, and behind which their Indian subjects might live at peace. Arthur explained of the Marathas that 'they well know that we shall found our claims to satisfaction and security on the fact that they were the aggressors'.[13] Nor were the British any longer to disguise themselves as agents of the Mogul emperor. They were to step forward as sovereign, claiming paramount power in their own right.

This empire was to be run as a military despotism, at least outside Bengal, the economic heartland whose prosperity would justify, as it would pay for, conquests elsewhere. Arthur encouraged Wellesley in the habit of employing soldiers as political agents at the courts of the Indian states, and even as revenue officers in Madras. Unlike Henry Dundas, however, who preferred to appoint soldiers to Indian governorships, Arthur believed that heads of government should be civilians with ultimate authority over the army on which they depended. Wellesley had been appointed captain-general by Dundas, an office Arthur later proposed to bestow on all governors-general. In the interval, he had decided that the militarisation of British India had gone too far, and was causing rather than preventing unrest as officers looked to crises to obtain the notice of the governor-general and possibly promotion. While prime minister, therefore, he agreed to order the government of India to appoint civilians to all civilian posts, including the agencies at the Indian states. The only exception permitted was the employment of soldiers as agents in the Middle East, evidence for the view that he thought of British interests in the area as strategic rather than commercial. The primacy of strategic over economic considerations in the Victorian official mind would owe much to the views of the world developed by Arthur Wellesley as the result of his career in India.

Wellesley's tie with India was not broken on his departure from Calcutta in March 1805. His Indian experience would influence his conduct in Portugal, as prime minister, and as commander-in-chief. The change between 1828 and 1834 in the British world view which set up Russia in place of France as Great Britain's most likely enemy derived partly from the introduction into English politics of the Wellesley brothers' Anglo-Indian notions of British national interests.

The influence of expansionism in India under the Wellesleys on British foreign policy was seen first in the Peninsula War, in their attempt to treat the kingdom of Portugal as if it were Hyderabad, by imposing upon it an Indian-style subsidiary alliance similar to the subsidiary alliance foisted upon the nizam in 1800. The nizam of Hyderabad had been guaranteed his independence against a challenge from the French and the Marathas, at the cost of surrendering it to the British. He was obliged to listen to, and usually follow, the advice of a British agent; to hire large numbers of British troops; to hand over to the British large amounts of territory to provide payment for them; and also to hand over the conduct of his foreign relations. In return, he and a group of his notables might – and did – survive beyond 1947.

So in Portugal between 1810 and 1812, when Wellington in the field could count on the support of Wellesley at the Foreign Office. The British notion of fighting for the independence of Portugal was to promise the regent and the notables safety in Brazil in exchange for control over the council of regency and through it over the resources of the state. To keep the Braganzas to their bargain required constant effort by Lord Strangford, the British ambassador at Rio de Janeiro, and Sir Charles Stuart, his deputy at Lisbon, as well as by Wellington himself, for the council of regency vigorously resisted the British demands. And well they might, given their extreme nature. The Portuguese army was placed under a British commander, taxes were raised dramatically, and the scorched-earth strategy implemented by Wellington as he fell back towards the defensive lines he had prepared outside Lisbon at Torres Vedras in the false hope of starving his opponent, Marshal Massena, brought social and economic disaster to Beiras and Estramadura.[14] No Indian state, not even Oudh, had had such heavy demands made on it.

Wellington's determination to thrust on Portugal a relationship identical to the relationships he had criticised when thrust by Wellesley upon the Indian states need not to be attributed solely to self-interest and to the demands of his own military career, and the family's political and social advancement, however well they were served by the Peninsula War and threatened by alternatives such as the Walcheren Expedition. The regent of Portugal met two of the requirements lacked by both Baji Rao II and Daulat Rao Sindhia. Out of the way in Brazil, he could be both more effectively protected and effectively overridden. And the British, using their navy to protect themselves as well as him, could ensure that the war was confined to his territory and would not spill over into theirs. They could retreat from Lisbon to London, as they retreated from Corunna, and as they could not have retreated from Poona to Madras. The subsidiary alliance, by which Wellesley had hoped to create a continental empire was better suited, in Wellington's opinion, to use by a peripheral power fighting a limited war in however savage a style.

Appeasement had such a bad name in England for so long partly owing to the excessively patriotic accounts written of the Napoleonic Wars and Great Britain's part in them. The Portuguese would have done better to make terms with Napoleon, as the Dutch and Italians, and even the Austrians, did, waiting for events elsewhere to free them from a burdensome yoke. The British, who could not defend them but rather used them as a defence of Great Britain, nevertheless cited the Peninsular campaigns in proof of their absurd claim that they had defeated Napoleon by their exertion and freed his other enemies by their example. In fact, between 1807 and 1812, while the Wellesleys and their friend George Canning were in command of policy making, the British had been dreaming dreams of an Anglo-Russian imperial condominium over Europe equivalent to the partition of Central Asia into two spheres of influence of which Wellesley had dreamed while dreaming of empires in India.

So obvious had the Anglo-Indian assumptions underlying the conduct of British foreign policy become by the end of the Napoleonic Wars that the king of Sardinia complained that the British 'consider me and all the rulers of Mediterranean islands as mere Indians and nabobs'.[15] Anglo-Indian habits of undermining the independence of an ally while seeming to buttress it, and of demanding protection from those to whom protection was supposedly being offered, brought back from India by the Wellesleys — and by their rival, Lord William Bentinck, commander-in-chief in the Mediterranean and formerly governor of Madras from 1804 to 1807 — would be exported again during the 1820s and 1830s to the Middle East, after Wellington had taken up the position of unofficial minister for India in the earl of Liverpool's administration.

Wellington's Indian experience naturally had less significance for his military career than for his subsequent role in British politics. His career as a statesman started at Vienna, continued as commander of the Allied army of occupation in France, and moved to a new plane with his entry into the cabinet in 1818. George IV, after Castlereagh's death in 1822, increasingly regarded the duke as the most reliable member of the government and in the end thrust him forward as prime minister. His particular contribution to the second phase of the Liverpool administration, after the bargain with the Grenville whigs, the death of Castlereagh, and the return of Canning to the Foreign Office, was to lend both countenance and support to the whig president of the Board of Control for India, Charles Williams Wynn, to whom neither Canning, nor an East India Company showing a surprising determination to flex its political muscles, would otherwise pay much attention. In defending Wynn's stand on two of the issues that split the government and divided it from the East India Company, Wellington revealed more of his conception of British India and the needs of its defence.

The first dispute arose over the East India Company's wish in 1825 to recall the governor-general, Earl Amherst, from India for his conduct of the First Burma War. Amherst had been appointed only because all the other nominees were unacceptable to either the East India Company or the government, and because Canning had supported him. Canning had now changed his tune, however, seeing in the recall of Amherst an opportunity to strengthen his own position in the government. If Amherst were replaced in India by the duke of Buckingham, the leader of the Grenville whigs, Wynn could be squeezed out of the cabinet to make room for Canning's friend William Huskisson. The plan misfired because neither Liverpool nor the East India Company would accept Buckingham. The company wanted Lord William Bentinck, which was one reason why, when Liverpool turned to Wellington to decide how to settle the dispute, Wellington recommended the retention of Amherst and persuaded the East India Company to accept him.[16] Defending Amherst also had the attraction of disobliging Canning.

Wellington's effective intervention on behalf of Amherst revealed his most important assumptions about British rule in India. Whereas he disliked Bentinck as too radical and likely to be too fidgety, he respected the East India Company for its local knowledge, and had made personal friends of two of its most senior and distinguished officials, Sir John Malcolm and Sir Thomas Munro. The company knew that it could count on Wellington's support against critics demanding the termination of its rule, because for Wellington chartered rights were the foundation of the British political and social system. To tamper with them was to invite anarchy. Wellington's ideas about Indian government derived from a Hobbesian conception of the anarchic state of nature. Accordingly, a strong central government was needed to maintain order and ensure to every man his rights.

Wellington's assumptions partly derived from his own experience: the orderly hierarchy of British India and army life contrasted with disorderly civilian society during the French Revolutionary era and life in Ireland, where an Anglo-Irish minority lived in isolation and fear among its Catholic tenantry. British India, where Anglo-Indians were even thinner on the ground, must be prepared likewise for rebellion and mutiny. Its stability would depend on its army, on a policy of non-interference with Indian custom, and on the maintenance of the outward symbols of British power. Politically, as well as militarily, the British must never be seen to retreat. For these reasons, the war in Burma must be fought to a successful conclusion, at whatever cost, and Amherst confirmed in office, whatever the East India Company might think of him. Recalling him would be tantamount to revolution, offering an invitation to disorder.

Until the late 1830s, when Wellington began to be criticised for being twenty-five years out of date and for having learned little of India since his return, he was treated as the authority on all Indian military affairs. Even when not commander-in-chief, his advice was asked before senior appointments were made to the Indian high command. Unlike his rival, Bentinck, who distrusted the Indian Army, both its sepoy rank-and-file and its British officers – perhaps owing to his recall from Madras in 1807 following the mutiny at Vellore – Wellington's attitude was ambivalent. While in India he had been highly critical of Indian Army officers who aped the aristocratic pretensions of their British Army colleagues by riding roughshod over Indians and refusing to pay their bills. Their search of fortune did not offend him, however; nor should it have done. Being too poor to sustain himself in England in the rank to which he aspired, he had gone out to India on the same quest.

Wellington's fear of unrest in India explains his support of Wynn in the second of the two Asiatic crises facing the government in 1826, the outbreak of the second Russo-Persian war. An argument between Wynn and Canning about Persia's right to British mediation under the terms of the treaty of Tehran of 1815 was referred to Wellington for resolution. In supporting Wynn's claim that Great Britain had 'fair grounds' for intervention rather than Canning's denial of it,[17] Wellington extended the significance of the dramatic change that had taken place at the end of the Napoleonic Wars in the world view of many of the men responsible for planning British foreign policy. According to Paul W. Schroeder, the assumption that Great Britain and Russia should share between them control of Europe and the Middle East, inherited by Canning and the Wellesleys from Grenville during the war of the Second Coalition, had been replaced under the guidance of the earl of Aberdeen, then British ambassador at Vienna and later Wellington's foreign secretary, by an unnatural 'natural' alliance with Austria. Instead of sacrificing herself to accommodate Russia, Austria would henceforth be expected to stand up to her to accommodate Great Britain.[18]

The line to be drawn by Austria in central and eastern Europe on behalf of the British might have to be drawn in the Middle East by the British themselves. What began for Wellington as a theoretical question, the need to deny the claim made by the tsar and accepted by Canning that Great Britain, not being a neighbour of Persia and the Ottoman Empire, had no reason to take an interest in their relations with Russia, turned after the treaties of Turkmanchay in 1828 and Adrianople in 1829 into the practical question of finding a way to prevent the two states from being turned into Russian protectorates. In Wellington's opinion, such a change in the status of Persia was likely to destabilise India, first the Indian states, later the territories under British rule, as soon as Persia with the encouragement of Russia sought compensation in Afghanistan and Sind for the losses she had suffered in the Caucasus. Wellington had no fear of an overland invasion. Few Englishmen feared a Russian invasion of India, however many may have talked as if they did. Their more immediate fear was of bankruptcy, following a prolonged period of civil unrest combined with a frontier war with the remaining independent Indian states or an attempt by the government of India's protectorates to recover their independence.

After Wellington became prime minister in 1828, his president of the Board of Control for India, Lord Ellenborough, hoping by dramatic victories in the Middle East to prove himself more worthy than Aberdeen of the Foreign Office, suggested that the best way to stabilise British India, and to forestall any potential challenge from Russia, would be by a demonstration of Great Britain's equivalent ability to destabilise the southern provinces of the Russian empire. Wellington, however, was quick to forbid any such attempt. Instability in all forms and all places ought to be discouraged: it spread. By using closer commercial links with the states of Afghanistan and Turkestan to create a stable buffer zone beyond the North-West Frontier, the government of India could demonstrate that Russian influence in Iran was unlikely to destabilise British India. As Kabul, Khiva, and Bukhara lay far from the frontier of Russia as well as of British India, Russia would not be able to claim, as a neighbour, a more important interest than Great Britain in what might happen there.[19]

When looking at the shah of Persia, Wellington saw Baji Rao II or Daulat Rao Sindhia, an ally too weak to be of use, who would try to take the British in tow as soon as he was allowed to assume that the stability of British India was thought to depend on the stability of Persia. Having criticised Canning for failing to insist that Great Britain had a right to be consulted about the terms of peace between Russia and Persia, Wellington took steps to re-establish Great Britain's claim to influence in Persia that seem at first glance to have been remarkably rash. Aberdeen was not permitted to warn the Russians, at Ellenborough's request, that further expansion southwards at the expense of Persia would be treated as an infringement of Great Britain's interests as an Asiatic state. Ellenborough, on the other hand, was permitted to tell the Persians that Great Britain would not permit the subjugation of Persia by Russia. One thinks of Sir Edward Grey during the Moroccan Crisis, warning Germany that Great Britain might support France in the event of war, while warning France that British support should not be taken for granted. Whereas Grey warned the stronger and discouraged the weaker, Wellington encouraged the weaker while failing to warn the stronger. He hoped, however, by re-establishing the British military mission in Persia, to make sure that the shah did not try to take advantage of the gesture. The mission would demonstrate Great Britain's determination to support her claim, without risking a new crisis in Russo-Persian relations. By increasing Great Britain's influence over the Persian government and the government's control over Azerbaijan, Wellington hoped to deprive Russia of the opportunity to deny Great Britain her legitimate role in Persian affairs. As soon as the heir apparent felt confident of British, as well as Russian, support for his accession, for example, he would have no need to offer further concessions to Russia in return for a promise of military support against his rivals for the throne.

Having set one precedent in Persia, by denying that a sea power had any less right than a neighbouring land power to claim an interest in developments inland, Wellington then set another precedent in Central Asia, one to be followed during the partition of Africa, by trying to ensure that Anglo-Russian disputes in the Middle East should be settled cheaply on maps, rather than expensively on the ground. Russia was to be told that a line would be drawn on a map to the north of Khiva and Bukhara and that her expansion towards, certainly beyond, the line would be treated as a European question. Given that the Middle East had been excluded from the terms of the Final Act of the congress of Vienna, one cannot be sure how Wellington supposed that this could be arranged. During the recent Russo-Turkish war he had explicitly denied the practicability of bringing pressure to bear on the Russians by calling up British ships from the Mediterranean to the Black Sea, which would have 'placed our fleet in a *rat trap*'.[20] The suggestion that Great Britain might risk a major international crisis on the continent for the sake of stabilising her Indian Empire harked back, however, to the decision taken by Henry Dundas and Pitt the Younger upon the collapse of the second coalition. In the autumn of 1800, the British army in the Mediterranean had been sent to Eygpt, to drive the French out of the Middle East without letting in the Russians. One suspects that in 1830 Wellington would have expected Prince Metternich to act as Great Britain's necessary ally, as Dundas and Pitt had expected Baron Thugut to act, and as Count Buol would be expected to act during the Crimean War, both of them receiving no thanks.

The instructions to promote trade with Central Asia sent in January 1830 by Ellenborough, acting with Wellington's approval, to the governor-general of India – as it happens, Lord William Bentinck, who had been appointed by Canning despite, or perhaps because of, Wellington's dislike of him – mark the beginning of the rivalry between Great Britain and Russia for influence in the Middle East known as the Great Game in Asia. Whether these instructions attest to the importance of the Indian Empire to the British sense of Great Britain's role as a world power, or whether Wellington led the British rather than reflecting their assumptions, is a question causing some dispute. The Indian lobby in the House of Commons in the 1820s numbered about seventy-five, more than a tenth of the membership, however, and the arguments over Indian affairs referred by Liverpool to Wellington show that the government was careful not to provoke its opposition. The rarity with which Indian affairs were debated in parliament may indicate that the importance of India was taken for granted rather than that few men thought much about it. Its importance had certainly been taken for granted by Pitt and Dundas thirty years ealier. Even if, as P. J. Marshall suggests, British India remained until the 1820s a largely autonomous state, pursuing its own purposes of safety and consolidation,[21] after Wellington's administration those purposes would be pursued on its behalf by the home government. Wellington's interest in Indian affairs turned him into a bridge leading from the excitement aroused by the conquest of Bengal in the late eighteenth century to the parallel excitement aroused by the debate over Indian defence a hundred years later.

That Wellington's decision to shift the responsibility for defending

British India from the government of India to the home government
would be acceptable to all groups in politics was shown during Earl
Grey's administration, when the Canningite foreign secretary, Lord
Palmerston, followed where Wellington had led. In 1833, he interpreted the treaty of Unkiar Skelessi in the manner in which Wellington
and Ellenborough had interpreted the treaties of Turkmanchay and
Adrianople, and the following year he moved quickly to ensure that
Russia could not turn the succession crisis in Persia to her political
advantage. Similarly, when Ellenborough proposed in 1835 to send a
Canningite member of the whig Board of Control, Henry Ellis, on a
mission to Persia to decide whether Afghanistan or Persia would make
the better outpost of British India, Wellington agreed and Palmerston,
on returning to office, confirmed the appointment. Henceforth, whigs
and tories would argue, sometimes bitterly, about how British India
could be most effectively and most cheaply defended. Neither would
question that its defence had become one of the government's most
important responsibilities.

The decisions to shift attention from Persia to Afghanistan and, if
necessary, to turn the stability of the Indian Empire into a European
question, would set Great Britain on the road to the First Afghan War
and the strategic system for the defence of India known in the late
nineteenth century as the Punjab School, associated with the name of
Sir John Lawrence and the phrase 'masterly inactivity'. Owing to the
notorious retreat from Kabul in 1840, to be found on the list of
landmark imperial disasters in company with Isandalwana, Gallipoli,
and Kut, the First Afghan War is often regarded as a British defeat.
From Wellington's perspective, however, the war proved a success. He
had agreed in 1838 that an invasion of Afghanistan might be unavoid-
able, if force seemed to be needed to open up trade routes to Central
Asia blocked by Russian influence in areas far from the Russian
frontier, well beyond the line drawn to the north of Khiva, and
therefore in which Great Britain must demonstrate her ability to
deploy superior strength. Such a military demonstration, if accompanied by the opening of the Indus to steam navigation, would achieve
the goal Wellington and Ellenborough had set ten years earlier. 'A
more decisive step will have been taken to establish the influence of
England, English commerce and manufactures in Central Asia, to the
detriment of Russia, than can be taken by any other means.'[22]

The invasion of Afghanistan appears at first glance to have been
such a disaster because of the way in which Englishmen interested in

India, including Wellington, were bound to interpret the significance of the retreat from Kabul. Since the turn of the century and the development by the Wellesleys and their coterie of the ideology of paramountcy, the British had always been afraid of arousing the resentment, or triggering what they took to be the religious militancy, of their Muslim subjects and dependants. The retreat from Kabul was followed by a campaign of retribution, lest Indians should aggravate the crisis by mistaking the determination as well as the power of Great Britain, in the way both the emperor of China and the supporters of the Indian Mutiny were to do.

Although the British pulled their troops out of Afghanistan in 1842, as a demonstration of British power the invasion had been the success Wellington supposed. The amir of Afghanistan took care not to take any step likely to provoke similar British intervention, maintaining a cautious neutrality even during moments of great embarrassment for the British during the Crimean War and the Indian Mutiny. The trade routes to Central Asia had been unblocked, for those who believed that they existed, and the Russians had pulled back from both Afghanistan and an expedition against Khiva. Wellington therefore supported the decision to evacuate taken by his friend Ellenborough, who had exchanged in 1824 the Board of Control for the governor-generalship of India. The corollary to the evacuation of Afghanistan, however, was British control over Sind. Wellington was one of the most important politicians to support the annexation of Sind in 1843, and would have resisted the demand successfully made by the East India Company the following year for Ellenborough's recall. That his support of Ellenborough proved unavailing may illustrate the decline in his political standing. Sir Robert Peel had never cared for Ellenborough, nor much for the Empire.

If Wellington may be said to be the precursor of the Punjab School of Indian defence, his old friend and former colleague in India, Sir John Malcolm, whom he appointed governor of Bombay in 1828, may be said to have been the precursor of its rival, the Bombay School. The beginning of the Great Game in Asia in 1829 may be said to be the beginning of the debate between the two. Both schools, looking back to the history of relations with Persia during the Napoleonic Wars, wished to isolate British India from the effects of instability in the European states' system. Whereas Malcolm and his associates looked to forward policies and the deployment in a crisis of military power in the Middle East, Wellington looked to the Continent and to cooperation with European allies under the aegis of the concert of Europe. Paradoxically, therefore, Wellington assumed that India could be separated from Europe only by connecting the two. His reliance on diplomacy rather than force, perhaps a tribute to his long experience of high command, contrasts strongly with Malcolm's reliance on military force, perhaps a tribute to Malcolm's feat in having risen to the rank of major-general, the highest rank in the Indian Army, without ever having commanded even a regiment in the field. Wellington was as unwilling as Wellesley had been during his term as governor-general to accept Malcolm's premise that the most effective military strategy in the Middle East for the defence of British India was to treat Persia as a military desert. The Indian Army, operating from a base in the Persian Gulf, should strike north at will, recruiting tribesmen as irregular cavalry and disregarding the Iranian government.[23]

Malcolm's strategy for the defence of British India derived from an application to Persia of the conclusion drawn by Wellington from the defeat of the Marathas in 1803, when compared with their success in 1804 and in the campaigns of the Third Maratha War of 1816–18. Although Wellington had been surprised by the excellence of the Maratha infantry and artillery, which would have overpowered any other Indian state and twice nearly overpowered him, nevertheless he thought that the Marathas would have been more effective against him, had they adopted a mobile strategy relying on superiority in cavalry. Malcolm thought the same of the Persian army, disparaging with good reason the performance of the infantry trained during the Napoleonic Wars by the French as well as the British. Asiatic states could resist European encroachment most effectively by turning their relatively higher level of political and social disorder, and relatively lower level of economic development, into a strategic asset. Such states made unreliable allies, however, owing to the difficulty of controlling them. By the time Wellington came to launch the Great Game in Asia, he preferred Great Britain's Asiatic allies to show a semblance of political predictability rather than claim a military capability likely to prove illusory.

Wellington's recognition that British power in India must rest on management rather than force, and that the more effectively the symbols of power were deployed, the less often would the British be called upon to demonstrate their resolution, was most clearly illustrated in his acceptance in 1835 of the selection of Lord

Heytesbury to succeed Lord William Bentinck as governor-general. Personally he would have preferred Lord Fitzroy Somerset, thus breaking his rule that the government of India ought to be headed by a civilian, but he told Ellenborough that 'there are several diplomatic servants who would answer your purpose'.[24] The choice of an ambassador to St Petersburg who had been dismissed by Ellenborough in 1829 as 'a mere Russian',[25] for his refusal to see any danger to British India from the expansion of the Russian Empire in the Middle East, shows that Wellington was more sanguine than Palmerston of the possibility of monitoring Middle Eastern politics in cooperation rather than in competition with Russia. The Indian Empire would prosper best if nobody in Europe remembered that it was there.

The duke of Wellington's eight years as a soldier in India, when he drew on political as much as on military abilities, governed much of his thinking as a politician called in the 1820s and 1830s to help solve the difficult security problems facing the British Empire in Asia. His awareness of the political fragility of the Indian Empire, and that the Indian Army was better suited to be a police force than a defence against foreign invasion, pointed him towards diplomacy and trade as a substitute for strategy. Effective diplomacy would persuade Russia to give in to Great Britain's demand for recognition of an interest equal with Russia's in developments throughout the Middle East and Central Asia. The most important development to require British supervision would be the expansion of her own trade. If enough merchants travelled beyond the frontiers of the Indian Empire, the government of India might never again need to send soldiers.

Were these choices representative rather than unique? The further one travels from the Industrial Revolution into post-industrial Thatcherite Britain, the more obvious it appears that manufacturers and merchants never told anybody what to do. Or that, when they did, nobody listened. Innocent diplomatists and soldiers were not asked to perform courtly dances overseas to disguise the nefarious activities of traders. The rule must be turned about. In the nineteenth century the vocabulary of trade and prosperity was employed to disguise the nefarious strategic and political activities of soldiers and diplomatists, followers of Arthur Wellesley, first duke of Wellington.

Notes

1 P. J. Marshall, 'Looking at the defence of India', *Times Literary Supplement,* 9 April 1982, p. 409; M. E. Yapp, *Strategies of British India: Britain, Iran and Afghanistan, 1798–1850* (Oxford, 1980), pp. 2–3.

2 Ricketts to Hawkesbury, 6 November 1801, Liverpool MSS, British Library, Add. MSS 38237, f. 172.

3 William H. Springer, 'The military apprenticeship of Arthur Wellesley in India, 1795–1805' (Ph.D. dissertation, Yale University, 1966).

4 WSD, i, 126.

5 *Ibid.*, ii, 408.

6 WD, i, 235.

7 WSD, ii, 255. For details of relations with the Marathas see A. S. Bennell, 'The Anglo-Maratha confrontation of June and July 1803', *Journal of the Royal Asiatic Society* (1962), pp. 107–31.

8 WSD, iv, 55.

9 Springer, p. 137. See also Randolf G. S. Cooper, 'Wellington and the Marathas in 1803', *International History Review,* xi (1989), pp. 31–8; and John Pemble, 'Resources and techniques in the Second Maratha War', *Historical Journal,* xix (1976), pp. 375–404.

10 H. Clinton to R. Clinton, 30 September 1803, John Rylands University Library, Clinton MSS 218/7/52. For the military culture of India see D. H. A. Kolff, 'An armed peasantry and its allies', (Ph.D. dissertation, University of Leiden, 1983).

11 See A. S. Bennell, 'Factors in the Marquis Wellesley's failure against Holkar, 1804', *Bulletin of the School of Oriental and African Studies,* xxviii (1965), pp. 553–81.

12 WSD, iv, 383.

13 *Ibid.*, p. 221.

14 See Donald D. Horward, 'Wellington and the defence of Portugal', *International History Review,* xi (1989), pp. 39–54; and Domingos Oliveira Silva, 'Wellington and the problem of legitimacy in Portugal, 1808–1811', delivered at the Wellington Congress, July 1987.

15 See John Rosselli, *Lord William Bentinck: The Making of a Liberal Imperialist* (1974), pp. 147–51, 168.

16 See Douglas M. Peers, ' "He looked at India with filial affection": The duke of Wellington and the administration of British India during the Liverpool administration, 1819 to 1827', *Journal of Imperial and Commonwealth History,* xvii (1988–9), pp. 5–25.

17 WD, iii, 539.

18 See Paul W. Schroeder, 'The collapse of the second coalition', *Journal of Modern History,* lix (1987), pp. 244–90, and 'An unnatural "natural alliance": Castlereagh, Metternich, and Aberdeen in 1813', *International History Review,* x (1988), pp. 522–40.

19 See Edward Ingram, *The Beginning of the Great Game in Asia, 1828–1834* (Oxford, 1979), ch. 3.

20 Aberdeen to Gordon, 30 October, 8 December 1829, Aberdeen MSS, Add. MSS 43210, ff. 114, 193.

21 P. J. Marshall, *Bengal: The British Bridgehead: Eastern India, 1740–1828* (Cambridge, 1988), p. 136.

22 Memo. by Wellington, 21 November 1838, WP 2/177/62.

23 See Edward Ingram, 'The role of the duke of Wellington in the great game in Asia, 1826–1842', *Indica*, xxv (1988), pp. 131–42.

24 WPC, ii, 278.

25 Lord Ellenborough, *A Political Diary*, ed. Lord Colchester (2 vols, 1881), ii, p. 88.

John K. Severn

3

The Wellesleys and Iberian diplomacy, 1808–12

When Sir Arthur Wellesley began his peninsular adventure in 1808, he did so as a general whose only credentials were those acquired in five years of successful campaigning in India. In an England struggling desperately with revolutionary France, few people took note of Wellesley's accomplishments in the subcontinent and those who did thought the experience an inadequate test of a general's worth. Five years later, he left the peninsula as Lord Wellington, a hero to his countrymen and an acknowledged captain of genius. This transformation from obscurity to celebrity led Wellington's biographers to take a close look at the Peninsular War and as a consequence the war itself has often been studied solely in the context of Wellington's career. Hence, political and diplomatic events became subordinate to the military ones and the achievements of other participants paled in the giant shadow cast by the great duke. The Wellesley name itself is obscured by Wellington's omnipresence. In fact, Arthur's early career was inextricably tied to the careers of his several brothers and much of what he accomplished in the peninsula was made possible by the work of Richard and Henry, and to a lesser degree, William Wellesley-Pole. These brothers, in the years 1808–13, were in positions to determine Britain's diplomatic agenda in Iberia, and to influence the political debate concerning Britain's commitment to the Peninsular War.

The eldest of the brothers, Richard, figures most prominently in Arthur's early career; in fact, he dominated and overshadowed Arthur until 1813. He became earl of Mornington on the death of his father in 1787 but he made his reputation as governor-general of India from

1797 to 1805, becoming the marquess Wellesley in the process. He went on to become foreign secretary from 1809 to 1812 and very nearly became prime minister after the death of Spencer Perceval. He was never enormously popular but it was he who provided the political base upon which Wellington built his career. And it was Richard who sustained Arthur during very difficult times. Henry, too, was closely tied to Arthur in these formative years. The fifth and last of the brothers, he had a highly successful career as a diplomat. As Lord Cowley, he became ambassador in Madrid, Vienna and Paris. The least aggressive of the clan, he was adored and trusted by all his siblings. William, the second brother, inherited the estates of a cousin, William Pole, and took the name as well. As William Wellesley-Pole, he served as a cabinet secretary and earned a peerage as Baron Maryborough. He served as something of a family business manager and political watchdog when his brothers were on assignment.[1]

The Wellesleys worked together first in India, where Richard built an empire, Arthur tasted military victory and Henry learned the art of diplomacy. There they complemented one another, demonstrating clearly the Wellesley character, which above all detested disorder, and at the same time was self-opinionated, arrogant and very clear-headed. Richard, believing Arthur and Henry were the most capable men at his disposal, entrusted them with his most important assignments despite repeated charges of nepotism.

Iberia was the next stage on which the Wellesley brothers displayed their talents in concert. Arthur got his taste of the peninsula in the summer of 1808, when he went to Portugal to fight the battle of Vimeiro. The battle concluded successfully for Arthur but his super-session by Sir Harry Burrard and Sir Hew Dalrymple prevented him from following up the victory and he ended up as co-signatory to the controversial Convention of Cintra. The convention, which provided for the French army's evacuation from Portugal on British ships, produced an uproar in England and resulted in Arthur's recall to face a court of inquiry. The sudden shift in Arthur's fortunes did not surprise Richard, who had recently faced an unsuccessful parliamentary challenge to his India policies and realised that his antagonists were turning their attentions towards Arthur. Samuel Whitbread, an enthusiastic Wellesley-hater, wrote to the gossip Thomas Creevey: 'I grieve for the opportunity that has been lost of acquiring national glory, but am not sorry to see the Wellesley pride a little lowered.'[2] William Cobbett was more succinct:

now we have the rascals on the hip. It is evident that he was the prime cause – the *only* cause – of all the mischief, and that from the motive of thwarting everything *after he was superseded*. Thus do we pay for the arrogance of the damned infernal family. But it all comes at last to the House of Commons.[3]

The Wellesley brothers, realising the gravity of the situation, planned Arthur's defence. At stake was nothing less than the family's future and perhaps Britain's involvement in the peninsula. The family determined that the best course was to encourage a comprehensive and open inquiry – one going at least as far back as Arthur's landing in Portugal. A thorough inquiry, they hoped, would lead to Arthur's vindication; over Portugal, he had the least to hide and the most for which to be proud. William wrote to Arthur: 'unless the public mind is restored to health, you never can recover your place in the public estimation; and to restore the public mind, I am sure it is necessary for you to take the pains of having your conduct placed fairly before the public'.[4] The Wellesleys were victorious. After a comprehensive and protracted investigation, ending in December 1808, Arthur was absolved of all wrongdoing.

Arthur would now wait and hope for another appointment. His opportunity came in the spring of 1809 when he took command of the British expeditionary force after the death of Sir John Moore. The marquess followed in July as ambassador to the Spanish government in exile known as the supreme junta, then operating out of Seville. Arthur owed his resurrection to his ability, to Richard's influence and to his friendship with Lord Castlereagh; the marquess owed his appointment to his political collaboration with George Canning. In fact, he was sent to Spain as an interim measure until he could be brought into the Portland ministry. Whatever the reasons, their arrival in Iberia ushered in an extraordinary period in British military-diplomatic history which could justifiably be labelled the 'Wellesley' era.

Sir Arthur's second foray to the peninsula was to prove more difficult and more successful than the first. His primary responsibility was to secure Portugal. Expelling France from the peninsula was a secondary goal to be undertaken only if it did not compromise the first. But Sir John Moore's campaign had further politicised the war in England. Gone was the sudden burst of enthusiasm which greeted the Spanish resistance following *Dos de Mayo*. The parliamentary opposition began to view the Spanish cause as hopeless and British support of it as reckless.[5] Such pressure led the government to question its own commitment and the degree to which it could support the Spanish – militarily, politically and financially. Arthur, therefore, had to act as both soldier and politician.

He made quick work of securing Portugal with a decisive strike at Soult, then occupying Oporto. His attentions then turned eastward to his Spanish allies. Since Moore's disastrous retreat in 1808, the Spanish had fought on alone; now they looked to Britain for help. Wellesley, therefore, made plans with the Spanish captain-general, Don Gregorio Garcia de la Cuesta, to attack in concert the army of Marshal Victor. From the start, Wellesley and Cuesta got on poorly. But plans went forward and battle was joined at Talavera on 27–8 July 1809. The result was a costly victory and Arthur's alienation from Cuesta specifically and the Spanish in general. Apart from the difficulty he found in trying to coordinate strategy, what annoyed him most was Spain's inability to supply his army. In a huff, he separated from the Spanish and threatened to retreat into Portugal. Mutual recrimination followed as each side came to distrust the other. It was at this juncture that Lord Wellesley arrived in Spain and it became his task to re-establish mutual trust.

The marquess went to Spain assured his stay there would be brief. It would prove, nevertheless, to be a valuable one. Though convined that Iberia was the ideal place to stop Napoleonic aggression, he soon discovered that the Spanish would not be easy allies. He first saw that the junta government was precisely what the term implied – an extraordinary government, with minimal experience and an uncertain base of support. Given that the country was impoverished and the military ineptly led, the junta, despite good intentions, could not always deliver what it promised. The government was, in addition, strongly nationalistic, the result being that while Spain had to depend on Britain for sustenance, she was sensitive to anything which smacked of a threat to national sovereignty.[6] This was not a natural alliance; England and Spain had been drawn together not by mutual interests but by the presence of a common foe.

Lord Wellesley conceded that the state of the Spanish government boded ill for the Anglo-Spanish alliance, but he was confident that the Spanish will to resist existed, and the potential for success was ever-present. His first task was to calm Arthur, who had publicly vowed never again to cooperate with a Spanish army.

His handling of both Arthur and the Spanish proved remarkably restrained and realistic. First establishing close communications with Arthur so that the two could be aware of one another's intentions, he then turned to the Spanish, insisting that measures be taken to supply Wellington's army. The Spanish responded with a proposal which Wellesley believed was a step in the right direction. 'I am inclined to believe,' he explained to Arthur, 'that this Government is disposed to make every effort compatible with its powers, with the state of the country, and with the inveterate defects of the military department in Spain.'[7] Acknowledging that deficiencies might persist, Wellesley urged his brother to remain in his present position.

But while Arthur waited, his army's condition grew more desperate. 'Either the British Army must be fed and supplied with the necessaries which they require,' he wrote to the marquess, 'or I shall march them back into Portugal.'[8] At this point, the future course of Anglo-Spanish relations became clearer to Lord Wellesley. He foresaw the necessity of bringing about military and governmental reform; yet as ambassador his immediate responsibility was to support his brother's army and to maintain harmony within the alliance. Meanwhile, the junta began to panic over the military situation. Spanish politicians and soldiers alike were horrified by the British commander-in-chief's repeated threats to retreat into Portugal. It was widely believed that this would create an untenable military situation, since it would leave southern Spain open to French attack. This prospect aggravated the junta's already declining popularity.

Wellesley's task, therefore, became more complicated. Arthur wished to withdraw while the Spanish demanded at the very least an English presence on Spanish soil. In desperation, they accused the British of ulterior motives. Wellington, they said, was withdrawing because Spain would not cede to Britain the cities of Cádiz and Havana as a condition for military assistance. At the same time, the junta glossed over its failure to provide provisions and transport for Wellington's army, and accused Wellington of misrepresenting the situation.[9] Concluding that the state of the British army was as bad as his brother described, Lord Wellesley realised the army would have to withdraw to a point within range of reliable depots or face dissolution. But the nearest such magazines were in Portugal, and he believed that a retreat of such magnitude would increase Spanish suspicions of British intentions at a time when the alliance more than ever had to be preserved in good harmony. Rumours of a Franco-Austrian armistice were rampant in Seville. Wellesley knew the rumours had substance and that Napoleon would shortly be concentrating his energies on Spain. With the prospect of the Anglo-French conflict being fought exclusively in the Iberian Peninsula, it was no time to jeopardise the Spanish alliance. Wellesley therefore set about to complete a plan which he had been nurturing for several days. He hoped simultaneously to alleviate the consternation of the Spanish government without exposing the British army to unnecessary danger and to allow both parties the time and means to reorganise, reform, and do whatever else was needed in order to prepare for another campaign.

On 21 August 1809, Lord Wellesley sent a two-part proposal to the Spanish foreign minister, Don Martín de Garay: first, a 'Plan to enable the British Army to procure the Means of Movement', and, second, a 'Plan for the British Army taking up a Position upon the Left Bank of the Guadiana'. The plan was brilliantly conceived, given its rather limited goals. On the one hand, it would keep the two armies separate but within reach of one another. The British position would provide sufficient protection for Portugal and have the added benefit of protecting Seville and the left flank of the Spanish army. At the same time, their positions would allow both armies temporary means of subsistence while a plan of supply was being implemented. Writing to Wellington, Lord Wellesley explained:

> Viewing, however, so nearly the painful consequences of your immediate retreat into Portugal, I have deemed it to be my duty to submit to your consideration the possibility of adopting an intermediate plan, which might combine some of the advantages of your return into Portugal without occasioning alarm in Spain, and without endangering the foundations of the alliance between this country and Great Britain.[10]

To Wellesley's dismay, the junta held his proposals for four days before responding, and then suggested a plan of their own. Enraged, Wellesley wrote to George Canning: 'A strict observation of the proceedings of the Junta and of its officers, has convinced me, that I had formed too sanguine an expectation of their exertions, and too favourable an opinion of their sincerity.'[11] He demanded that the junta should act on his proposals and when no answer was forthcoming, informed them of his decision to advise Wellington to retreat. At the same time, Wellesley hoped his brother would proceed cautiously: 'The longer you can delay your actual passing the Portuguese frontier, the less will be the ill-temper and alarm in this quarter; that if you can take up your position within the Spanish frontier, it will be more satisfactory here.'[12] The junta made a desperate attempt to forestall the retreat by declaring its adherence to Wellesley's proposals but the marquess informed Martín de Garay that the retreat would continue. However, he assured the foreign minister that the bulk of Wellington's army would remain in Spain, near Badajoz, and, in an effort to re-establish British credibility, publicly and privately, he explained the necessity for Wellington's retreat.[13] Ultimately, Wellington withdrew to the Portuguese frontier, but the retreat came about slowly and was completed only after Wellesley convinced himself and the Spanish that it was absolutely necessary. While not all Spaniards were convinced, the public reaction was restrained and no irreparable damage had been done to the alliance. In this light, the marquess's negotiations were timely, and they contrast vividly with Wellington's. It was the difference between the experienced statesman and the young commander-in-chief; Arthur defended his army while Richard set the stage for future campaigns.

Meanwhile, this unfortunate postscript to the battle of Talavera had become common knowledge in London, and George Canning, in turn, grew discouraged, so much so that he became convinced that it would ultimately be necessary to abandon Spain. Writing privately to Wellesley, he explained that the best to be hoped for was to keep the British army intact, behind the Portuguese frontier. He saw in the Spanish nothing but ineptitude, and even suggested abandoning the alliance.[14]

Wellesley was not so disillusioned and avoided following his suggestions. Writing to Canning, he argued that:

> A relaxed state of domestic government, and an indolent reliance on the activity of foreign assistance, have endangered all the high and virtuous objects for which Spain has armed and bled. It must be now evident, that no alliance can protect her from the inevitable result of internal disorder and national infirmity; she must amend and strengthen her Government; she must improve the administration of her resources, and the structure and discipline of her armies, before she can become capable of deriving benefit from foreign aid; the matchless enterprize and skill of her most powerful, generous, and active ally, have been rendered fruitless in victory by the inefficiency of her own Government and army; and Spain has proved untrue to our alliance because she is not true to herself.[15]

But change did not come easily. The supreme junta's receptiveness to the ambassador's suggestions generally varied in relation to Britain's response to Spanish demands and the general state of the military situation in Spain. Success usually depended upon Wellesley's ability to keep diplomatic initiative in his own hands, but problems between the allies meant that he was constantly frustrated in his efforts to maintain that initiative.

Surprisingly, Wellesley did not initiate discussion on the subject of governmental reform. In mid-August, Martín de Garay, in private discussions, requested Wellesley's opinion of the state of the Spanish government. In a series of private meetings which followed, the marquess outlined his ideas. First, the supreme junta should immediately nominate a council of regency composed of not more than five members to assume executive power. Second, the junta should call a prompt election and assembling of the Cortes, the election to be superintended by those members of the junta not serving in the regency. Third, the junta should decree 'a redress of grievances, correction of abuses and the relief of exactions in Spain and the Indies, and also the heads of such concessions to the colonies, as shall fully secure to them a due share in the representative body of the Spanish Empire'. Finally, the regency's first act should be to improve Spain's military system. Apparently Garay expressed agreement with most of Wellesley's suggestions but an official response was not forthcoming.

Apprehensive, the marquess officially presented his suggestions to the supreme junta in a note sent on 8 September 1809. He informed the junta that the British army would not return to Spain until the military department was revised to cope with the various problems of logistics and strategy. This, he explained, could not be effected unless there was a correction in the executive power of Spain. And to employ the human and natural resources of Spain effectively, Wellesley believed it necessary to provide the people with a voice in government.[16]

The supreme junta, however, was not much interested in being hoist with its own petard and responded in vague and evasive terms. Wellesley's negotiating position was never strong in the weeks of September and October due in part to French inactivity and to the fact that he was attempting to negotiate the purchase of specie in the Spanish American colonies. Only when he intervened to prevent an attempted *coup d'état* did he feel he possessed much diplomatic leverage. The junta, however, remained recalcitrant. The marquess told Wellington:

> They were all gratitude *for an hour*, but *now* that they think themselves secure, they have begun to cheat me again. . . . I told Garay this evening that I would not trust the protection of a favourite dog to the whole Spanish army. It is some satisfaction to abuse such miscreants, if you cannot reform them.[17]

In October the junta, manoeuvring to conclude a treaty of subsidy with Great Britain, presented its own plan for reform. In the end, they would agree only to cosmetic changes and before these could be implemented, the marquess was recalled to assume the Foreign Office. Before departing, he tried to set Britain's Spanish affairs in order. There was a lengthy consultation with Arthur, now Lord Wellington, who had been busy constructing the lines of Torres Vedras. The result was a memorandum which reflected the 'Wellesley' view of Spain and Portugal. It called for a vast reinforcement of the British army, renovations in the Spanish government, and the consolidation of Spain's military forces under Wellington's command. A sensitivity towards Spanish opinion was apparent as was a realistic appraisal of British domestic politics. But at the heart of the document was a commitment to Spain. Following his conversation with Arthur, Richard wrote that:

> However the conduct of the Spanish government may increase the difficulties of cooperation, alienate the spirit of the English from their cause, and even apparently justify a total separation of the interests of the two nations, yet it must never be forgotten that in fighting the cause of Spain, we are struggling for the last hope of continental Europe.[18]

Among his contemporaries, Wellesley was one of the first to perceive the value of nationalism. Napoleon, he knew, sustained his power in France through the exploitation of nationalism, and expanded it throughout Europe through suppression of the same sentiment. He knew also that the spasmodic and ineffectual resistance posed by Austria and Prussia was the response of jealous monarchs, not enraged nations. The reaction in the Iberian Peninsula, on the other hand, was a revolt on the part of the citizenry, and the fact that it continued despite the repeated failures of Spain's armies, demonstrated to him, as it should have to others, the value of a nationalistic response.

Lord Wellesley took up the seals of office confident that the struggle against Napoleon in Iberia could be won. Assured by Wellington that

Portugal could be defended, he would focus much of his attention on Spain. To implement his policy, he counted on his brother Henry's presence in Spain. Wellesley knew from experience that the Spanish responded to the British point of view only after strenuous pressure. That there were few available means to bring such pressure to bear was obvious. Still, he believed that the negotiations could be greatly influenced by the strength and skill of the British representative in Spain. As brother of both the foreign secretary and the commander-in-chief, Henry would possess extraordinary influence. The marquess had employed this method of diplomacy in India, where he entrusted Henry with several critical negotiations. 'As his brother,' Henry explained, 'I would have greater advantages ... than could be possessed by any other individual in India excepting himself, and this was, I believe, his principal reason for entrusting this important mission to me.'[19] It was India all over again only this time the stakes were higher and the drama would be played out on the centre of the stage.

It was a curious and fortuitous occurrence that for three years the fortunes of Anglo-Iberian relations and Iberian independence lay in the hands of the Wellesley family. Between 1809 and 1813, they would, for the first time, marshall the British war effort against Napoleonic France on one theatre. They worked together in difficult circumstances as no other three men could have done to produce a relatively unified policy. While the marquess shielded his brothers from sceptics in London and promoted Britain's commitment to the struggle in Iberia, Wellington planned France's expulsion from the peninsula and Henry worked to keep Spanish resistance alive. The three trusted one another implicitly, allowing each of them extra-ordinary freedom of action at a time when decisions had to be made quickly and decisively.

Lord Wellesley sent his brother out with a set of general instructions reflecting the aims of his own embassy. To begin, Henry should do all he could to secure a change in government in Spain. In advocating the election and convocation of the Cortes and the formation of a regency to serve in an executive capacity, the marquess was really trying to accomplish two things. First, from a practical point of view, a change was necessary. Second, anything which appeared to resemble a liberalisation of Spain's political institutions could only help the foreign secretary's position in parliament. Next, Henry was to pro-mote fundamental changes in Spain's military establishment. The reforms he had in mind were sweeping in nature – from training and commissariat to the structure of command. Wellesley viewed these various tasks as all directed to the primary benefit of Spain herself. A stronger Spain would, of course, benefit England in her struggle against Napoleonic France. But the remainder of Henry's instructions were designed to strengthen England directly. Henry's first task was to negotiate with Spanish authorities for a licence to purchase specie from the Spanish colonies, needed not only for the support of Spain but for Wellington's Portuguese operations. Of long-term importance, Henry was instructed to begin negotiations for a trade agreement which would open Spain's colonial ports to British trade. The marquess knew from his own experience that specific instructions would more than likely be invalidated by rapidly changing political and military conditions, and so he did not burden his brother with them. And, while this might cause an envoy some anxious moments, Henry quickly came to appreciate his brother's foresight.[20] Eager to pursue the broad goals of his embassy, young Wellesley was plagued from the start by minutiae.

He arrived in Cádiz to discover that this ancient port was all that remained of free Spain. Late that autumn an ill-advised Spanish offensive had resulted in a series of disastrous defeats, first at the Battle of Ocaña and then at the Battle of Alba de Tormes. On 20 January 1810 the passes of the Sierra Morena were taken, exposing Seville and Cádiz to French assault. The immediate result of these events was the abolition of the supreme junta, the creation of a regency council and a retreat to the confines of Cádiz, on the Isla de Leon. Chaos ensued. The junta of Cádiz and the regency council had difficulty in defining their individual responsibilities, given the fact that Cádiz was all that remained of free Spain. Henry promptly stepped into the breach:

> The government too are following the example of their worthy predecessors. . . . owing to some misunderstanding with the Junta of this place, they cannot be prevailed upon to take up their residence here, but remain at the Isla de Leon conducting themselves more like the Junta of a miserable village, than the Regents of a Kingdom a condition to require all the energy and exertion of the most vigorous minds.

First he negotiated the transfer of the regency's headquarters to Cádiz from the environs of the Isla de Leon. Next, he convinced the regency that there were areas of responsibility which were distinctly theirs, particularly issues involving security and the military. He was able to arrange such matters as the military reinforcement of Cádiz and the Isla de Leon, and the transference of French prisoners of war and the Spanish fleet to areas of greater security.[21]

From the beginning, Henry Wellesley realised that negotiations with the Spanish would be difficult. Like Lord Wellesley, he would run up against the fact that despite Spain's dependence on Great Britain, she was tenacious over issues relating to national independence and honour. The presence of British soldiers in Cádiz, suggestions for centralising Spanish military command in British hands and granting 'privileged' status to British trade, all provoked suspicion. He wrote soon after his arrival that 'a party at Cádiz hostile to the British nation was endeavouring to instil into the minds of the lower classes of the inhabitants, that all the measures we proposed . . . were so many steps towards retaining permanent possession of Cádiz'. With the solid backing of his brother in London, he was prepared to deal with most circumstances, if sometimes only in a limited way. His primary diplomatic tool was the yearly subsidy to Spain. This subsidy, voted annually by parliament, was used to provide Spain with operating capital and to pay the costs of military supplies sent to the Spanish government. Most of the subsidy went towards the latter as this transaction was handled in England and therefore involved only the exchange of paper currency. The cash subsidy had to be paid in specie which was in desperately short supply. Whenever possible, the young envoy would respond to problems with solutions which, though expensive, would not involve direct payment of specie. This, however, was not always an effective expedient, especially in the more important matter of securing reforms in Spain's government and military establishment.

Meanwhile, Lord Wellesley faced a difficult situation in London. Severe economic stress coupled with the failed Walcheren expedition and latent pessimism over the Peninsular War made Perceval's government less than decisive in its prosecution of the war. As Lord Liverpool explained to Wellington:

> The expenditure of this country has become enormous, and if the war is to continue, we must look to economy. I do not believe so great a continued effort has ever been made by this country, combining the military and pecuniary aid together, as his Majesty is making for Portugal and Spain. The respective governments of these countries should be made sensible of the truth of this position, and should feel the necessity of making extraordinary exertions for their own support.[22]

Wellesley cautiously took measure of the situation confronting him, but he entered the political fray enthusiastically. The parliamentary opposition revealed its hand early, during a debate on a vote of thanks to Wellington for the victory of Talavera: ministerial ignorance and neglect and the nature of Spanish resistance would be issues on which the government would be challenged. What Lord Wellesley discovered in this first debate was that the government would only be in a secure position if it pursued a policy of openness. The more information it could produce, the better off it would be. To his mind, the government had done nothing to discredit itself. With a full-scale debate on the war in Spain a certainty, Wellesley urged the publication of the government's Spanish papers. Perceval, reticent and fearing the worst, advised against such a course. The marquess, however, was adamant.

> The moment is now arrived . . . we must satisfy both Spain and England that our conduct has been right, and that the causes of past misfortunes are not irremediable, because those causes are to be traced to errors and faults, which may be corrected, and which we are resolved to correct by the utmost efforts of our infuence. If the Spanish and Portuguese papers are to be suppressed, I confess that it appears to me, that we shall deprive ourselves of our main advantage in the conflict with the opposition. They will not be able to withstand the intrinsic and honest strength of our cause as founded on that information. But we shall be subject to every kind of prejudice, misrepresentation, and calumny if we refuse to produce evidence, of what we must assert.[23]

In the end, Perceval gave way and the papers were laid before the public.

But Spain's failures and her reduction to Cádiz heightened the current pessimism. The opposition, though willing to vote funds for the Portuguese effort, was less cooperative about Spain. Samuel Whitbread explained the opposition's position in the House of Commons:

> Spain has not done its duty – no matter from what cause – the people, had, however, some excuse – they had been under the selfish sway of an aristocracy, that only wanted to use them as an instrument to effect their own narrow purposes; their implicit confidence had been abused by the blind bigotry of an intolerant priesthood – a priesthood, that whatever it preached, practised not the gospel it ought not alone to preach but practise; they often had had the sword in their hands as often as the crosier – and that they had had, he feared, in their hearts any thing but the meekness, humility, charity, and peace that their blessed master

had inculcated by his pure precepts, enforced by the example of his apostle's [sic] life, and sealed by the last sufferings of his all atoning death.[24]

In simple terms, the opposition could not stomach supporting the Spanish inquisition and social injustice.

These debates were instructive. Wellesley realised that if he was to enlist support for the war effort he would have to concentrate on reforms in Spain's government. But while he could deal with this, he had a more difficult time with his ministerial colleagues' timidity. Neither Liverpool nor Perceval could overcome their fears of military failure in the peninsula, financial disaster at home, and political defeat in parliament. He could do nothing more than preach the wisdom of commitment on the first, but he could be more active with the other two. With regard to Britain's financial difficulties, Wellesley decided to procede with efforts to acquire trading concessions from the Spanish. As for the ministry's political vulnerability, Wellesley proposed overtures to Canning, Castlereagh and Sidmouth.

At the same time, Henry was playing his part in Cádiz. In March he had secured, after complicated negotiations, a licence to export desperately needed specie from Veracruz, and had initiated discussions on trade. He realised that these negotiations would be delicate in that 'the city of Cádiz is more connected with South America than all the rest of Spain put together'. But it was the Spanish who first brought up the issue. In early April 1810, Don Eusebio de Bardaxi y Azara, the new secretary of state for foreign affairs, informed Wellesley that the Regency was without funds and would require substantial and immediate assistance from Great Britain. Taken aback, Henry explained that such aid would have to be submitted to parliament, 'which would occasion discussions, which in the actual condition of Spain, it would be very desirable to avoid'. The Spanish promptly pursued another course, suggesting a trade agreement in exchange for an agreement on subsidies. Henry wrote excitedly to his brother:

> This is the moment for concluding a commercial arrangement with the Spanish government, which should be so formed as to make it easy to prove that, while it is advantageous to the interests of Great Britain, it is not injurious to those of Spain. ... I am certain that the Spanish government and Bardaxi are anxious to meet me half way in any arrangement which may have for its object the mutual benefit of the two kingdoms. I shall therefore wait with anxiety for your instructions upon this subject.[25]

The marquess, however, had different notions. Convinced that successful diplomacy in Spain required flexibility in the granting of aid, he was determined to keep separate the promise of British assistance from the conclusion of a trade agreement. If the subsidy were to be formalised by treaty, there would remain few incentives for the Spanish to comply with British suggestions. As it happened the issue lapsed, clearly proving Lord Wellesley's point. On 2 May, two Spanish ships, the *Algeciras* and the *Asia,* arrived from Veracruz with $7 million in specie thus relieving the regency's financial anxieties and bolstering its sense of independence. Discussions on a trade agreement were dropped.

Despite these initial disappointments, the diplomatic agenda remained unchanged for the Wellesleys. The heart of Lord Wellesley's peninsular policy was the introduction of military reforms in Spain similar to those in Portugal. Specifically, Wellesley called for the creation of a Spanish army of 30,000 men under British command. These soldiers would be raised, equipped, paid, and commanded by British authorities with no interference on the part of the Spanish government. The cost of such a project Wellesley estimated at nearly £3 million per year, a considerable amount indeed but less expensive than maintaining a British contingent of equal size. He realised, however, that he would have to obtain allies both in and out of government before his plans could be fulfilled. He therefore sought to enlist support for the Peninsular War through the forthcoming inquiry into the government's handling of the war in Spain, through the conclusion of a trading agreement with Spain, and through a general strengthening of the cabinet by the inclusion of Canning, Castlereagh and Sidmouth. In Cádiz, Henry, would negotiate for the commercial agreement and at the same time press the Spanish for political and military reform.

Though the Wellesleys entered into their projects enthusiastically and energetically, they encountered disappointment on many fronts. The first came at the opening of the parliamentary inquiry with the news from the peninsula that Masséna was laying siege to Ciudad Rodrigo. London newspapers responded with dire predictions of Wellington being chased into the sea – hardly the atmosphere for debate for which Wellesley had hoped. Nevertheless, the debate went on as he had planned and before concluding his own analysis of the situation, Wellesley reminded his colleagues:

The brightest prospect which had offered itself for several years of reasserting the independence of Europe, and with it the security of this country, opened at the moment when Spain magnanimously rose to maintain her legitimate monarchy, and to resist the most unprincipled usurpation of which history affords an example.[26]

The government emerged from the debate unscathed but Wellesley realised it would still have to be strengthened if he hoped to proceed with his ambitious plans. In fact, Liverpool informed him that even the reinforcement of Wellington's army would be impossible unless Spain aided by supplying specie. This was indeed a dilemma, with Liverpool insisting that Spain help with the costs of the British effort while in fact she could not support herself. Discussions with Sidmouth, Castlereagh and Canning were begun, but they yielded nothing, and the marquess found himself in a position of fighting to maintain the status quo while dreaming of an expanded effort.

Henry Wellesley's task in Cádiz was now to hold the alliance together while bolstering a regency council beset with problems. He was operating in an atmosphere of renewed anglophobia. An unfortunate article had appeared in British newspapers suggesting the seizure of Ceuta to protect British commerce in the western Mediterranean. In light of this, it is not difficult to understand why the Spanish began to suspect British motives in all that they suggested. More importantly, it played into the hands of Cádiz's merchant community which was determined to oppose the granting of trading concessions, convinced that they would only promote a British conspiracy to destroy the economic power of Cádiz. Not surprisingly, Henry avoided the issue of trade until emotions settled.[27]

There were, however, other problems. By mid-June, the Regency again found itself in financial trouble. Solicitations for a loan were renewed, and Henry, aware of the reality of Spain's distress, was eager to help. Because of Perceval's concerns over Britain's financial position, he proceeded cautiously, suggesting to the marquess that the application be given serious consideration. The regency's concerns soon turned to panic. Henry himself concluded that the government's financial position had deteriorated to such an extent that unless Spain received immediate pecuniary assistance she might be forced to terminate her military activities for the rest of the summer. Still, he took no action. By the end of June Bardaxi was again suggesting a commercial agreement in exchange for a loan. This too was rejected and Bardaxi came back with a moderate request for a short-term loan of $1.5 million on the condition that if London did not approve the more substantial request, the amount could be paid from the first specie received from South America. Lacking the authority to grant such a request, Wellesley again declined, but as time went on, he began to give the request greater consideration, concluding that the disintegration of Spanish armies still in the field would have a disastrous impact on Wellington. On his own authority, he granted the short-term loan.[28]

Perceval, already disturbed by the Wellesley family's willingness to commit Britain to projects which he felt the country could not afford, was horrified. 'I tremble for the effect of it,' he exclaimed and believed the occasion called for a strong reprimand.[29] Lord Wellesley disagreed and insulated his brother from Perceval's wrath. He simply advised caution.

Henry's decision led to more positive relations with the regency and he sought to exploit his new status by opening the subject of trade again. Thinking that any type of trade was better than none and that once started, it would naturally expand, his strategy was to suggest a type of circuitous trade with the colonies, which would go through Cádiz. The Spanish responded by demanding that British goods be transported in Spanish ships and that a trade agreement be linked with a treaty on subsidies. Wellesley retorted that Britain would not negotiate on this premise and unless the linkage were abandoned, he would send nothing on to London. Surprisingly, the regents agreed and Henry subsequently sent the proposals to his brother.

The marquess, for his part, was becoming desperate on the issue of trade. On 19 April 1810, led by the city of Caracas, Venezuela had declared its independence from Spain and had applied to Great Britain for support. Britain's military governor in Curaçao, General Layard, rashly entertained requests for muskets, ammunition and naval protection. The revolt did not catch the marquess by surprise but it did place him in a very uncomfortable position. Britain was committed by treaty to the support of Spain and her colonial empire. But failure to help the Venezuelans would probably cause them to turn to the United States or France. English commercial interests would never tolerate government assistance in suppressing the revolt, for it would jeopardise not only future dealings in America but also some existing illegal arrangements. Clearly, it was in Britain's interest that disputes between Spain and her colonies should be resolved peacefully. Meanwhile, Layards's response to the revolt did not comply with the spirit of the alliance and was sure to evoke a vigorous protest from Cádiz. Before a protest could be formed, Liverpool sent him a harsh reprimand and copies were sent to the Spanish embassy and Cádiz. But the larger problem of mediating on the dispute and heading off further revolts remained.[30]

For the marquess, the key to mediation was a commercial agreement between Spain and Great Britain since the immediate cause of the Venezuelan rebellion, in his mind, was economic distress caused by the sharp drop in trade since Napoleon's usurpation of the Spanish throne. The best way to eliminate the cause of revolt, and prevent the spread of revolutionary activity, would be for Spain to open her colonial ports to British commerce. Such a move would also enhance Britain's ability to support Spain. He was not so naive as to see economic conditions as the sole cause of colonial discontent, but he apparently believed that restoring favourable economic conditions would postpone further revolutionary activity, at least until the end of the war. He favoured an agreement which would permit Britain direct trade with the Spanish colonies, but he allowed his brother the flexibility of negotiating a circuitous trade for British ships. That was further modified in August to allow the use of Spanish vessels. The evolution in Lord Wellesley's thinking can be attributed to the fact that he had been paid a visit by two representatives from Venezuela, Simón Bolívar and Luis Méndez. The Spanish embassy protested against the meeting vigorously, reminding the marquess of his delicate position between Spain and Venezuela.

Henry Wellesley, meanwhile, attempted to deal with his brother's instructions. While he appreciated the new flexibility on the nature of a trade agreement, he was dismayed by the fact that Britain was offering Spain little in the form of incentive to conclude an agreement. In response to Spain's request for an advance of £2 million and a loan of £10 million, Britain offered only £1 million in aid, including military stores. 'If Perceval had taken a credit for six million instead of three,' he complained, 'he might have been enabled to assist the Spaniards effectively but the assistance they are prepared to give them will be of little or no use.'[31] As he feared, the negotiations quickly bogged down over the issue of financial assistance, and they eventually degenerated further as each side accused the other of faithlessness towards the alliance.

Wellesley had other issues with which to deal. The regency

government had found itself under attack from several directions, resulting in near political paralysis. It was blamed for Spain's wretched financial position, the deteriorating military situation, and attempting to open colonial trade to Great Britain. Yet what cut across Spain's political lines, attracted the attention and aroused the ire of the people were the circumstances surrounding the forthcoming meeting of the Cortes. Spaniards clamoured for the Cortes, originally scheduled to meet in March and then postponed to August. A second postponement to September made many people feel that the regents were delaying the meeting because the Cortes's first act would be their removal. The delays were a cause of concern to Wellesley, who, like his brother, believed the assembling of the Cortes was absolutely essential if Spain were to continue in the struggle against France. The problem was that the regents were being besieged by complaints from all sides over the method by which representatives to the Cortes were selected. The situation was further complicated by the intrigues of the duke of Orleans, who had mysteriously arrived in Cádiz and who saw himself as a suitable regent. Wellesley, therefore, opened discussions with various influential delegates to the Cortes, quietly working to negotiate existing problems and to remove Orleans from Cádiz. His steady diplomacy succeeded; the Cortes calmly convened on 24 September 1810.

The marquess, too, found himself in a difficult situation. Increasingly frustrated in his efforts to meet Spain's requests for arms, money and reinforcements, he became insistent that Perceval should strengthen his government. 'Perceval came and passed two hours here,' wrote Lord Sidmouth, 'but I cannot say that our meeting was satisfactory: Lord Wellesley's difficulties were the beginning, middle and end of what he had to say.'[32] Wellesley urged Perceval to bring Canning into the cabinet as soon as possible. The prime minister agreed, provided Castlereagh could be persuaded to join as well. Wellesley could not object to this, but to his disappointment, Castlereagh declined. Without Castlereagh, Perceval would not agree to a new arrangement, and for the time being the issue was dropped. Wellesley, sick and irritable, besieged by the innumerable complaints and requests from the Spanish embassy, perplexed by the revolts in South America, disappointed over the failure to strengthen the ministry, also had to deal with the reality of Masséna's steady advance into Portugal after the fall of the border fortresses of Ciudad Rodrigo and Almeida. There is evidence that he considered resigning at this time, but military events in Portugal, the summoning of the Cortes in Cádiz, and political events in Britain persuaded him to stay.

September 1810 proved to be a good month for the Wellesleys; on the 24th, the Cortes assembled amid hopes for more effective government and three days later Wellington defeated Masséna on the heights of Bussaco. Wellington's victory was particularly gratifying to Lord Wellesley because it confirmed in his own mind the reasons for Britain's involvement in Iberia. 'The wisdom of maintaining the war in Spain and Portugal,' he wrote, 'has been fully proved by the shade it has cast on the military and political character of Bonaparte.'[33] He believed that overall success could be achieved only when the peoples of Europe rose in revolt against the power of France, and he was realistic enough to see that such insurrections would not take place unless the possibility of success was clearly demonstrated. Therein lay the value of the Peninsular War apart from the importance of freeing Portugal and Spain of French domination. The opening session of the Cortes gave equal cause for celebration. The marquess believed that given the necessity of an interim government in Spain, a representative assembly would be necessary to overcome local jealousies and give it public support, but he was also sensitive to the opposition's demand for a liberalisation of Spain's political, economic and social systems. The Cortes represented a visible first step in this process.

He was, however, spared little time to savour this turn of events. On 15 October 1810 it was announced that George III had again slipped into the mental incompetence that had visited him several years earlier. To his advisers, it was clear that it would be necessary to establish a regency, with the Prince of Wales as regent. The prospect struck alarm throughout the Tory party and especially with Lord Wellesley, since the Prince's Whig sympathies ran counter to his own political philosophy and therefore to the family fortunes. Perceval sought to delay any decision on a regency and when he could avoid the issue no longer, brought in a bill modelled on that drawn up by William Pitt in 1788. Debate on that bill was to be long and heated, but in the end the government had its way.

With these distractions, the advantages created by the assembling of the Cortes and the victory at Bussaco quickly faded. British diplomacy became static in the next few months; Wellesley sought only to maintain Britain's existing commitment and to keep relations functioning smoothly. While he was certainly disappointed by this turn of events, the regency question also served to distract potentially hostile attention from the government's Bullion Report and Wellington's retreat behind the Lines of Torres Vedras. The Bullion Report recommended the resumption of payments in specie and the abolition of paper currency, which, if adopted, would have crippled the war effort. Fortunately, debate on the report was delayed until the regency question was settled and by that time Wellington was preparing to take the offensive and military success seemed within reach. Nevertheless, the report had a chastening effect on the government. William Hamilton, permanent under-secretary in the Foreign Office wrote:

> 30,000 men more would ensure success – but unluckily men are scarce & money still more so. The distress in the city (individually) is very great, & foreign (European) trade is at a very low ebb, & as if B. Parte [Napoleon] had the Devil's own luck, this bullion report has gone well nigh to convince him of the final efficacy of the measures w^h he has long been taking to destroy our commerce.[34]

Preoccupation with the regency question also shielded Wellington from widespread criticism. His decision to withdraw behind the lines of Torres Vedras was based on the knowledge that Masséna could not attack and that a dearth of subsistence would ultimately force him to withdraw. In essence Wellington believed he could force the French out of Portugal, without risking his army in pitched battle. His was a wise policy, but it was one which required time and patience, the latter a mood distinctly lacking among critics at home.

It was, therefore, business as usual at the Foreign Office with Wellesley continually spurning Spanish requests for increased aid, and trying to find a way to mediate in the revolts of the Spanish colonies. This situation was further complicated by the fact that the Argentine had joined Venezuela in rebellion, and that there were reports of revolts in other colonies. Wellesley, believing that compromise was the only reasonable solution, urged the Spanish to come to terms with the rebels, even offering himself as mediator. But the Spanish solution to colonial problems was suppression, and they would agree to discussions only after the rebellious colonies publicly conceded that their actions were a mistake and had restored the authority of the regency. Wellesley warned that Britain would not condone or assist any attempt to subdue the colonies by force and began considering a strategy to engage the Spanish in mediation.

Henry Wellesley experienced frustrations in Cádiz as well. The deliberations of the Cortes were not living up to his expectations. To begin with, the assembly severely restricted the regency's executive authority, and then, to make matters worse, passed a resolution prohibiting anyone who had signed Napoleon's Constitutional Act at Bayonne from serving on the council of regency. The act served to eliminate several capable people who were now staunch opponents of the Bonaparte regime. The result was the appointment of a mediocre regency council which included an outspoken anglophobe, General Joaquin Blake. While Henry was promoting reforms in Spain's army, the Cortes concerned itself with constitutional issues, often functioning as little more than a debating society. Even when he proposed the creation of a new Spanish army of 10,000 to be raised, trained, clothed, and armed by Great Britain and commanded by a British officer, the Spanish were uncooperative. Still, Wellesley was persistent and eventually secured approval for the creation of two new army corps commanded by Major General Whittingham and Colonel Roche.[35]

The Cortes, however, failed to make much progress on important issues, and, when it turned its attention again to constitutional questions, Henry's frustration turned to despair. When he suggested that the Cortes should address itself to the more immediate problems of war and finance, he was told that: 'it was in vain to call to the people to enlist into their armies until they are assured, that after they had risked their lives to secure the independence of their country, they shall return to live under a government the abuse of which had been corrected.'[36]

Despite his anger over these proceedings, Wellesley continued to assist the Spanish as much as possible, extending short-term loans when appropriate, directing British aid to its most effective use, and purchasing specie for Wellington. Here his relationship with the marquess was decisive in that he often lacked the authority to make such decisions. It is not suggested that he flaunted his independence. Certainly he often acted contrary to Perceval's wishes, but in so doing he was generally responding to crises which called for bold and imaginative responses. It seems clear that, in many cases, Wellesley's presence in Cádiz was decisive for the survival of independent Spain. Thus, though refusing to grant Spain the large sums she routinely requested, he continued to subsidise the government with small amounts of cash for specific projects or when he sought favours in return.

At this juncture the Spanish were forthcoming with very few favours. Discussions on trade ceased and bitter disagreement over military reform became common. Henry was becoming desperate over the issue of military reform as he had received word that Masséna had begun withdrawing from Portugal. Since Wellington would soon be operating in Spain, the question of coordinating allied operations was imminent. Accordingly, on 15 March, Henry formally asked the regents to place Wellington in temporary command of the provinces contingent to Portugal. Bardaxi's response bore the mark of General Blake's xenophobia:

> As the war in which Spain is engaged had from the beginning a national character, so decisive, as that there is scarcely an example in history of another war declared by the unanimous consent of a whole population, abandoned to themselves; and the free will of the said people, being its principal foundation, who aspire to independence, this will must necessarily suffer a very sensible change, upon the fact of seeing, that the command, although it should be temporary, of some Provinces, is confided to a foreign General.[37]

While the regents referred the request to the Cortes, that body had little choice but to veto Wellesley's request. The episode was instructive for Wellesley, since he came to realise that behind the developing acrimony between the two allies was General Blake, who opposed everything in which Britain was involved. In the weeks to come, he was to take every opportunity to secure a change in regents. To be effective, however, he needed considerable diplomatic leverage, obtainable only through the promise of increased subsidies.

There was, unfortunately, little prospect of that. Though the regency question had been resolved, and the ministry had the support of the prince regent, Perceval was still reluctant to commit himself to an increase in war expenditures. British public opinion was turning against Spain. Reports had reached London of the Cortes's nebulous debates on constitutional issues, annoying many Britons who felt that its attentions would be better directed towards military and fiscal reform. More annoying still was Spain's refusal to grant trading privileges. Another factor was Britain's predilection for Portugal, where Wellington was about to assume the offensive. Lord Wellesley's position, as a result, remained unchanged. The marquess by this time was beside himself with frustration. He had a clear vision of where his policy would take Britain but he lacked the resources to implement it. The placement of French power within acceptable limits, he speculated in the spring of 1811:

could be accomplished only by creating so powerful a diversion in the Peninsula as might enable the powers on the Continent to oppose the views of France, according to their respective means, so that France might be reduced to the alternative, either of relinquishing her designs in the Peninsula or elsewhere, or of making an imperfect effort in two quarters.

But Perceval remained cautious, and in his frustration, Lord Wellesley withdrew from his ministerial colleagues, treating them with scorn and seldom attending their meetings.

Conscious that aid for Spain would not be substantially increased, and of Spain's reluctance to follow his advice, Henry became more selective in choosing the projects which he would support. Specifically, he was prepared to support only enterprises over which Britain had some control, such as financing Spanish armies under British command and providing funds to Spanish armies operating in areas crucial to general military operations in the peninsula. In so doing, he was remarkably open minded, even advancing $60,000 to General Blake so that he might take an army to aid General Beresford in the siege of Badajoz. When crises arose, to Perceval's dismay, he resorted to waiving Britain's right to repayment of loans when the granting of new loans proved inadvisable. Writing to the marquess, he clarified his actions:

> I have frequently had occasion to mention in my dispatches the pecu-
> niary distress of the Sp. Gov't. It is now arrived at its full height, the
> treasury is entirely empty, the Gov't. has not credit sufficient to raise a
> dollar in the town, nor is there any prospect of their soon receiving a
> supply from the colonies.[38]

The second half of 1811 seemed to promise an improvement in Anglo-Spanish relations. Wellington was on the move, the French were on the retreat and rumours of an impending split between Russia and France were rampant. In short, the prospects for liberation were brighter than ever. Still, disagreements between the allies became more common, more acrimonious and potentially more damaging to the alliance. The issues of the colonial revolts, military reform and British aid were no closer to resolution than they had ever been.

The question of the Spanish American colonies was the most complex and bewildering of the issues confronting the Wellesleys. First, and most obviously, the rebellions were causing economic disruption in both the colonies and in Spain. Second, they placed Lord

Wellesley in an increasingly untenable position between London commercial interests and Britain's responsibility as an ally. For Henry Wellesley, the colonial issue further fuelled Spanish fears of Britain's ultimate intentions. Indeed, much of General Blake's success in spreading his anglophobia around Cádiz was due to the belief that Britain was encouraging the revolutionary activity. 'The irritation and discontent excited by these suspicions,' explained Henry, 'tend considerably to weaken the influence of Great Britain here; to retard the conclusion of any commercial arrangement, and to impede the adoption even of those measures, which I have recommended as necessary to the successful prosecution of the War in the Peninsula.'[39] The situation became even more complicated with the spread of the revolts to Chile and New Granada (Colombia). Lord Wellesley responded to the dilemma by insisting on mediation. While there is every reason to believe that Wellesley hoped to effect a reconciliation, it is also clear that a prolonged negotiation suited his immediate need to remove the colonial dispute until after the war. He soon discovered, however, that the two parties were far apart as to the points of the mediation, most significantly over Spain's insistence that Britain should assist in suppressing the rebellions if the mediation failed.

Sensing no prospect for cooperation from the Spanish, Henry Wellesley decided to pursue the outstanding issue of military reform on his own. The heart of his project was the one initiated by the marquess of raising an army of 30,000 Spaniards to be placed under Wellington's command – a project similar to that accomplished by General Beresford in Portugal. The Spanish could have no objections, Henry reasoned, if Britain assumed full financial responsibility for the project. If this army were then combined with those being trained by Whittingham and Roche, an army of 50,000, upon which Britain could depend, would be available. Wellesley acknowledged the high cost of the project, but thought the investment well worthwhile.

Though the mood in London was becoming more optimistic, the tight-fisted Perceval rejected the project. Henry, therefore, returned to his routine of waiving repayment of loans and subsidising small projects. But his spirit was beginning to break. Writing to Wellington, he explained: 'I think, between ourselves, that there is a very bad spirit prevailing here, and that it is increasing daily, and I am sure I know not what to do to correct it. I do not see how things are to go on here unless England furnishes some pecuniary assistance.'[40] In fact, anglophobia was on the rise, the newest rumour being a revival of an old one, that

Britain's ultimate goal was the seizure of Cádiz. 'In the name of the British Government and the whole British Nation,' Henry wrote vehemently to Bardaxi, 'I most solemnly and distinctly disclaim all views of aggrandizement, of acquisition of territory or of property either in Europe or America, at the expense of the Spanish nation.'[41]

But he worked on, establishing a military depot in Cádiz under the command of Brigadier General William Doyle, to train Spanish officers and soldiers to replace field casualties. The depot was to maintain a constant strength of 2,000 to 3,000 recruits, for whom Britain would assume the responsibility of supplying, arming and clothing. To this the Spanish did not object and certainly Henry savoured every minor success. But the major issues of military reform, the colonial problem, governmental decisiveness and revenue raising remained, and Henry could address them only through the exertion of constant diplomatic pressure. Unfortunately, the only pressure the Spanish understood was pecuniary.

The reality of the situation was that Henry Wellesley was on his own; Lord Wellesley was locked in a bitter political struggle with Perceval and had time for little else. In the summer of 1811 he started to work through the prince regent. At the very least, he hoped the prince regent would apply pressure on Perceval to increase the government's commitment to the war. In the long term, Wellesley hoped that he might take Perceval's place as prime minister.[42] While all of this was developing, Wellesley did meet with a Spanish confidant, Don Andres Angel de la Vega, who was about to depart for Cádiz to assume a seat in the Cortes. Their discussions were about designing a strategy to bring in a new, more pro-British regency council. 'The Cortes should take without loss of a moment,' Vega wrote to Henry on his arrival in Cádiz, 'the resolution of constituting a Regency, with competent and independent faculties to act, without being constrained in its operations, however, liable to be called to an account in due time.'[43]

Henry, of course, was enthusiastic about the prospect of a fresh set of regents. Blake's hostility, in particular, was beginning to wear him down. He and Vega met regularly in the next weeks but before long it became clear that the process would be both long and difficult. In the midst of all of this, Bardaxi informed Wellesley that the government planned to send a military expedition to South America to suppress the colonial revolts. Henry protested vigorously, pointing out that it went against the spirit of the mediation proposed by Lord Wellesley and

would detract from Spain's efforts in the war. Wellesley's anger was
further fuelled by the fact that Spain intended to send troops which
had been fitted out and supplied by Great Britain and would be
transported on ships which had recently been refitted in London at
Britain's expense. The marquess was equally appalled at the prospect
of Spanish soldiers going to America. He decided, in response, to
appoint three British commissioners of mediation and send them to
Cádiz. Then, either the Spanish would agree to sail to America to begin
mediation on British terms or they would be held responsible for the
failure of the mediation. While Lord Wellesley was really seeking to
buy time, he enjoyed being on the offensive. Charles Stuart, George
Cockburn and Philip Morier were nominated as commissioners and
directed to prepare for departure.[44]

In Cádiz, Henry, recently raised to the rank of ambassador extraordinary and minister plenipotentiary, saw no improvement in his
own situation. General Blake, beginning to feel pressure around him,
rallied his supporters to head off any change in the regency council,
using his most effective tool, anti-British propaganda. Henry reacted
calmly and continued with plans to create a large Spanish army for
Wellington and to build support for Britain in the junta of Cádiz. As
usual, his projects required financing; this time he dispatched his
secretary, Charles Vaughan to London to present the case in person.
Vaughan's trip was to no avail. He wrote to Henry:

> I am afraid that there is no hope . . . of obtaining larger succours –
> notwithstanding the liberal views of Lord Wellesley – and I have
> therefore ventured to state, that from such limited supplies and from the
> manner in which it is thought proper to grant them, no great expecta-
> tion ought to be entertained by the Govern't at home of a material and
> permanent improvement in the temper of the Government of Spain.[45]

The marquess knew that though this would come as no surprise to
Henry, his brother would be disappointed. As for other
matters, Lord Wellesley advised Henry to separate himself from the
issue of changing regents, believing that results would not warrant the
effort. Henry was to proceed as he always had done, dispensing what
aid Britain was providing with care. He had a yearly subsidy of
£600,000 at his disposal and it could be expended on anything other
than hostilities against Spanish America. He was 'to require positive
assurance that no similar misapplication of the British supplies shall
again be attempted'.

To Henry's suprise, on 12 January 1812, the Cortes passed a decree calling for a change in government with the hope that Britain would be satisfied with the new regents. He was subsequently informed that at least two regents would be of his choosing. His despair quickly turned to optimism. Even without an enormous increase of support from London, he could now count on greater cooperation from the Spanish government. On 22 January 1812 the Cortes announced the appointment of a new regency, consisting of the duke of Infantado, General Henry O'Donnell, Admiral Villa Vicencia, Don Joaquin Masquera, and Don Ignacia Ribas. Henry was delighted. The new regency, he wrote, 'promises to afford to Great Britain the influence which she ought to possess in the Councils of Spain, and to be productive of that change of system without which it is in vain to hope for a successful issue to the contest.'[46] His enthusiasm was enhanced by the news that Wellington had forced the surrender of Ciudad Rodrigo three days earlier. What he did not know was that the 'Wellesley Era' in Anglo-Spanish relations was about to come to an end.

The marquess Wellesley was no longer in a position to share his brother's optimism. By the end of December 1811, relations between Wellesley and Perceval had broken down and the proper course for the foreign secretary was clearly resignation. He was, however, encouraged to stay on until the prince regent was at liberty to change ministers. On 17 February 1812, he resigned as foreign secretary. But putting together a new ministry proved a difficult task and Perceval remained as prime minister until his assassination in May 1812. This seemed to open the door for Wellesley, but his premiership foundered on his inability to coalesce with the opposition leaders Grey and Grenville. It was Lord Wellesley's great misfortune that he slipped into political obscurity just as Wellington began the march which was to bring him everlasting glory. The road from Lisbon to London would pass through Almeida, Ciudad Rodrigo, Salamanca, Madrid, Vitoria and Waterloo.

Harsh criticism has fallen on Wellesley for his inability to get on with ministerial colleagues. It cannot be denied that he treated them with scorn and for most of this tenure, refused to attend their meetings. But while such behaviour cannot be excused, it can be explained. The fact is that Lord Wellesley took office assuming he would play a leading policy-making role in the Perceval cabinet. Perceval's desperate solicitations for his services in October 1809 pursuaded him that his presence in the cabinet was essential. Moreover, in the absence of Canning and Castlereagh he was, aside from Perceval, certainly the cabinet's most distinguished member. He believed also that Perceval and his colleagues supported his views on Portugal and Spain. Not only was he the former ambassador to Spain, but his anti-French sentiments had never been a secret, and in the past he had been vocal in urging an extension of Britain's effort in the peninsula. He doubtless believed that Perceval would not have offered him the foreign office had the cabinet entertained different views.

From the beginning, however, he found that his approach differed from the cabinet's. Spencer Perceval, by nature a cautious man, was determined to move slowly and carefully in all that he attempted, especially the war in the peninsula. He faced several problems: a tenuous parliamentary majority, a blockade that was beginning to weigh heavily on Great Britain, and a vulnerable military position in the peninsula. Later, George III's madness and the subsequent creation of the regency compounded his problems. He was not, therefore, willing to give Wellesley a free hand in the peninsula and in fact sought to contract Britain's commitment.

The marquess had little appreciation of the prime minister's position and ·was rankled by what was to him the timidity of the cabinet. For his part, he continuously pushed for an increased commitment in both Spain and Portugal in the form of money, supplies and soldiers. Perceval held back, fearing drastic political, economic and military consequences should Britain over-extend herself. The inability to act as he saw fit brought out the worst in Wellesley. Autocratic and arrogant by nature, he was not what would today be called a 'team player'. He liked to be in control of all things – to be the centre of attention. Moreover, he was something of an idealist and not given to compromise. As a result, rather than trying to work out a course of action agreeable to his colleagues, he turned his back on them.

In a strange way, Wellesley, though not cut out for a subordinate role, was the right man at the right place at the right time. At this very difficult juncture of the Peninsular War, when defeat was as imminent as victory, his uncompromising stand goaded the government into at least maintaining its level of support for Spain and Portugal. In the absence of the marquess, it is fair to speculate that Perceval, supported by his minister of war, Lord Liverpool, might have made a slight, yet potentially fatal retreat in the peninsula. As it was, the Spanish did hang on and Wellington had to beg, borrow and steal to support his efforts.

Though Anglo-Iberian relations, especially Anglo-Spanish relations, were always difficult, this was not because the Wellesleys' policy was ill-conceived or poorly executed. In dealing with the Spanish, they employed a maximum of diplomatic leverage, short of withdrawing British support. Henry Wellesley's appointment to the embassy in Cádiz was a part of this effort. Nevertheless, despite Henry's power and Spain's dependence on Britain, the Spanish remained remarkably independent. Though they changed governments three times at Britain's insistence, they were obdurate on key issues. Still, the Wellesley brothers were persistent and much of the credit for continued Spanish resistance belongs to them. And, because of their work, Wellington was able to maintain his army adequately while in Portugal, and find a smoother road on which to campaign when he entered Spain.

Notes

1 Basic family history can be found in: Iris Butler, *The Eldest Brother: The Marquess Wellesley, 1760–1842* (London, 1973); Elizabeth Longford, *Wellington: Years of the Sword* (1969); John Severn, *A Wellesley Affair: Richard Marquess Wellesley and the Conduct of Anglo-Spanish Diplomacy 1809–1812* (Tallahassee, Florida, 1981).

2 Thomas Creevey, *The Creevey Papers: A Selection from the Correspondence and Diaries of the Late Thomas Creevey, M.P.* (New York, 1903), Whitbread to Creevey, 25 September 1809, I, 89.

3 *Ibid.*, Cobbett to Folkestone, 9 October 1809, I, 89.

4 WSD, William Wellesley-Pole to Arthur Wellesley, 27 October 1808, vi, 170–73.

5 Parl. Deb., first series, xii, 106–7, 133–58.

6 Severn, *A Wellesley Affair*, pp. 46–87.

7 Great Britain, Public Record Office, Foreign Office, 72/76, Richard Wellesley to Arthur Wellesley, 23 August 1809.

8 WD, Arthur Wellesley to Richard Wellesley, 13 August 1809, iii, 417–18.

9 PRO, FO 72/76, Richard Wellesley to Canning, 24 August 1809; Wellesley Papers, British Library, Add. MSS. 37, 287, Richard Wellesley to Canning, 24 August 1809.

10 PRO, FO 72/76, Richard Wellesley to Arthur Wellesley, 22 August 1809; Add. MSS. 37, 287, Richard Wellesley to Arthur Wellesley, 22 August 1809.

11 Add. MSS. 37, 287, Richard Wellesley to Canning, 24 August 1809; PRO, FO 72/76, Richard Wellesley to Canning, 24 August 1809.

12 WSD, Richard Wellesley to Arthur Wellesley, 29 August 1809, vi, 337.

13 PRO, FO 72/76, Richard Wellesley to Canning, 15 September 1809; Add. MSS.

37, 289, Richard Wellesley to Canning, 15 September 1809; PRO, FO 72/76, Richard Wellesley to Garay, 8 September 1809; Add. MSS. 37, 287, Richard Wellesley to Garay, 8 September 1809.

14 Add. MSS. 37, 286, Canning to Richard Wellesley, 12 August 1809.

15 PRO, FO 72/76, Richard Wellesley to Canning, 2 September 1809; Add, MSS. 37, 287, Richard Wellesley to Canning, 2 September 1809.

16 Add. MSS. 37, 287, Richard Wellesley to Garay, 8 September 1809; Severn, *A Wellesley Affair*, pp. 75–8.

17 WSD, Richard Wellesley to Wellington, 19 September 1809, vi, 372–73.

18 Add. MSS. 37, 288, memorandum by Richard Wellesley, 4 November 1809.

19 Cowley papers, Great Britain, PRO, FO 519/67, Diary.

20 Add. MSS. 37, 291, notes from Richard Wellesley, 25 January 1810; PRO, FO 185/19, Notes from Richard Wellesley, 25 January 1810.

21 PRO, FO 72/94, Henry Wellesley to Richard Wellesley, 21 March 1810; Add. MSS. 37, 291, Henry Wellesley to Richard Wellesley, 21 March 1810.

22 Liverpool Papers, British Library, Add. MSS. 38, 244, Liverpool to Wellington, 15 December 1809; WSD, Liverpool to Wellington, 15 December 1809, vi, 441.

23 Add. MSS. 37, 295, Richard Wellesley to Perceval, 12 February 1810.

24 *Parl. Deb.*, first series, xvi, 10–11.

25 Add. MSS. 49, 981, Henry Wellesley to Richard Wellesley, 7 April 1810; PRO, FO 72/94, Henry Wellesley to Richard Wellesley, 7 April 1810.

26 *Parl. Deb.*, first series, xvii, 484–97.

27 Cowley Papers, PRO, FO 519/35, Henry Wellesley to Wellington, 9 June 1810; Add. MSS. 37, 292, Henry Wellesley to Richard Wellesley, 12 June 1810.

28 PRO, FO 72/96, Henry Wellesley to Bardaxi, 5 July 1810, to Richard Wellesley, 11 July 1810; Add. MSS. 49, 981, Henry Wellesley to Richard Wellesley, 11 July 1810.

29 Add. MSS. 37, 295, Perceval to Richard Wellesley, 14 July 1810.

30 PRO, FO 185/18, Liverpool to Layard, July 1810; Spain, Archivo Histórico Nacional, Sección de Estado, Legajo 5462, Albuquerque to Bardaxi, 4 July 1810; Richard Wellesley to Albuquerque, 21 June 1810; PRO, FO 185/18; Richard Wellesley to Henry Wellesley, 13 July 1810.

31 Cowley Papers, PRO, FO 519/35, Henry Wellesley to Wellington, 16 August 1810.

32 George Pellew, *The Life and Correspondence of the Right Honourable Henry Addington, 1st Viscount Sidmouth* (1847); Sidmouth to Bathurst, 17 July 1810, 27.

33 Add. MSS. 37, 292, Richard Wellesley to Smith, 12 October 1810; PRO, FO 185/18; Richard Wellesley to Henry Wellesley, 8 December 1810.

34 Vaughan Papers, Oxford, All Souls College Library, C:49:6, Hamilton to Vaughan, 8 December 1810.

35 Add. MSS. 49, 982, Henry Wellesley to Richard Wellesley, 24 October 1810; PRO, FO 72/98, Bardaxi to Henry Wellesley, 24 October 1810; Henry Wellesley to Richard Wellesley, 24 October 1810.

36 PRO, FO 72/98, Henry Wellesley to Richard Wellesley, 16 December 1810.

37 PRO, FO 72/110, Bardaxi to Henry Wellesley, 25 March 1811; Add. MSS. 49,

983, Henry Wellesley to Richard Wellesley, 25 March 1811; A.H.N. Sección de Estado, Legajo 5613, Bardaxi to Henry Wellesley, 25 March 1811.

38 PRO, FO 72–110, Henry Wellesley to Richard Wellesley, 15 April 1811; Add. MSS. 49, 983, Henry Wellesley to Richard Wellesley, 15 April 1811.

39 PRO, FO 72/110, Henry Wellesley to Richard Wellesley, 30 March 1811; Add. MSS. 49, 983, Henry Wellesley to Richard Wellesley, 24 April 1811; A.H.N., Sección de Estado, Legajo 5463, Apodaca to Bardaxi, 30 April, 25 June 1811, Bardaxi to Apodaca, 17 May 1811.

40 WSD, Henry Wellesley to Wellington, 26 July 1811, vii, 187.

41 PRO, FO 72/112, Henry Wellesley to Bardaxi, 5 August 1811.

42 Carver Papers, University of Southampton Library, Papers of Richard Wellesley ii, Political Diary, 1810–1814.

43 PRO, FO 72/113, Vega to Henry Wellesley, 4 September 1811.

44 Add. MSS. 37, 293, Richard Wellesley to Henry Wellesley, 30 September 1811, to Infantado, 30 September 1811; PRO, FO 72/156, Croker to Hamilton, 1 October 1811; A.H.N., Sección de Estado, Legajo 5464, Regency to Infantado, 4 December 1811, Infantado to Bardaxi, 5 October 1811.

45 Vaughan Papers, E:11:6, Vaughan to Henry Wellesley, 10 January 1812.

46 Add. MSS. 49, 984, Henry Wellesley to Richard Wellesley, 22 January 1812; PRO, FO 72/129, Henry Wellesley to Richard Wellesley, 22 January 1812.

Charles J. Esdaile

4

The duke of Wellington and the command of the Spanish army, 1812–14

The duke of Wellington's command of the Spanish army is perhaps the least-known aspect of a long and distinguished military career that has otherwise been covered to exhaustion. Yet the subject is too important to be passed by in this fashion, the acquisition of the supreme command of the Spanish forces having been a central goal of British policy since at least 1809. When the Cortes of Cádiz voted to offer it to the duke on 19 September 1812, it also seemed that a new era had opened in the history of the four-year struggle for Iberian independence.

Until that point the record of Anglo-Spanish cooperation in the common cause had been distinctly unhappy. In the military sphere the air had been thick with an atmosphere of mutual recrimination after a series of fruitless campaigns which had almost invariably ended with the British and the Spaniards accusing one another of betrayal.[1] Even when the fighting had produced a more fortunate result, as was the case with the campaigns of Albuera and Arroyo Molinos in 1811, the Spaniards had infuriated the British by arrogating to themselves the lion's share of the glory.[2] Meanwhile, in the field of diplomacy, relations between the two allied governments had been strained by the linked questions of aid, trade and the Latin American revolutions. After 1810 the French overran an ever-greater area of patriot Spain, thereby depriving its government of considerable revenue. At the same time, the outbreak of revolution in Mexico and South America had ended the copious financial support that had initially come from the Spanish empire. Increasingly destitute, the Spaniards naturally turned to Britain for assistance. Yet it was beyond the means of the British government to meet these demands, as it was itself very short of specie. To make up its own wants, it was constantly urging that the Spaniards should open the American colonies to British commerce, a demand in which it was encouraged by powerful domestic interests. Needless to say, the Spaniards could not possibly have contemplated such a concession, for they had always regarded a trade monopoly as the foundation both of their own prosperity and of the very survival of the empire. Nor were their suspicions assuaged by the policy adopted by the British with regard to the American rebels. Fearful – or so it claimed – that the *criollos* would turn for support to the French, and alarmed at the disruption that had been caused to the flow of bullion, the Court of St James sought to achieve a reconciliation between Spain and her colonies by offering to mediate between the two. Naturally enough, the Spaniards came to the conclusion that this was merely an attempt to achieve the independence of the colonies by covert means, an impression that could only be strengthened by the friendly attitude that was adopted by certain British representatives in the Caribbean and South America towards the rebels, and the refusal of the British government to promise military assistance to the Spaniards should the talks break down. Furthermore, it should also be remembered that during the long years of war between Britain and Spain before 1808, London had provided a home to inveterate revolutionaries such as Francisco de Miranda, just as a British expeditionary force had invaded Argentina in 1806–7. Finally, as if this was not enough, from 1810 to 1813 the Spanish capital was situated at the port of Cádiz, a city whose prosperity had been founded upon the American trade and which was possessed of a lively and influential press. In such an atmosphere the question of Latin America could not but bulk large and unhappily in Anglo-Spanish relations.

Underlying all the military and political disagreements, of course, was the historic enmity that prevailed between Protestant Britain and Catholic Spain, as well as a distinct sense of cultural rivalry. Arriving in the peninsula, British officers everywhere encountered a standard of living that was far below that of Great Britain. Just like many English tourists of the present day, they were shocked by Spanish dirt, cruelty and chaos. In searching for an explanation of their experiences they pitched upon the supposed defects in the Spanish national character, the duke of Wellington describing his allies as 'the most incapable of all useful exertion of all the nations that I have known, the most vain, and at the same time the most ignorant, particularly of military affairs, and above all of military affairs in their own country'.[3] As to why the Spaniards should have been so lazy, ignorant, vain, dirty, proud and quixotic, the answer was found in the influence of the Catholic Church, which was held to have retarded the development of both Spain and Portugal through its superstition and obscurantism, whilst at the same time underming the morals of the population; so profound was this idea, indeed, that some British officers even welcomed the Napoleonic invasion as having dealt a crushing blow to clerical domination. Never inclined to a charitable view of the Catholic Church at the best of times, Protestants were strengthened in their prejudices by the numerous clergy whom they encountered everywhere, who in their view were dissolute parasites and shirkers who should have been serving their country in the ranks of the army. At the same time, the peninsular army was universally bemused by the instition of the convent. Diarist after diarist is found to be unable to comprehend the monastic ideal, or to be convinced that most nuns were immured against their will, often at the behest of cruel stepfathers and the like. Disgust was mingled with romantic fascination, for the same writers often dream of rescuing the 'fair creatures' from their supposed imprisonment. Indeed, on at least one occasion, they actually attempted to do so: for example, George Bell describes how a group of his friends got very drunk one night and decided to liberate the nuns in one of the convents of Trujillo, only to be driven off by its redoubtable chaplain.[4] Nor were such incidents isolated: whether it is Leach and Kincaid pelting their clerical hosts at Robledillo with snowballs, Lawrence tricking the owners of his billet into eating some meat during Lent, or the officers of the Twenty-third Light Dragoons parading a mock bishop through the streets of Badajoz, peninsular memoirs and diaries are redolent with a malicious anti-papism that Wellington's strictures could do little to restrain.[5] Unfortunate though such behaviour was, it was hardly less wounding to the Spaniards than the messianism frequently affected by their allies, as witness the reaction to the numerous proposals that the Spanish army be placed in the hands of British officers.[6]

The fault was not entirely restricted to the forces of 'perfidious Albion'. Whatever special pleading may be made on its behalf, the Spanish army's performance on the battlefield was rarely distinguished. As the British moved across Spain, moreover, they discovered considerable evidence to suggest that the famous 'people's war' against the French had been considerably exaggerated. Guerrillas notwithstanding, it was apparent that the bulk of the population had taken no part in the struggle: hate the invaders though they might, they had done little to resist them and had merely tried to live at peace with both sides.[7] Yet paradoxically, when the Spaniards did go to war, it was in a style that aroused universal revulsion amongst the British. Just as the Spanish regulars failed to meet the standards set by Wellington's army, the latter was disgusted by the refusal of the Spaniards to honour the conventions of civilised warfare: picquets were fired upon, isolated Frenchmen murdered in circumstances of revolting brutality, prisoners and wounded massacred or allowed to die of starvation, and the very graves of the enemy violated.[8] It was, therefore, small wonder that off the battlefield the British actually got on better with their French opponents than they did with their Spanish allies, their frustration and disgust finding ample expression in the sack of the unfortunate cities of Ciudad Rodrigo, Badajoz and San Sebastián in 1812 and 1813. Once again, it might be argued that such behaviour was explained, if not precisely warranted, by the unfriendly reception given by the civilian population to the British, or by the failure of the Spanish authorities to provide the duke of Wellington with adequate supplies. Yet considerable evidence exists to suggest that the British were as often welcomed with open arms as they were treated with indifference and hostility, and that the Spanish authorities were as genuinely unable to meet their needs as they were unwilling to do so.[9] With some exceptions, treatment of the British seems to have worsened with experience, which, as Sherer, perhaps the most sensitive of the peninsula writers, noted, was hardly surprising:

> It is with pain that I am compelled to confess that the manners of my . . . countrymen soon wrought a change in the kind dispositions of this people. When they saw many assume as a right all which they had accorded from politeness, and receive their respectful attentions and cordial services as expressions of homage due to the courage, wealth and power of the British nation, when the simplicity of their manners, their frugality, the spareness of their diet, the peculiarities of their dress and their religious prejudices were made the subject of derision and ridicule, when they witnessed scenes of brutal intoxication, and were occasionally exposed to vulgar insult from uneducated and overbearing Englishmen . . . they were often very soon disenchanted, and the spirit which we had awakened in them manifested itself in various acts of neglect, rudeness and even resentment. The English . . . will not bend

with good humour to the customs of other nations. . . . No, whereever
they march or travel, they bear with them a haughty air of conscious
superiority, and expect that their customs, habits and opinions should
supersede . . . those of all the countries through which they pass.[10]

Prejudices, misunderstanding and sheer stupidity having combined
to create a most unhappy alliance, it would be foolish to pretend that
the appointment of the duke of Wellington to the command of the
Spanish armies could instantly dispel the looming tension. Yet as an
important demonstration of Spain's good faith and of the trust that
she placed in her ally, it might have done much to reassure the British,
and thus to ameliorate their scorn for their allies. By ending
Wellington's inhibitions about undertaking full-scale operations in
the interior of Spain, it would in turn have shown the Spaniards that
the British were in earnest in their commitment to the Spanish war,
and encouraged them to take a more accommodating view of Britain's
wishes on the diplomatic front. Far from realising these hopes,
Wellington's appointment precipitated a crisis in Anglo-Spanish relations that at times seemed to threaten the very survival of the alliance.
    The idea of some centralisation of the military command in the
hands of Great Britain was almost as old as the war itself. In the
aftermath of the Spanish uprising of 1808 political power had fallen
into the hands of a large number of separate provincial juntas and
petty military dictatorships, each of which had its own independent
army. It very soon became apparent that the restoration of some form
of central government was essential, but it was only after a convoluted
period of intrigue and negotiation that such a body emerged in the
form of the Junta Suprema Central (in 1810 this was replaced by the
first of four councils of regency). To the horror of British liaison
officers and Spanish generals alike, however, the new government
refused to appoint a commander-in-chief, arguing that the control of
strategy was the responsibility of the civil power. Events in the field
soon made it apparent to British observers that some form of central
military authority was essential, but it was equally clear that even if the
Spanish government had been willing to countenance such a prospect,
its generals were so jealous of one another that they could never have
agreed on a candidate for the post of commander-in-chief. As the
British had no intention of letting their forces serve under a foreign
general, the idea emerged that the command should pass to Great
Britain, a goal that was rendered all the more attractive in the light of

Sir John Moore's near-disastrous 'Retreat to Corunna' of December 1808–January 1809, not to mention the subsequent political furore. When the marquess of Wellesley was despatched to Seville as British ambassador in June 1809, the British foreign secretary, George Canning, therefore instructed him to examine the possibility of the command being offered to the then Sir Arthur Wellesley, although he stressed that 'this cannot be required'.[11]

In adopting this line, Canning was encouraged by developments in Spain itself: in a desperate attempt to save Madrid from the advance of Napoleon's armies in December 1808, certain un-named Spaniards appear to have suggested that Moore should be offered the command if only he would march to save the capital. In view of the angry reaction of the Junta Central to the British attempts to secure the admission of a British garrison at Cádiz, it is hard to see how this offer could have been taken seriously, despite the fact that the marquess Wellesley's predecessor, John Hookham Frere, was claiming that Britain's friends in the junta were eager to repeat it. At all events, its intended beneficiary was distinctly unimpressed, writing to Frere in June 1809 that, however desirable it was that he should be appointed to the command-in-chief, it was an object 'more likely to be attained by refraining from pressing it, and leaving it to the Spaniards themselves to discover the expediency of the arrangement than by any suggestion on our parts'.[12] Though the disagreement and want of cooperation that marred the subsequent Talavera campaign – which incidentally owed at least as much to Wellington as it did to his Spanish allies – confirmed Canning in his opinion that the command-in-chief was a desirable object of British policy, Wellington's retreat into Portugal removed the need to pursue the project any further. Although it remained a subject of discussion, the issue of the command was not revived until the duke had forced the invading army of Marshal Massena to retreat from before the lines of Torres Vedras in March 1811. Believing that he would soon once again be free to operate in the hinterland of Spain, Wellington's younger brother, Henry Wellesley, who had been appointed as ambassador to Spain in the autumn of 1810, proposed that the duke should be appointed Captain General of the Spanish provinces bordering upon Portugal, only for a storm of protest to dispel any notion that the Spaniards were ready to surrender their military independence.

Although the supreme command remained an object at least of the marquess of Wellesley, who had returned from Spain to become foreign secretary, this eruption did not lead to an immediate crisis. For the rest of 1811 the French proved able to prevent Wellington's army from advancing any distance into Spain. It was only with the capture of the crucial border fortresses of Ciudad Rodrigo and Badajoz in the early part of 1812 that Wellington was once again able to penetrate into the interior. By that time, however, the growing respect which many Spanish generals felt for the duke had brought a partial solution to the problem. As the British diplomat, Thomas Sydenham, wrote to Henry Wellesley on 28 September 1812:

> The fact is that from the respect and confidence which all the Spanish officers place in his military talents and . . . unassuming character, he now exercises almost as much authority as he could do under a regular commission from the government. All his wishes and suggestions are received as commands, and are obeyed with as much punctuality and zeal as Spaniards are capable of.[13]

Sydenham's estimate was to prove more than somewhat optimistic even in so far as it related to the army. As for the rest of society, there were powerful obstacles in the way of the appointment of any commander-in-chief, let alone the duke of Wellington. The national uprising of 1808 had unleashed a revolution led by the urban and rural *bourgeoisie*, supported by some elements of the clergy and the aristocracy. Although the aims of this coalition were often divergent, ranging as they did from a simple reform of the government to the wholesale restructuring of Spanish society, the bulk of its members shared a determination to overthrow the privileged position which had been enjoyed by the Spanish army under the *ancien régime*. Once the army had been humbled, there was great reluctance to do anything that might restore its influence, especially in the light of the knowledge that many generals harboured every intention of establishing a military dictatorship. Hence the refusal to appoint a commander-in-chief in 1808, and then in 1810 the creation of a general staff, the Estado Mayor General, as a means whereby the government could enforce its control of strategy.

The subordination of the army to the civil power was not the only strand in Spanish military policy, however. On numerous occasions in the first half of the war, the Spanish government had been deeply frustrated, not to say embarrassed, by its inability to exert any control over the operations of the British army. Time after time their allies had left the Spaniards alone to face the French, or failed to follow up such victories as had been won. Unable to comprehend so fabian a strategy, the regency was understandably eager to find some means of bringing Wellington under their sway. Henry Wellesley's suggestion that the duke should be given the command of the frontier provinces had therefore been countered with a proposal for a convention under which the duke would be commited to a prearranged plan of operations in return for a guarantee of all the logistical and military support which he might require. A year later another attempt was made to achieve this aim through the establishment of a *junta de generales* at Cádiz whose task was supposed to be the formulation of a plan of operations for the allied armies. Not surprisingly the duke would have none of it, writing to Lord Liverpool that 'the consequence of entering into such a convention would be that I should bind myself . . . to perform a certain operation even after my own judgement should have convinced me that I ought to discontinue it'.[14]

Given the fact that the Spanish generals were responsible to the regency, and ultimately to the Cortes, the Spaniards evidently came to the conclusion that by appointing Wellington as commander-in-chief they would at last have put an end to his autonomy. Nevertheless, the proposal would have remained unthinkable had it not been for the events of the summer of 1812. Following the great victory which he won at Salamanca on 22 July 1812, Wellington had gone on to liberate Madrid, which he entered in triumph on 12 August, whereupon the French were forced to evacuate La Mancha and Andalucía. Wellington's stock among the Spaniards shot up dramatically, and certain anglophile deputies at last felt able to suggest that he should be given the command. The growing support that they received amongst the liberals who dominated the Cortes was not only the product of a desire to gain control of Wellington's army. The Spaniards had only to look back to the events of 1808 for an object-lesson in the need for a united command. Exactly as had occurred in 1812, the victory of Bailén had cleared the French from all of central Spain, only for Napoleon to exploit the divisions in the patriot ranks to launch a great counter-offensive that came within an ace of knocking them out of the war. Meanwhile, the political situation in Cádiz also made it imperative that the liberals should do something to secure the support of Great Britain. The regency had just been thrown into considerable disorder by the resignation of one of its five members, namely the Conde del Abisbal. As Abisbal had been by far the most liberal of the regents, the balance of power in the government had tilted in favour of the traditionalist interest headed by the Duque de Infantado. To make matters worse, as usually occurred at any sign of instability in the government, the partisans of Fernando's elder sister, María Carlota, the wife of the prince-regent of Portugal, had begun to put forward her claims to assuming the presidency of the regency as the only member of the immediate royal family to have escaped the clutches of Napoleon in 1808. A fanatical absolutist, María Carlota was supported by the traditionalists in the Cortes, who looked to her to overthrow the liberal revolution that had culminated in the famous Constitution of 1812. Faced by the urgent necessity of forming a new regency to resist the conservative challenge, a number of the liberal leaders called upon Henry Wellesley to seek his opinion on the course of action that they should adopt. Determined to force the Spaniards to acquiesce in the appointment of his brother, the ambassador replied that he would not give any government his approval unless he first received assurances that it would immediately appoint a commander-in-chief of 'all the military operations to be undertaken in the peninsula', with the 'powers necessary to render the army efficient'. Confronted by this *diktat,* the very next day the Asturian deputy, Andrés Angel de la Vega, returned to Wellesley with the news that 'a notion would very shortly be made in the Cortes for appointing Lord Wellington Generalissimo of the Spanish armies'.[15]

The motion was duly introduced in a secret session of 16 September 1812, and met with little opposition, except from a group of Catalans who were concerned that Britain's growing influence in Spain would prove detrimental to the nascent Catalan cotton industry. They were soon overwhelmed, however, and on 19 September the Cortes voted that the command of all the Spanish armies in the peninsula should be offered to the duke of Wellington for the duration of the war. The conditions under which this offer was made are crucial to an understanding of later events. As far as the Spaniards were concerned, Wellington's role was solely to direct the military operations of the Spanish armies in conjunction with those of his own forces in accordance with the directions that he would be given by the Spanish government. Beyond that, however, he was to have no power either with regard to the organisation and composition of the forces under his command or to their supply, both matters having been placed firmly in the hands of the civil power by the Constitution of 1812. Yet to the British, Wellington's accession to the command meant something entirely different. In the first place, the duke certainly had no intention of letting the Spaniards have any say in his operations.[16] Nor were the duke's conditions limited to the retention of his strategic independence: for reasons that were as personal as they were military, the armies whose command he had just been given had to be placed in a state in which they could be put to good use. As Wellington later wrote to Vega:

> I am fully alive to the importance which has been attached throughout Spain, as well as in England and the other parts of Europe, to . . . my having been entrusted with the command of the Spanish armies. . . . But I have a character to lose, and in proportion as expectation has been raised by my appointment will be the extent of the disappointment at finding that things were no better than they were before. I confess that I do not feel inclined to become the object of these disagreeable sensations, either in Spain, in England, or throughout Europe.[17]

Wellington's determination that he be invested with the powers that he felt necessary to protect his own reputation and to turn his new appointment to advantage was reinforced by the result of the autumn campaign of 1812. If Salamanca had compelled the French armies to evacuate many of their conquests, it also enabled them to bring the full weight of their numerical superiority to bear against him. With his forces badly over-extended, Wellington was driven into a headlong retreat for the safety of the Portuguese frontier. The French were unable to follow up their advantage, but Wellington had still been in what he himself described as 'the worst scrape I ever was in'. Rather unfairly, the duke blamed all his misfortunes upon the Spaniards, whose armies had not been able to provide the suport which he had expected. Only a small fraction of the large number of troops which they theoretically had under arms had been able to take the field for want of food, money, clothing, footwear and transport, whilst those that did appear were composed almost entirely of ill-trained infantry witn neither cavalry nor artillery. Though some of the Spanish generals had done their best to cooperate with the duke, others had been obstructive and dangerously self-willed. Finally, even the much-vaunted guerrillas had proved of little use when it came to the conduct of regular operations. Yet at the same time the very odds which he had been forced to face convinced Wellington that, as he wrote to Beresford on 10 December 1812: 'It is obvious that we cannot expect to save the Peninsula by military efforts unless we can bring forward the Spaniards in some shape or other.'[18] In the mind of the duke, such an aim would not be achieved solely by accepting the nominal rank of commander-in-chief. Instead, he was convinced that his authority would have to be reinforced by political and administrative power of a nature sufficient to set about rectifying the army's abiding deficiencies.

Acting on the encouragement of Henry Wellesley, who assured him that the Cortes was still ready to grant whatever he should ask of it. Wellesley outlined his position in an uncompromising letter to the war minister, General Carvajal. After describing the many ills that afflicted the Spanish army, he declared that had he realised the extent of its problems, 'I should have hesitated before I should have charged myself with such a herculean labour as its command.' In order to remedy matters, he went on to demand certain powers that he considered to be indispensable, namely that officers should only be appointed to the command of higher formations at his recommendation, that he should be given the power to dismiss officers from the service, that the military budget should only be spent as he himself should indicate, and that the government should only communicate with the army through Wellington's headquarters, which should henceforward be the residence of the chief of the Spanish general staff. Wellington also proposed a complete reorganisation of the army's unnecessarily cumbersome and expensive command structure, but by far the most controversial part of his requirements concerned the supply system. In accordance with the liberal determination to eradicate the political power of the army, the Constitution of 1812 had deprived the military commanders of any power to intervene in the civil government. Though no lover of military rule, the duke believed that, given the chaotic state into which much of Spain had fallen, civilian officials would never be able to exert the sort of authority that they would require if they were to provide for the wants of the army. Convinced that his first task was to ensure that his new subordinates were paid and fed, he demanded that the military commanders should once more be invested with the civil power.[19]

It was as well that Wellington's intentions had remained secret: however apposite his analysis of the army's problems, his demands would still have been anathema to many Spaniards. Had his terms been known in September, it is difficult to see how he could have been offered the command. For the liberals who dominated the Cortes, it was axiomatic that the military and civil authorities should be kept entirely separate, for to do otherwise was to incur the risk of despotism. Nor had the liberals any desire to see Wellington rebuild the Spanish army in the same style as the Portuguese, as they not only regarded professional armies as the inveterate enemies of liberty, but also genuinely believed them to be inferior to a whole nation fighting for its liberty. In their eyes, therefore, Wellington's conditions were both politically dangerous and militarily counter-productive: they would overthrow Spanish liberty, and thereby undermine the popular fervour which acted as the motor of the war effort.

Yet the liberals, who were only a minority in the nation as a whole, were not the only Spaniards who were likely to object to Wellington's demands. It was not simply that the duke was a foreign heretic, nor even that his command of the army threatened to place Spain under the tutelage of a foriegn power. The country was completely unprepared for the brutal manner in which he had brought her face to face with the realities of her military situation. The collapse of the *ancien régime* had swept away all the restraints that had hitherto been imposed on the Spanish press, with the result that the war had witnessed a tremendous upsurge in the number of newspapers and periodicals. Their contribution to the struggle had not been entirely negative, for the unfailing optimism of their editors had helped to keep a spirit of resistance alive even in the darkest days of the war. Yet by the same token they had done little to inform the public of the real ills of Spain's situation. Not all Spaniards were so insouciant, but it was clearly going to be difficult to persuade public opinion of the need to invest the duke with such sweeping powers. Matters were particularly delicate with regard to the army itself, for whom his appointment could be construed as a calculated insult. Though many officers were threatened by the proposed reforms, the damage to their *amour propre* was far more significant. Indeed, the commander of the Fourth Army, General Francisco López Ballesteros, was so angry that he 'pronounced' against the government by writing an open letter of protest to the war minister in the hope of persuading his fellow commanders to veto the appointment. In the event none of them showed any willingness to follow his lead, and Ballesteros was arrested and banished to the penal colony of Ceuta. Nevertheless, the controversy that ensued showed that he was not without his supporters, both inside and outside the army: not only were numerous pamphlets published in support of the rebel general, but the governor of Ceuta treated him more as an honoured guest than as a prisoner.

The French reoccupation of Madrid having dealt a grievous blow to Wellington's prestige, it would perhaps have been advisable to tread carefully. Yet when the duke visited Cádiz to finalise the details of his appointment towards the end of December, he made no attempt to moderate his demands, and threatened to refuse the command unless all his conditions were granted. It is impossible to determine what would have occurred had the Spaniards called his bluff, but in the event Wellington's threatening behaviour paid off: by the time of the duke's departure on 9 January 1813, the regency and the Cortes had between them agreed that no generals would be appointed to the command of higher formations without the government's having first consulted his opinion, that all communications with the army should pass through his headquarters, that he should have control of the military budget and the power to suspend such officers as failed to meet his standards, that both the structure of the army and its supply system should be reorganised along the lines he had suggested, that 90 per cent of the revenue should be devoted to the upkeep of the army, and that the civil power should be subordinated to the military authorities in those matters pertaining to the conduct of the war.

Armed with these powers Wellington set about, as he put it, 'bringing forward the Spaniards in some shape or other'. Amongst other measures he reduced the number of soldier-servants that were allowed to each officer, and engaged in a long correspondence with General Castaños and the Conde del Abisbal with regard to the reorganisation of the Spanish infantry with a view both to reducing the number of regiments (and thus making a more cost-effective use of such soldiers as were available) and to keeping the ranks up to strength. For the most part, however, Wellington did not directly intervene in the organisation or regulation of the Spanish forces. Nor did he make any attempt to place them under the command of British officers. Instead, he was prepared to leave them as they were in the firm belief that the measures that he had taken to ensure that the Spaniards received adequate logistical support would in themselves be enough to enable them to take the field. These hopes, however, were soon to be disappointed. In the first place, Wellington seems simply to have underestimated the sheer scale of the chaos into which Spain had fallen since 1808. Such areas of the country as had been liberated from the invaders were in a state of complete devastation, especially as the retreat of the French had everywhere been marked by the destruction of whatever supplies the invaders had not been able to carry with them. In addition, the countryside was infested with large numbers of bandits, amongst whom were numbered, be it said, many erstwhile guerrillas. Space does not allow for a detailed discussion of this subject, but it is apparent that from the earliest days of the 'little war' against the French personal gain had been a major motive in the minds of many of its participants. Indeed, a certain number of the *partidas* had never been formed of guerrillas at all, but of bandits and deserters who preyed upon both sides equally. With the retreat of the French, the incidence of crime became that much more marked. Once the invaders had been cleared from a given province, the patriotic course for its guerrillas would have been either to follow the retreating enemy to fresh scenes of harrassment, or to have incorporated themselves into the regular army, either as individual volunteers or in formed units. A number of guerrilla regiments, such as Julián Sánchez's Lanceros de Castilla, were added to the regular army, but many bands simply turned to banditry, whilst those units that were taken into the order of battle seem to have suffered a high rate of desertion.

In coping with these problems, it has to be said that Wellington did not have the whole-hearted cooperation of the Spanish government. The decision to subordinate the civil authorities to the Captains General had certainly contravened the spirit, if not the letter, of the Constitution of 1812, and had aroused a storm of protest among extreme anglophobes and liberals. Furthermore, as the tide of warfare finally began to turn against Napoleon, so the Spaniards began to acquire a greater measure of self-confidence. Not only did the allied resurgence in the rest of Europe offer them the hope of Napoleon's downfall, but they considered that they themselves bore the chief share of the glory: in response to the idea that the Spanish struggle had reanimated the rest of the continent, articles began to appear acclaiming Spain as 'the liberator of Europe'.[20] As if this was not enough, the Russian campaign seemed to offer one more proof of the efficacy of the 'people's war' so beloved by the liberals. As 1813 wore on so the British came under ever-greater criticism, particularly as fresh factors emerged to stimulate Spanish anglophobia. For example, when months went by without any advance on the part of the Anglo-Portuguese army, it was claimed that the British were needlessly prolonging the war to undermine Spain's position in the world. Similarly, nothing could have been more calculated to upset the liberals than a foolish plan that was foisted upon Wellington by a British secret agent to introduce a Russian expeditionary force into the peninsula. Most damagingly of all, a rumour spread that a plot was afoot to make him King Arthur the First of Spain.[21]

Thus fortified, the Spanish government found itself able to revenge itself upon the duke for the over-bearing tactics which he had employed at Cádiz. Having only made the concessions that he had demanded under duress, it was only natural that the regency should have attempted to restrict their scope, and in particular to delay the implementation of the various practical reforms that had been agreed with regard to the supply of the army. Spanish bankruptcy and exhaustion were such that it must be doubted whether these ever could have made any real difference, but the fact remains that the army's logistical problems remained unresolved. Left with little more Spanish support than he had received the previous year, it is hard to see how Wellington could ever have liberated Spain had it not been for the guerrillas. At the very same time that the sometime guerrillas of Andalucía and the Castiles were causing such havoc in the areas that had been wrested from French control, their counterparts in northern Spain were attaining their maximum effectiveness. Formed into regular units and equipped with light artillery pieces, they became such formidable opponents that the Emperor ordered a large part of the forces that had been containing Wellington in the western marches to join the struggle against them. By doing so he opened the way for a fresh offensive, which this time culminated in the decisive battle of Vitoria, and the eviction of the French from what remained of their conquests.

Paradoxically, as the duke of Wellington rendered patriot Spain ever-more secure, so the potential for a crisis in Anglo-Spanish relations grew ever greater. With the French armies in full retreat, there was less reason why Wellington should retain the command. If the regency did not actually become committed to provoking the duke's resignation, it certainly showed few inhibitions with regard to actions that might incur his displeasure. Relations between the two were at a low ebb for most of the first half of 1813. Already angered by the Spanish government's attempts to sabotage his logistical arrangements, Wellington had been further provoked by its attempts to interfere in the military command. The regency that had been in power when Wellington had been offered the command was essentially reactionary in its politics, whereas the Cortes had continued to be dominated by the liberals. Early in 1813 rumours began to spread that its president, the Duque de Infantado, was planning to overthrow the assembly by force. Whether or not this was actually the case, on a variety of pretexts the regency ordered a number of regiments to move to the vicinity of Cádiz and appointed a general loyal to itself to their command. However, on 8 March it was itself voted out of office by the Cortes, and a new regency established that was wholly in thrall to the liberals. In order to ensure that the constitutional system was not imperilled again, the new regency went on to declare the establishment of a new Captain Generalcy at Cádiz whose commander, the noted liberal, Cayetano Valdés, was placed solely at its own orders.

Though none of these intrigues were primarily directed at the duke of Wellington, the actions of both regencies had contravened the conditions under which he had accepted the command. He was soon threatening to resign, but the Spaniards showed no signs of heeding his anger. On the contrary, in June 1813 the regency dismissed two of the duke's most loyal Spanish subordinates, Generals Castaños and Girón for their suspected connections with the traditionalist opposition that had been aroused by the Cortes' abolition of the Inquisition. Wellington could not object to this action in itself, for he had never aspired to a veto on the dismissal of generals. What he did seize upon, by contrast, was the government's appointment of two new generals to replace those who had been dismissed. An angry correspondence ensued, but the Spaniards would not give way, with the result that on 30 August 1813, Wellington formally resigned the command on the understanding that he would continue to exercise it until such time as his resignation had been formally accepted by the Cortes.[22]

Matters were still in this state when events at the front once more intervened to disturb the course of Anglo-Spanish relations. On 31 August 1813, the Anglo-Portuguese army had stormed the city of San Sebastián which was then thoroughly sacked. In the course of these events the city caught fire and was burnt to the ground. Understandably, the Spanish reaction was one of complete revulsion, particularly as supporters of the government and anglophobes of every stamp lost no time in spreading the most lurid propaganda with regard to the atrocities committed by the British, even going so far as to allege that Wellington had ordered the city's destruction to remove it as a threat to British commerce.[23] Demonstrably farcical as these allegations were, they probably did less harm to Wellington's cause than they did good: at all events, the Cortes eventually voted to confirm the duke as commander-in-chief with the full powers that it had been agreed that he should have during his visit to Cádiz in December 1812. Yet the campaign against his authority had not been without its effects. Encouraged by the obvious hostility of the regency, the authorities in

northern Spain had in many places withdrawn their cooperation from
the allied army, refusing to provide it with transport, billets, store-
houses and hospitals. Even the supply route to the Pyrenean front was
not sacrosanct: customs officials insisted on searching the cargoes of
allied ships for contraband, and the major staging post of Santander
was placed in quarantine after dubious allegations were made that the
British hospital there was suffering from a dangerous epidemic.[24]

Meanwhile trouble had also erupted in the army. For the most part
such Spaniards as actually reached the front in 1813 fought very well:
indeed, on the very day that the Anglo-Portuguese had been wreaking
such havoc at San Sebastian, an outnumbered Spanish force had
gained a considerable victory over Marshal Soult at San Marcial. Yet
the Spaniards continued to be looked down upon by many of their
allies, whilst they received no reward for their efforts. Once they had
reached the Pyrenees, moreover, their tenuous logistical system broke
down under the strain of attempting to feed large numbers of troops in
a mountainous region whose scarce resources were also the prey of
two other armies. To feed themselves the Spanish soldiery had no
option but to pillage the countryside, an activity in which they were
encouraged once they were across the frontier by a natural desire to
revenge themselves upon the French for all the evils that had befallen
Spain since 1808. Fearing that he would himself have to face a
guerrilla war of the type that had so crippled his opponents, in the
middle of November Wellington ordered that almost all the Spanish
troops attached to his army should be sent into cantonments in Spain.
When the few that he retained continued to misbehave, they were
severely disciplined. Denied the glory to which they felt themselves
entitled, irritated at the superior demeanour of their allies, and convinced that their troops were being deliberately humiliated, the
Spanish generals were furious.[25]

By the end of 1813, Anglo-Spanish relations were in a state of crisis.
At root the alliance remained intact, as witness the Spaniards'
indignant rejection of Napoleon's efforts to offer them a separate
peace in exchange for the release of the imprisoned Fernando VII. Yet
the situation became grave enough for Wellington seriously to have
considered overthrowing the Spanish government. In moving against
the government, of course, Wellington was also moving against the
liberals, there being ample evidence to suggest that he hated the
Spanish revolution. Barely one month after the opening of the Cortes
of Cádiz in September 1810, he had written to Henry Wellesley, 'I am

apprehensive that the Cortes are becoming a national assembly, and they will ruin the cause!'[26] Nor did his opinion improve as the war went on. After his visit to Cádiz at the end of 1812, for example, he had written several letters denouncing the Constitution of 1812, in part on the grounds of its supposed impracticality but chiefly because it failed to provide any protection for private property, and especially the property of the aristocracy. The result could only be mob rule, which he already professed to see in Cádiz. Not only did this conjure up nightmarish visions of another jacobin revolution, but it would materially interfere with the conduct of the war – in marked contrast to his liberal opponents in Cádiz, the duke refused to believe that popular fervour could form the motor of the war effort; indeed, if anything, he believed enthusiasm to be antithetical to military success. Finally, like many Spanish conservatives, Wellington could not see the relevance of the liberals' stress upon political reform to the struggle against the French. Stung by the constant opposition to his command, in July 1813 he complained to Lord William Bentinck, 'Neither the government nor Cortes appear to care much about the foreign wars. . . . All that they care about is the praise of their stupid constitution and how to carry on the war against the bishops and the priests.'[27]

All these factors convinced Wellington that it was essential for the British government 'to discountenance by every means in their power the democratical principles and measures of the Cortes'.[28] It is clear from the tenor of his correspondence that he would have liked to strike a direct blow against the Cádiz régime, but prudence dictated other-wise. The most obvious means of ousting the liberals would have been for the British to have thrown their weight behind the conservative opposition, but Wellington judged that to do so would be fatal, for the Spaniards were so jealous of foreign intervention that to have inter-vened on behalf of reaction would have been to condemn it to instant failure. Though urged by the secretary of state for war and the colonies, Lord Bathurst, to pursue this very course, the duke advised the British government to remain neutral, and consistently rebuffed the attempts of the Spanish conservatives to win his support. In adopting this policy, however, Wellington had no intention simply of submitting to the liberals. On the contrary, it is apparent that he believed that the 'violent and democratical principles' espoused by the liberals would sooner or later provoke a civil war, whose outbreak 'would be the time for the British government to come forward, particularly if its support or its opinion should be asked for'.[29]

Though initially ready to wait on events, the duke was goaded beyond endurance by the events of the autumn of 1813. Claiming that a breach between Britain and Spain was inevitable under the latter's existing government, Wellington suggested that Britain should threaten to withdraw from the peninsula in the hope that this might provoke the population – which he believed to be firmly pro-British – to rise up against the regency and Cortes and install a friendlier régime at Cádiz.[30] The proposal was never adopted, it was not long before Napoleon's release of Fernando VII had achieved a similar effect. When the king returned to Spain in the spring of 1814, he very soon realised that the opposition to the liberals was so strong that there was no need to swear allegiance to the Constitution of 1812. Provided with an army by the 'pronunciation' of the Spanish forces in eastern Spain in favour of the restoration of absolutism, Fernando sent his troops to occupy Madrid, and had soon secured the dissolution of the Cortes and the arrest of many leading liberals (10–11 May 1814). By this time, of course, the Duke of Wellington was far away in France so that he was at first spared the need to play a direct role in the crisis. It so happened, however, that the Spanish forces who were attached to his army were reputed to be less disaffected than those who had been left behind in Spain, whilst they were also commanded by men who were sympathetic to the liberals. As a result rumours soon spread that they were planning a counter-coup. The idea seems distinctly far-fetched, but Wellington certainly took the possibility seriously enough to take action to ensure that no such event took place. The Spanish troops in France therefore remained quiescent, leaving Fernando to enjoy his triumph in peace. The Spanish revolution was over, and Wellington had, in the words of Brian Hamnett, 'ratified' its downfall.[31]

To conclude, it is impossible to pretend that Wellington's command of the Spanish army was the greatest success of his career. Not only was he unable to extract much profit from his appointment in the military sense, but he presided over a dramatic deterioration in Anglo-Spanish relations. Conflict was inevitable from the very moment that the duke was offered the command, for the conditions which he played upon his acceptance simply could not be accommodated within the political system that had emerged in patriot Spain. If the liberals were suspicious of both military power and foreign influence, Wellington despised the constitution which they had created. Furthermore, whereas the duke regarded popular enthusiasm as anathema, for the liberals it was the most important weapon in their armoury. At the same time, unreasonable and intransigent though the Spaniards may have been, Wellington's character was not calculated to assuage their pride, which was wounded by the very presence of a foreign general at the head of the armed forces. His habitually haughty and intolerant behaviour may have been acceptable in his dealings with his own army, but it was unsuited to the conduct of relations with an allied power. As time wore on there are signs that Wellington became more aware of the sensibilities of his Spanish subordinates – hence his decision not to relieve the beleaguered defenders of San Marcial with British troops – but in so far as his relationship with the Cádiz régime is concerned, it must be said that his prescience was not matched by a realisation that politics was the art of the possible. Yet during the Waterloo campaign and the subsequent allied occupation of France, the duke proved to be an able diplomatist and coalition general. The contrast is so glaring that we are forced to conclude that in reflecting upon his Spanish command, Wellington came to the same conclusion which he reached about his first taste of military experience in Flanders in 1794: 'Why – I learnt what one ought not to do and that is always something.'[32]

Notes

1 E.g. Graham to Liverpool, 9 March 1811, Public Record Office, War Office Papers (hereafter WO) 1/252, 119–22; M. La Peña, *Representación hecha a las Cortes por el Capitán General de Andalucía y General en Jefe interino del Cuarto Ejército, Don Manuel La Peña* (Cádiz, 1813), 18, 23–8.

2 E.g. Graham to Liverpool, 27 May 1811, WO 1/252, 331–2; Graham to Bunbury, 29 May 1811, WO 1/252, 336–9; c.f. also *Diario de las discusiones y actas de las Cortes* (Cádiz, 1811–13), vi, 64–5; *Gazeta de la Junta Superior de la Mancha,* 16 November 1811, p. 349, Servicio Histório Militar, Colección Documental del Fraile (hereafter SHM CDF) cxxxv.

3 Weelington to Bathurst, 18 August 1812, WP 1/347–9.

4 G. Bell, *Rough Sketches of an Old Soldier during Fifty Years' Service,* ed. B. Stuart (1956), pp. 33–4.

5 W. Lawrence, *The Autobiography of Sergeant William Lawrence, a Hero of the Peninsular and Waterloo Campaigns,* ed. G. Bankes (1886), pp. 60–1; J. Kincaid, *Adventures in the Rifle Brigade* (1909), pp. 49, 186–7; J. Leach, *Rough Sketches of the Life of an Old Soldier* (1831), pp. 243–4; A. Schaumann, *On the Road with Wellington: the Diary of a War Commissary in the Peninsular Campaigns,* ed. A. Ludovici (New York, 1925), p. 210.

6 C.f. *El Redactor General,* 23 July 1811, 139–40, Hemeróteca Municipal de Madrid (hereafter HMM) 6/3; *Semanario Patriótica,* 19 December 1811, p. 83,

HMM AH1–6(199).

7 E.g. Sydenham to H. Wellesley, 12 September 1812, WP 1/361.

8 Kincaid, *op. cit.*, pp. 83–4; E. Costello, *The Adventures of a Soldier, or Memoirs of Edward Costello* (1841), pp. 205–6; J. Donaldson, *Recollections of the Eventful Life of a Soldier* (1856), p. 62; R. Porter, *Letters from Portugal and Spain Written during the March of the British Troops under Sir John Moore* (1809), pp. 229–30.

9 E.g. proclamation of the Junta of Plasencia, 3 July 1809, US WP 1/267; Eguia to Ureta, 18 August 1809, US WP 1/291.

10 J. Sherer, *Recollections of the Peninsula* (1823), pp. 36–7.

11 Canning to Wellesley, 27 June 1809, (hereafter FO) 72/75, 25–40.

12 Wellington to Frere, 10 June 1809, WP 1/265.

13 Sydenham to H. Wellesley, 28 September 1812, WP 1/361.

14 Wellington to Liverpool, 12 March 1812, WP 1/346.

15 H. Wellesley to Castlereagh, 17 September 1812, FO 72/132, 46–50; H. Wellesley to Wellington, 25 September 1812, WP 12/2/3.

16 Sydenham to H. Wellesley, 28 September 1812, WP 1/361.

17 Wellington to Vega, 3 April 1813, WP 1/370.

18 Wellington to Beresford, 10 December 1812, WP 1/355.

19 Wellington to Carvajal, 4 December 1812, WP 1/355.

20 *Diario de Gobierno de Sevilla*, 16 June 1813, pp. 1107–8, SHM CDF cxlii.

21 *El Redactor General*, 18 September 1813, p. 3377, HMM 6/3.

22 Wellington to O'Donoju, 30 August 1813, WP 1/375.

23 E.g. *El Duende de los Cafées*, 27 September 1813, FO 72/146, 139–41.

24 E.g. Wellington to Alava, 19 August 1813, WP 1/375; Wellington to Kennedy, 26 October 1813, WP 1/377; Wellington to H. Wellesley, 19 January 1814, WP 1/396.

25 Cf. Freyre to Wellington, 13 November 1813, WP1/382; Morillo to Freyre, 21 December 1813, WP 1/381; Morillo to Freyre, 30 December 1813, WP 1/391.

26 Wellington to H. Wellesley, 21 October 1810, WP 12/1/2.

27 Wellington to Bentinck, 8 July 1813, WP 1/373.

28 Wellington to Bathurst, 5 September 1813, WP 1/377.

29 Wellington to Bathurst, 12 July 1813, WP 1/373.

30 Wellington to Bathurst, 27 November 1813, WP 1/381.

31 Wellington to San Carlos, 21 May 1814, WP 1/417; Wellington to Castlereagh, 25 May 1814, WP 1/417; Wellington to Stuart, 25 May 1814, WP 1/417; B. Hamnett, *La política española en una época revolucionaria, 1790–1820* (México ÐF, 1985), p. 199.

32 *Cit.*, A. Bryant, *The Years of Endurance, 1793–1802* (1942), p. 103.

Donald D. Horward

5

Wellington as a strategist
1808–14

The third son of the earl of Mornington, Sir Arthur Wellesley, the future duke of Wellington and certainly one of England's greatest generals, has often been ignored when considering military strategists of the Napoleonic period. His strategy has been examined by non-British military scholars primarily to explain the failure of French operations in the Peninsular War. There is continued interest in his tactical use of linear formation against the French column, but students of military history have not replaced the study of the Auster-litz or Jena campaigns with that of Portugal or Spain. Nevertheless, careful examination of his campaigns reflects a bold and sophisticated understanding of the elements of strategy. Indeed, as he matured as a strategist, Wellesley assumed the responsibility of formulating strategy on all levels – operational, national, and coalition – and adapting it to the unique conditions of the Iberian Peninsula.

In examining Wellesley's military education, there is little in his background reflecting serious military training. His early military experience was undistinguished and limited to service in Holland. Through a series of purchased promotions and family influence, young Wellesley was able to secure advancement. His introduction to the formal study of warfare and strategy came from a library of military books that he purchased before sailing for India in 1796. Upon his arrival in India, although only a lieutenant-colonel of the Thirty-third Foot, he enjoyed the support of his elder brother, Richard, Lord Mornington, governor-general of India. Pressed into service as a temporary quartermaster, he performed effectively by

Spain and Portugal at the time of the Peninsular War

organising a commissariat to supply a small army waging war against Tipoo, sultan of Mysore. When this army marched, he led his Thirty-third Foot successfully into a campaign that saw Tipoo killed and his capital occupied. In 1803 during the Second Maratha war, Wellesley commanded a large independent force; he developed a campaign strategy that led to the conquest of the Maratha lands and a treaty of peace ending the war. In addition to his success on the battlefield, he was often called upon to function as a diplomat; he acquired valuable insights into the interrelationship between war and diplomacy and their role in achieving peace. Hence, when he left India, he took with him a variety of military experiences; an unusual understanding of tactics, strategy, logistics; as well as an appreciation of the pitfalls of coalition warfare.

Following his return to Britain, Wellesley spent the next three years as a member of parliament, in part to defend his brother Richard who was under attack for his policies in India. During the political intrigue, he acquired an appreciation of power politics and formed valuable relationships with men who would one day guide the destinies of England. He was soon named chief secretary to the lord lieutenant of

Ireland. From Dublin Castle he laboured through a maze of appointments and duties, dispensing both civil and military patronage. His tenure in Dublin was interrupted when he was named to command a division in the summer of 1807 against Denmark. In a major operation he assumed the offensive and employed his division against an enemy relief column of militiamen which resulted in the capitulation of Copenhagen and the surrender of the Danish fleet. Hence, Wellesley again returned to England with new laurels and a growing martial reputation. It was not long before his advice was sought on military matters by government ministers, including Lord Castlereagh, secretary of state for war.

After his return from Copenhagen, Wellesley was approached by George Canning, the foreign minister, with a scheme to send British troops to Spanish America. In November 1807, while he was planning the campaign, the French invaded Portugal. By the spring of 1808 the French occupied northern Spain. Insurrection erupted on 2 May and soon the provinces began organising armies to resist the French occupation. As a consequence, the British government, hoping to capitalise on events in the peninsula, considered a possible diversion of forces to the Iberian Peninsula.[1]

In response to appeals from the Spanish and Portuguese insurrectionaries, the 'Red Squadron' was sent to the Tagus under Admiral Charles Cotton, followed by a convoy carrying a small contingent of 5,000 British soldiers under General Brent Spencer. Wellesley expressed a strong interest in peninsular operations and the possibility of diverting his command from South America to the peninsula. Indeed, he realised the implications such a revolt might have upon the French empire. In a memorandum dated 1 June, he firmly recommended British military intervention 'to alarm Bonaparte in France,' since his armies were 'spread in all parts of Europe'. For Wellesley, it was 'an opportunity which ought not to be passed by'. By these comments, he demonstrated a grasp of a vital principle that would later guide his strategy in the peninsula. Fortunately, these views on grand strategy, both perceptive and realistic, were shared by others in the cabinet, including Canning and Castlereagh.[2]

On 14 June, Wellesley, the most junior lieutenant-general in the army, was given command of almost 10,000 men for service in the Iberian Peninsula. He spent long hours organising the commissariat and supply train for his new command. However, he did have some time for relaxation. One evening while attending a dinner party just before his departure for the peninsula, Wellesley made a particularly perceptive observation on the success of Napoleon's armies: 'They have . . . a new system of strategy, which has out-manoeuvred and overwhelmed all the armies of Europe. 'Tis enough to make one thoughtful; but no matter: my die is cast, they may overwhelm me, but I don't think they will out-manoeuvre me.' Confidently he explained, 'First, because I am not afraid of them, as everybody else seems to be; and secondly, because if what I hear of their system of manoeuvres be true, I think it a false one against steady troops.' Wellesley would soon have an opportunity to test his theories. At the end of June he received final instructions to provide Spain and Portugal 'every possible aid in throwing off the yoke of France'.[3]

The last days of July were devoted to final preparations for the embarkation of the troops. Recalling his operations in India, he carefully orchestrated the collection and organisation of adequate logistical support, an adequate medical system, and sufficient finances, food, and fodder. Despite adverse winds which delayed the little fleet from sailing, Wellesley's ship, *HMS Crocodile*, slipped out to sea on 12 July and set a course for Corunna. Reaching Spain within a week, he landed to confer with Spanish revolutionaries; after evaluating their intentions and commitments, he rejoined his convoy at Mondego Bay.

Although Castlereagh's strategy called for an attack on the Tagus as his primary objective, Wellesley resolved to modify his instructions. Learning that a French force, estimated at 12,000 troops under General Jean Junot, was concentrated near Lisbon, he made a decision to 'land at a distance from Lisbon'. The Portuguese fortress of Peniche was a possible landing site, but Wellesley decided to go ashore at Figueira da Foz where Admiral Cotton had posted some four hundred marines.[4]

On 1 August, British troops began to disembark at Mondego Bay, followed by horses, artillery, equipment, and foodstuffs. Even before his army was ashore at Figueira da Foz, Wellesley began making arrangements to take the offensive, as he had done so often in India. A rudimentary supply train was organised for his small army, soon reinforced by Spencer's 5,000 men. Advacing along the coastal road towards Lisbon, escorted by 2,000 Portuguese cavalry, he maintained contact with the supply ships sailing along the coast. The French were first sighted at Obidos, and two days later their rear guard was overthrown at Roliça.

Junot, meanwhile, struggled frantically to concentrate his army; less than 13,000 men were available since many of his troops garrisoned the frontier fortresses. Marching northward to confront the British, he found Wellesley's army on 21 August near the village of Vimeiro. Taking advantage of the excellent topographic position, Wellesley posted his troops behind ridges, trees, and other natural defences. The French attacks were repulsed in detail and they were driven from the battlefield; Wellesley prepared to take up the pursuit and advance on Lisbon, but he was superseded by General Harry Burrard who halted the pursuit. The next morning General Hew Dalrymple arrived to supersede both generals. Within a few hours a French negotiator arrived at British headquarters; later that day an armistice was arranged, sparing the demoralised French a crushing defeat.

Nevertheless, Vimeiro was a decisive British victory and Wellesley's campaign strategy had proved highly effective; his decisions to land at Mondego Bay, to enlist the aid of Portuguese forces, to take the offensive and advance immediately on Lisbon, and his success in luring Junot on to his very formidable positions at Vimeiro all proved highly successful. With the French army defeated, demoralised, and without hope of reinforcements, Junot ultimately consented to the Convention of Cintra, an agreement which provided for the evacuation of the French army and its baggage to France aboard a fleet of British transports.[5]

The three generals involved in the Convention of Cintra were recalled to London to answer for several highly questionable provisions of the agreement. The members of the court of inquiry did not fix the guilt, but they seemed critical of Burrard's conduct. By contrast, they readily complimented Wellesley on his successful campaign, culminating in the battle of Vimeiro.

While Wellesley was undergoing interrogation by the board of inquiry, his former army, reinforced and commanded by Sir John Moore, moved to support a massive Spanish counter-attack against the invading French armies. However, Napoleon's personal intervention led to the defeat of the Spanish armies and the pursuit of Moore's army. Driven across the snow-covered mountains of northwest Spain, the British army was evacuated from Corunna on 16 January 1809 after the bloody battle at Elvina and the death of Moore. This humiliating defeat led to animated debate in parliament about the withdrawal of the British army from the peninsula. Moore's opinions and his failures in the peninsula reaffirmed the belief of many that the allies could not win this war. Indeed, if the struggle were to be continued, an infusion of new ideas, strategy, and leadership would have to be introduced into the allied war effort.

In England, meanwhile, Wellesley was convinced that the struggle could be successfully carried on in the peninsula. He arranged to go to London for the meeting of parliament and, more significantly, to seek reappointment to the army in the peninsula. He appealed to Castlereagh, and, aided by his supporters and relatives, he was reassigned to the peninsula.

In the meantime, the British cabinet, after sending supplies and armaments to sustain the Portuguese army, agreed to subsidise its troops and appoint a British general and regimental officers to command it. The British government, with Canning's prodding, had made a major decision to continue the fight for the peninsula, and, more particularly, for Portugal. Wellesley was of the same opinion. On 7 March 1809 he wrote a memorandum carefully detailing his strategy; he insisted that Portugal could be defended, whatever the results of the struggle in Spain. With a small British army of 20,000 men, supplemented by Portuguese regulars and the militia, he was convinced that Portugal could be defended against any French force of under 100,000 men. Therefore, he proposed that financial and political support be provided to aid in rebuilding the Portuguese army.[6]

Still, many in England could not forget Moore's ominous prediction that Portugal, indefensible against a superior force, could not be held if Spain fell. Moore's words haunted Wellesley. He was convinced they did not accurately reflect the situation. He was not alone; his assessment of Portugal coincided with that of Canning, Castlereagh, and other prominent members of the cabinet. Accordingly, on 2 April, Wellesley received his fromal instructions:

> The defence of Portugal you will consider as the first and immediate object of your attention. . . . His Majesty . . . leaves it to your judgment to decide when your army shall be advanced on the frontier of Portugal [and] how your efforts can best be combined with the Spanish as well as the Portuguese troops in support of the common cause.[7]

Sailing from Portsmouth on 15 April, Wellesley landed a week later in Lisbon along with many of the 9,000 reinforcements ordered to Portugal. Arrangements were quickly completed to organise a wagon train, and soon some 20,000 troops were equipped, provisioned, and ready to march. His strategy called for an immediate offensive, but he faced two options: he could advance to the Spanish frontier to support General Gregorio Cuesta and attack Marshal Claude Victor who threatened central Portugal, or he could move north and expel the army of Marshal Nicolas Soult occupying Oporto. Within two days he had decided to attack Soult and drive the French out of Portugal. Once this had been accomplished, Wellesley would move to cooperate with Cuesta against the French. If this venture were successful, it would relieve pressure on Seville and Lisbon, and open the route to Madrid. This strategy was ambitious and bold, but it would have to be implemented with dispatch and precision since Lisbon would only be protected by a weak force of 6,500 troops posted behind the Tagus.[8]

Within a week of Wellesley's arrival, the first of his troops left Lisbon, following a predetermined itinerary towards .Oporto, approximately 150 miles away. Meanwhile, a partially resurrected Portuguese army of some 6,000 troops marched along a parallel route to outflank Soult's army. Despite appeals from the Spanish junta at Seville for aid to protect southern Spain, Wellesley replied firmly that his main responsibility was to preserve the kingdom of Portugal. He did, however, express the hope that he would soon have an opportunity to cooperate with Cuesta's army.[9]

While the Portuguese regiments marched eastward to outflank the French, the British troops advanced directly toward the Douro River and Oporto. When the first fighting broke out on 10 May at Grijo, Soult had all the boats removed from the south bank of the Douro and almost every bridge on the river was destroyed; this would prevent a British crossing until the city could be evacuated. Although troops were posted along the Douro from Oporto to the sea, Soult neglected to have the river guarded above the town. On 12 May the British seized four barges on the north bank of the Douro. The army was immediately transported to a partially completed seminary building above Oporto. The British army advanced down the river immediately; each French counter-attack was repulsed and Oporto was captured.

Deserting his hospitals, Soult evacuated Oporto and withdrew towards the mountains, pursued by the British army, while the Portuguese troops raced to cut their escape route. To elude his pursuers, Soult abandoned his baggage train and artillery, taking a narrow mountain trail that ultimately led him across the Spanish frontier to Orense. Despite the relentless pursuit of the Ango-Portuguese army, and the loss of almost 5,000 men and their artillery, Soult's army did escape destruction. Wellesley, on the other hand, had achieved his first strategic goal by driving the French from Portugal. He had waged an aggressive and well-executed campaign; he had surprised the French, defeated their forces, and hounded them out of Portugal with heavy losses in both personnel and equipment. An unexpected benefit of the campaign had been his opportunity to observe Portuguese troops in action; Wellesley was reassured since they were to be an integral part of his strategy for the defence of the kingdom.

As Soult's army was retreating into Spain, Wellesley learned of the capture of the bridge at Alcantara and the threatening movements of Victor on the eastern frontier of Portugal. Orders were issued immediately to counter the French success and, in accordance with his strategy, his army marched to join Cuesta. The army slipped through the mountains despite the heavy rains of late May. Wellesley was anxious to overtake Victor, but the French marshal retired across the Tagus to safety.[10]

The vicissitudes of coalition warfare quickly became apparent when Wellesley and Cuesta first met to discuss campaign strategy. Wellesley, with authorisation to carry his operations into Spain as long as they did not endanger the safety of Portugal, was ready to enter Spain. Cuesta proposed several complex and impracticable schemes, and Wellesley countered with plans for a flanking movement against Victor. Additional revisions compounded the complexities of the project until the army of General Francisco Venegas was included in a scheme to cut Victor's communications while Cuesta and Wellesley advanced on Madrid. Such a diverse plan was feasible only under the most ideal conditions, and only with the complete commitment of each of the army commanders. Victor, in the meantime, aware of his untenable position, retired to within supporting distance of King Joseph's forces at Madrid.

The campaign was delayed three weeks while Wellesley awaited the arrival of army funds; it was only on 27 June that 23,000 men of the army marched. Moreover, without adequate transportation and supplies promised by Cuesta, the advance was further slowed. Distrust and reservations accompanied the initial movements and, with each passing day, there was more and more anguish over the lack of provisions. After frustrating delays the two armies finally united on 22 July. Contact was made with Victor's 46,000 troops beyond the town of Talavera. The vital manoeuvre by Venegas's army to cut Victor's communications never materialised, undermining allied strategy.

Wellesley's poorly-deployed forces were surprised on 27 July, and one of his divisions was temporarily routed. Retreating deliberately to a series of hills just north of Talavera, his troops successfully repulsed a French attack during the night, but the right wing of the allied army, commanded by Cuesta, apparently panicked. The following day, the vicious battle of Talavera was fought. Victor's troops assaulted Wellesley's positions for twelve hours; the British line was temporarily broken several times, but the enemy attacks were ultimately driven off late in the afternoon. It was a savage struggle – British losses totalled almost 5,400 casualties, or one-quarter of the army; the Spanish suffered over 1,200 casualties; and the French sustained at least 7,000 losses.[11]

The battle of Talavera was clearly a British victory, but Wellesley was furious over the behaviour of Cuesta and the Spanish army. Not only had he been abandoned, but his army had been allowed to languish without food or fodder. Resentful of the Spanish complaints that he would not pursue Victor's defeated army, he lashed back bitterly, 'I can get no assistance of any description from the country'. Prompted by a report announcing that Soult, with 15,000 Frenchmen, was advancing from Plasencia towards his line of communications, Wellesley fell back to Oropesa on 3 August. There he learned the true strength of Soult's force was in excess of 50,000 men. When Cuesta received this information, he withdrew to join Wellesley, abandoning more than 4,000 British wounded. Wellesley quickly retired across the Tagus at Puente del Arzobispo, but Cuesta lingered too long and was driven across the river. The allied armies continued their retreat to Jaraicejo where Wellesley established temporary headquarters.[12]

As Wellesley contemplated his options, it was obvious that Talavera had been a Pyrrhic victory and the campaign strategy had failed. It was only with the opportune arrival of his brother Richard at Seville as ambassador to Spain that he saw the slightest hope of restoring the situation. He bombarded his brother daily with complaints, confident that they would be relayed to the Spanish government. Richard pressed the junta for supplies; promises were made, but they went unfilled. Wellesley wrote to his brother on 13 August threatening: 'Either the British army must be fed and supplied with the necessaries which they require, or I will march them back into Portugal'. Describing the Spanish army as 'really children in the art of war', he withdrew his forces to the valley of the Guadiana on 21 September 1809.[13]

It is clear that by this decision, Wellesley – named Viscount

Wellington for his victory at Talavera – had given up his strategy to wage war in Spain. He admitted to his brother:

> By going within the Portuguese frontier, I clear myself entirely of the Spanish army; and shall have an opportunity hereafter of deciding whether I shall cooperate with them at all, in what manner, and to what extent, and under what conditions, according to the circumstances of the moment.

Wellington was not alone in his determination to retire into Portugal. In London, Canning expressed similar views and supported his decision.[14]

Almost as soon as Wellington had retired to Badajoz, along the Portuguese frontier, the Spanish junta again began making proposals for joint ventures against the French. He ignored their appeals, convinced that they were motivated by politcal rather than military factors. Relations deteriorated until the junta refused to provide him with accurate information on either Spanish or French movements. Richard attempted to persuade the Spanish government that England would not abandon the struggle, but they were hardly convinced. When he was recalled to London to become foreign secretary, he instructed his temporary replacement, Bartholomew Frere, not to commit Wellington's army to any joint operations with the Spanish. As soon as Richard assumed his new position, he appointed his younger brother, Henry, as ambassador to Spain. With Henry in Seville, Wellington's strategy would be firmly represented and, if necessary, defended to the junta – this was not what the Spanish wanted to hear.[15]

It is not surprising that friction developed between the two allies. Although there was talk of mutual cooperation, it could not erase several centuries of hostility. The British still occupied Gibraltar and their commercial activities sought to encourage revolutionary activity in the Spanish colonies. On the other hand, the Spanish, who could draw on a large reservoir of manpower and the wealth of their colonies, were unwilling to permit British political, military, and economic influences to permeate the country; indeed, they initially refused to allow British troops to land at Cádiz, fearful of their motives. The Portuguese, however, had been a close ally and trading partner for centuries; they were obviously incapable of resisting a French invasion so they had no alternative but to turn to England, whatever the costs, if they were to preserve their independence.

Despite Wellington's continuing controversy with Cuesta and the Spanish junta, he took time to consider the defences of Portugal. In a letter to Castlereagh dated 25 August, he recommended that the British should not 'have anything to do with [the Spanish army] in their present state'. On the contrary, he believed the Portuguese army could be revived. He declared, 'My opinion is that we ought to be able to hold Portugal, if the Portuguese army and militia are complete.' The entire frontier was obviously indefensible, but he was convinced that Lisbon could be defended. He was only apprehensive that some ill-conceived venture with the Spanish army or a transfer of his forces to defend Cádiz, might undermine his strategy for Portugal.[16]

While Wellington's army was posted in the vicinity of Badajoz, he travelled to Lisbon to consider the defensibility of the Lisbon peninsula. His staff had already collected 'a great deal of information' on the position; yet he wanted additional details before a specific strategy was developed for the capital. He received a lengthy report and a map drawn up by a Portuguese engineer, Major José Neves Costa; this document analysed the scores of defensive positions that could be fortified to form a series of defensive lines.[17]

With Neves Costa's report in hand, Wellington travelled to the Montechique mountains with Lieutenant Colonel Richard Fletcher of the Royal Engineers. They spent several days visiting villages, and noting roads, rivers, hills, and other topographic features that could be fortified. Upon his return to Lisbon, Wellington drew up his famous memorandum of 20 October. Extrapolating on Neves Costa's report, he carefully outlined the plans for what became known as the Lines of Torres Vedras – one of the most important fortified lines ever constructed. Wellington's strategy was simple. According to his memorandum: 'The great object in Portugal is the possession of Lisbon and the Tagus, and all our measures must be directed to this object. There is another also connected with that first object . . . the embarkation of the British troops in case of reverse.' Hence, all subsequent elements of his Portuguese strategy centred on these objectives.[18]

Wellington visualised a series of defensive positions extending across the Lisbon peninsula to control the roads leading to the capital. By the time the French finally reached these positions, there were three lines of fortifications extending from the Tagus River across the twenty-nine-mile peninsula to the Atlantic ocean. These independent fortifications, conforming to the surrounding topography, were dissimilar in size, configuration, and firepower, but each had parapets, a ditch, palisades, a garrison, and from three to forty cannon.[19]

The roads between Lisbon and the north were barricaded and the bridges destroyed; trenches were dug and hills scarped; trees were cut and rivers blocked; valleys and passes were obstructed with abatis; a lateral road was constructed along the lines to enhance troop movement; a semaphore system was raised atop the highest hills along the lines; and gunboats were anchored in the Tagus to support the right flank of the line. Thousands of Portuguese workers and *ordenanza* were transported from all over the province to labour on the lines under direction of British and Portuguese engineers. By mid-October 1810, when the French army arrived, the lines included 126 redoubts and 249 guns manned by 29,750 militiamen and *ordenanza*. In the event the French were able to breach the first line, Wellington hoped his field army would be in a position to launch a counter-attack. All else failing, the third line, centring on Fort São Julião, would provide cover for the embarkation of the British army.[20]

Although the Lines of Torres Vedras were a vital element in Wellington's strategy for the defence of Portugal, his memorandum of 20 October called for the mobilisation of the kingdom to thwart the enemy's advance. With the support of the Portuguese government, arrangements were completed to reinforce and resupply the major frontier fortresses and repair their defences to sustain a major siege. Anticipating the enemy's invasion route, the roads were broken up and destroyed, while those to be utilised by Wellington's forces were improved and defended. Vital passes, river crossings, and bridges along the anticipated invasion route were fortified to delay the French, and the rivers, possible routes of entry, were stripped of all boats and skiffs to the Spanish frontier; boat bridges were dismantled and transported to safety. To deny the enemy transportation, orders were issued for the removal of all forms of wheeled-vehicles and animals that might fall into their hands.[21]

In addition to the defensive elements of his strategy, Wellington had signified early in 1809 that he could save Portugal from all but a massive invasion. This was based upon the assumption that he could rejuvenate the Portuguese army and restore the militia regiments. By April 1808 it was well under way. The regency council, functioning in the absence of Prince Regent Dom João, had begun to recall the disbanded troops; voluntary contributions were solicited and French property was seized to generate revenue for the army, but those efforts were woefully inadequate.[22]

To support the Portuguese government, the British had supplied a small subsidy, arms, and a loan during the summer of 1808, but in November, Canning agreed to provide a subsidy of £226,000 to field 10,000 Portuguese troops and £135,000 to pay their officers. Early in 1809 the subsidy was increased to £450,000 to sustain 20,000 Portuguese in the field; this figure was later increased to £980,000 to field 30,000 auxiliaries for service with the British army.[23]

To rebuild the Portuguese army, the Regency Council appealed to Britain for leadership. Early in 1808, with Wellington's blessing, the Portuguese government had named William Carr Beresford marshal of Portugal and commander-in-chief of their army. Known as a disciplinarian and an effective administrator, Beresford began to reorganise the Portuguese army. With Wellington's firm support, he purged the officer corps. Old and physically impaired officers, as well as those guilty of absenteeism, dereliction of duty, or incompetence, were retired or cashiered; during the spring and summer of 1809 several hundred officers were replaced by promising young soldiers who were, for the most part, commoners.[24]

By January 1810 the army had reached a level of professionalism that prompted Wellington to remark, 'I have had opportunities of seeing fifteen regiments in the Portuguese service, and I have great pleasure in informing Your Lordship that the progress of all these troops in discipline is considerable [and] some of the regiments are in very good order'. A few weeks later he boasted, 'The Portuguese army . . . is better than I ever expected it would be'. British and Portuguese regiments were soon brigaded together under the command of British officers. The British commissariat began to assume responsibility for the transportation and distribution of arms and equipment, so order was slowly established in each branch of the Portuguese army. The militia was activated and soon between 52,000 and 70,000 more troops were under arms. They were employed to garrison fortresses, depots, cities, and provinces; some militia were also posted behind the lines of Torres Vedras and, on occasion, units served with Wellington's field army.[25]

Although Wellington relied primarily on the line regiments and militia to fight the enemy, his strategy also called for the implementation of an ancient Portuguese law to mobilise the *ordenanza,* similar to the French *levée en masse.* Composed of all able-bodied males between sixteen and sixty, they were expected to arm themselves and operate as guerrillas to 'do the enemy all the mischief in their power'. Although the *ordenanza* usually served locally, it had a devastating effect upon the French.

Turning to more revolutionary elements of his strategy, Wellington stunned Europe by methodically imposing the 'scorched-earth policy' upon the provinces that were under threat of French invasion. The Portuguese government had issued a series of inflammatory decrees inciting the peasants to resist the French. Such proclamations were hardly necessary since French foragers and stragglers had already committed appalling excesses along the frontier. Yet, with Wellington's 'Proclamation to the Portuguese People', he laid the foundation for the 'scorched-earth policy'. Promising to protect as much of the country as possible, he declared, 'It is obvious that the people can save themselves only by resistance to the army, and their properties only by removing them'.[26]

Wellington threatened to use his full power and authority 'to force the weak and the indolent to make an exertion to save themselves from the danger which awaits them, and to save their country'. Anyone who communicated with the enemy or aided them in any way would be considered traitors to the state and punished accordingly. To reaffirm this policy, he wrote to his cavalry commander, 'Send round to the people that they must retire from the villages, and let the magistrates know if any of them stay, or if any of the inhabitants have any communications with the enemy, they will be hanged'. The immediate success of his drastic action prompted him to write:

> The people of Portugal are doing that which the Spaniards ought to have done. They are removing their women and properties out of the enemy's way, and taking arms in their own defence. The country is made a desert, and behind almost every stone wall the French will meet an enemy.[27]

Another element of Wellington's strategy centred on the belief that the Portuguese economy could be modified to absorb much of the defence costs. Indeed, England had assumed the commitment to subsidise 30,000 Portuguese troops, provide arms, clothing, and other equipment, but it was soon abundantly clear that additional revenue would have to be generated for the war effort. As early as January 1809, a *Carta Regia* had been issued by the prince regent with instructions for the regency council to reform public finance by modifying old imposts and raising new taxes. By June the regency council imposed an 'Extraordinary Contribution for Defence', which was in fact a forced-loan on various segments of society. Proposals were made for increased land taxes and for a graduated income tax on the professional and commercial classes. At the same time it was agreed that Wellington or his representative would be permitted to attend all sessions of the regency council dealing with military or financial matters.[28] Nevertheless, by 1810 defence expenses borne by the Portuguese government produced a deficit of more than a million pounds, driving the country deeper into debt.

Consequently, Wellesley began to exert political pressure on the regency council for economic reform through the British ministers in Lisbon – John Villiers and, after February 1810, Charles Stuart. The subsidy became a matter of continual review. Whenever the regency council requested additional funds, Wellington and Stuart demanded tax reform and administrative changes, initially with little success, to increase revenue.

In January 1810 Prince João proposed a series of fiscal reforms to increase the revenues of the kingdom. In addition to taxes on the rents from ecclesiastical and crown lands, a stamp tax, sale of some crown lands, reform of the paper money, and a lottery, he recommended a duty reduction on British manufactured goods to stimulate trade. Wellington endorsed these proposals enthusiastically, but most were only enacted after long months of heated debate. In fact, during the last months of 1810, this economic crisis was usually ignored as members of the regency council attacked his strategy for Portugal. By December a frustrated Wellington, blaming the inadequate Portuguese tax structure for the miserable condition of the Portuguese army, admitted to Stuart that unless the regency council adopted a new tax system, 'I shall state my opinion to our Government that the war cannot be carried on as long as things remain as they are'. On Wellington's recommendation, Stuart proposed a series of new imposts in December, but they were postponed until the spring of 1811.[29]

Despite these efforts, the condition of the Portuguese army continued to deteriorate for lack of supplies and transports. Describing the starving condition of some 12,000 Portuguese troops and the lack of necessary medicine, Wellington appealed to the cabinet to raise the subsidy. A few months later, the House of Commons voted to increase it to £2,000,000. When Wellington learned of the increase, he cautioned Stuart that the Portuguese government 'should not be informed of [this] addition in the subsidy till it shall be absolutely necessary'. With the additional funds now available, he sought more effective control over the Portuguese economy. With judiciously applied pressure, he was able to force economic reform and increase revenues.[30]

In 1811 and 1812, through his application of the subsidy and threats to withdraw the British army, Wellington induced the Portuguese government to continue their tax reforms to produce additional revenue. He never lost sight of the fact that the Portuguese army was a necessary component of his peninsular strategy, so he conintually pressed for its improvement. Although it caused serious economic dislocation in Portugal, he was undeterred in his commitment to maintain the Anglo-Portuguese army in Portugal, whatever the cost. The British subsidy continued into 1814, but as the threat of French invasion receded and the army operated further from the kingdom, financial support declined drastically.

Another element of Wellington's strategy for the defence of Portugal centred around the Royal Navy. With control of the seas and easy access to the Tagus, the British navy guaranteed the arrival of reinforcements, supplies, and information as well as a means of escape if Wellington's strategy were to fail. In addition, Royal Marines were landed to support the army and defend the Tagus forts. Warships patrolled the lower Tagus, protected the right flank of the lines, and transported men and equipment along the coast and up the rivers. Also of vital importance was the success of the British merchant fleet in transporting massive quantities of food and supplies to Lisbon to feed the tens of thousands of Portuguese refugees who fled before the advancing French army. This remarkable record of cooperation was carried out with Admiral George Berkeley, an unusually capable officer who seconded Wellington's strategy in almost every instance, insuring its ultimate success.

This mobilisation of Portugal, considered in part or in its entirety, was a monumental undertaking, never before attempted on such a comprehensive scale. Taken in conjunction with the efforts of the Spanish armies and guerrillas, it presented obstacles that no invading French army could overcome. Yet, there were risks involved. For the British, the fate of their last viable army was at stake; for the Portuguese the heartland of their country would be sacrificed without any guarantee of success. The risks were great, but if Wellington's strategy proved successful, the independence of Portugal would be preserved, British foreign policy would be justified, and the victorious Anglo-Portuguese army would serve as an example – for people not only of the peninsula, but throughout Napoleonic-dominated Europe.

In Wellington's efforts to implement such drastic strategy, he encountered many in the British and Portuguese governments, as well as within his own army, who expressed various degrees of opposition to his plans. No sooner had he begun to formulate his strategy during the fall of 1809, than opposition began to surface. Lord Liverpool, secretary for war and colonies, was anxious about the evacuation of the British army and cautioned against 'sacrificing' the army. After Wellington visited Lisbon in October 1809, however, he was even more convinced of the practicality of his strategy than he had been six months earlier and he told Liverpool so. 'I do not think they [French] will succeed with an army of 70,000 or even 80,000 men.' Regarding the safety of the army, he declared, 'I am convinced we could embark after defeat.' His views were more circumspect in a letter to Villiers in January 1810; he claimed that he would 'fight a good battle for the possession of Portugal' with 30,000 British troops. 'If the Portuguese do their duty,' he declared, 'I shall have enough [troops] to maintain it; if they do not, nothing Great Britain can afford can save the country'.[31]

Although Wellington carefully apprised Liverpool of efforts to implement his strategy, he found the government, ever-mindful of Moore's disastrous campaign, critical and even fearful that his plans might cost England its last army. In a series of letters to Liverpool, Wellington tediously spelled out his precautions to ensure the safe evacuation of the army, but they were apparently unconvincing. Wellington was not immune from such criticism so he bluntly asked Liverpool if 'an effort should be made to defend this country to the last'; or, considering the deteriorating situation in Spain, should he 'seriously' contemplate 'the evacuation of the country'.[32]

Meanwhile, Wellington's request of 45,000 tons of transports and a battle fleet met with immediate approval. Transport in the vicinity of Portugal set a course for Lisbon; by February 1810 vessels totalling almost 24,000 ton were anchored in the estuary of the Tagus. Other transports from Cádiz, Malta, and Gibraltar were en route, and by March six ships-of-the-line, accompanied by ordnance and horse transports, were preparing to sail from England. Regimental baggage was stowed aboard the transports as they arrived with reinforcements.

Each regiment was assigned to specific vessels anchored in the Tagus. In event of embarkation, longboats were ready to transfer both British and Portuguese troops to the waiting vessels, equipped with food and water, for a trip to Cádiz or some other port. By 1 May there was enough British tonnage in the Tagus to evacuate the entire British army, ordnance, stores, and 2,000 horses; there were also enough Portuguese ships in the habour to embark the Portuguese army.[33]

Despite the criticism from England, Richard, Wellington's brother in the Foreign Office, remained a strong supporter of his strategy. Acutely aware of the importance of continued Spanish resistance if Wellington were to succeed, he encouraged a resurgence of Spanish military activity by sending funds and equipment for their armies. Indeed, if the Spanish armies collapsed, he realised that the French might be able to mobilise all their peninsular forces against his brother and drive him into the sea. In this endeavour, he was seconded by Henry in Spain who was always aware of Wellington's interests in Portugal. Another brother, William Pole, as secretary to the lords of the Admiralty, was always alert to naval policies that would affect Wellington, conscious that the Royal Navy was his lifeline.[34]

The discussion over Wellington's Portuguese strategy continued until the end of April when the private secretary of King George III, Colonel Herbert Taylor, wrote to Liverpool indicating that the king firmly supported Wellington's general plan of operations; moreover, he expected his ministers to let Wellington 'proceed according to his judgment . . . unfettered by any particular instructions which might embarrass him in the execution of his general plan of operations'.[35] With this decision Wellington was relieved of governmental interference and, more significantly, his authority and flexibility were reaffirmed. His meticulous planning, unswerving determination, and careful judgment had triumphed. Liverpool and the other critical ministers had no alternative but to accept his daring strategy unless they wanted to defy the wishes of the king, recall their most victorious general, risk attacks from the Wellesley clan, inflame the public, and undermine British foreign policy.

Another major effort to sabotage Wellington's strategy centred on a number of very influential Portuguese leaders. This opposition, led by José António de Menenzes e Sousa, known as the Principal Sousa, and António de Castro, the Patriarch, both members of the regency council, carried on a bitter struggle to alter his plans, especially the 'scorched-earth policy' which would turn the kingdom into a wasteland. Many loyal Portuguese condemned Wellington for his willingness to devastate Portugal, its people and resources, fearing he would ultimately abandon the country to the French. Consequently, they supported a strategy that would stop the French at the frontier rather than allow them to lay waste the heartland of the kingdom. During the fall and winter of 1810, Wellington's representative on the regency council, Charles Stuart, was under constant attack from the Patriarch, the Principal Sousa, and their followers. Hence, many pressing issues including tax reform, the British subsidy, administrative reform, and military mobilisation were ignored while they debated Wellington's strategy.[36]

Even as Wellington struggled with his Portuguese opponents, the French were preparing for the invasion of Portugal. By the first week of September, Marshal André Masséna's army had captured Almeida on the frontier and was poised to invade central Portugal. With some 65,000 men he advanced through a hostile land, stripped of all resources and defended by bands of *ordenanza*. Wellington's mobilisation plans, implemented with great care, caused unexpected suffering and frustration among the French. The allied army retired through the Portuguese mountains for 120 miles until they reached one of the most defensible positions in Portugal – the Serra de Bussaco. There Wellington concentrated his army to make a stand. His primary goal was to turn back the French and spare the country from further devastation. Even if he failed, he would silence some of his Portuguese and British critics who clamoured for battle, he would gain time to complete work on the lines, and he would give the Portuguese troops their baptism of fire. As usual, Wellington made excellent use of his formidable position. His army and artillery were partially concealed along the crest of the mountain and a road was constructed along the summit to facilitate the rapid movements of troops to repulse the French attacks. On 27 September 1810 Wellington watched two French corps struggle up the face of the mountain only to be overthrown by furious allied counter-attacks. French losses totalled almost 5,000 men while Wellington's casualties were 1,200. It was a brilliant tactical victory that would have major ramifications for the campaign. Nevertheless, the immediate result of the victory were negated by Masséna who turned Wellington's flank by the Boialvo road and forced his army to retreat.[37]

As planned, the allied army fell back toward Lisbon, drawing the French toward the lines of Torres Vedras. Masséna's advance guard reached the lines on 12 October where they were forced to halt – just twenty miles from the Lisbon suburbs. After several probes along the first line, Masséna, recalling his defeat at Bussaco, rejected suggestions that he should attack what appeared to be impregnable positions. He resolved to settle down before the lines while an aide was sent back to Napoleon with a request for reinforcements and siege artillery. Within a month, Masséna retreated thirty miles to the formidable positions at Santarém where he deployed his army. There the French army languished for almost four more months awaiting aid that would never come. On 5 March, Masséna finally issued orders for the retreat of his army, already reduced to 42,000 men and under constant threat from an ever-increasing allied army. Although Masséna hoped to establish a new defensive position in the less devastated provinces, Wellington's brilliant pursuit manoeuvred the French army from position to position until the Spanish border was reached three weeks later.[38]

Masséna made one last attempt to defeat Wellington's army at Fuentes de Oñoro on 3–5 May 1811, as he advanced to relieve the French garrison at Almeida. Fighting raged around the village for two days, but the French were finally repulsed with some 2,600 casualties; Almeida fell and the liberation of Portugal had been achieved. With this victory, Wellington had successfully completed the first phase of his peninsular strategy. It was unquestionably a monumental achievement for the allies. Despite the overwhelming strength of the French in the peninsula, the Anglo-Portuguese Army had defeated Napoleon's greatest marshal and driven him out of Portugal; this was achieved in conjunction with the Spanish forces who absorbed the bulk of the enemy forces so they could not concentrate for an all-out attack on Wellington.

To implement the second phase of Wellington's strategy – the expulsion of the French from Spain – Portugal would have to be retained as a base of operations for the army; from this sanctuary, Wellington would be able to strike at isolated French armies in Spain and infuse new enthusiasm into the long-suffering Spanish armies and people. This strategy was predicated on Wellington's ability to maintain the Portuguese contingent of his army; without it he could neither defend Portugal against another French invasion nor wage war in Spain. Consequently, Wellington, supported by Stuart in the regency council, carried on his struggle in the Poruguese political arena during 1811–13 to raise funds for Portuguese troops. Although the opposition forces in the regency council were less vocal as a result of his military victories, they were not anxious to accept an additional tax burden when the war seemed won. However, when revenue collections faltered and the Portuguese troops were without adequate food, supplies, or transport, Wellington withheld the subsidy payments, threatened to withdraw the British army, and appealed to Prince João in Brazil for continued support.[39]

With Portugal no longer under threat of invasion, Wellington was determined to take the offensive and invade Spain. This involved the capture of two old fortresses guarding the two main routes into Spain – Ciudad Rodrigo in the north and Badajoz in the south. Once he was convinced that Masséna's beaten army was no longer a present threat, Wellington left 28,000 men to watch them while he marched southward with two divisions to reinforce Beresford, already beseiging Badajoz. As soon as Soult learned of Wellington's movements, he appealed to Masséna's successor, Marshal Auguste Marmont, for aid. In one of the few instances of cooperation between French marshals in the peninsula, Marmont immediately collected his army and marched south across the boat bridge at Almaraz toward Badajoz. When Wellington learned of the arrival of Marmont's force, which increased French forces to over 60,000 men, he retired from Badajoz. What he had always sought to prevent had occurred; the French had united, achieving vast superiority over his forces. He hoped that his withdrawal into Portugal, coupled with a Spanish attack in Andalucia, would force Soult to withdraw his troops. His plan succeeded and Marmont, too weak to confront Wellington alone, gave up his position and moved to the Tagus valley. This was not the first but certainly it was a most graphic demonstration of Spanish contributions, indirect though it may have been, to Wellington's strategy.[40]

Apprehensive that another attack on Badajoz would bring Soult and Marmont together again, Wellington marched seven divisions of his army northward to threaten Ciudad Rodrigo. This was temporarily checked by Marmont, but in January 1812 Wellington moved quickly to invest Ciudad Rodrigo. Although the siege-work was incomplete, Wellington, anxious that Marmont should not have time to mobilise his troops and raise the siege, ordered a premature assault. On 19 January, long before Marmont could concentrate his army, the fortress was captured after a savage attack that cost the allies over 1,300 casualties. With the first route into Spain firmly under his control and Marmont's army back in cantonments, Wellington moved quickly to secure the second major route into Spain. Marching with the great bulk of his army, he arrived before Badajoz on 16 March. The trenches were opened immediately and soon artillery batteries were in place. Again time was a major factor; the siege had to be completed before Soult, and perhaps Marmont, could concentrate an adequate force to raise the siege. Within three weeks a breach had been pounded in the city walls; orders were issued for a premature assault. On 6 April the attack on the breach was beaten back in a violent hand-to-hand conflict, but a diversionary attack succeeded; losses were appalling with almost 4,000 casualties. The troops avenged themselves on the citizens and defenders of the town in a bloody orgy of sack, pillage, and rape. Wellington, however, had achieved his goal. With the two main routes into Spain under his control, his army would be able to invade French-occupied Spain.[41]

In addition to Wellington's operations in Portugal in 1810–11, and his sieges of the two frontier fortresses in 1812, Wellington was continually involved in the decisions being made to support the Spanish government and its armies. Through his brother's Richard and Henry, and various members of the British cabinet, his views were carefully considered in relation to Spanish operations. Hence, he played a significant role in various other military operations going on in Spain, especially when they had an impact upon his own.

During the spring of 1812 as Wellington contemplated proceedings in Spain, he came to the obvious conclusion that whichever route he followed into Spain, he might always be outnumbered as long as Marmont's forces in the north could reinforce Soult's army in the south or vice versa. To prevent such a junction in the future, he decided to attack the French positions on the Tagus near Almaraz and take up the boat bridge there, thereby destroying the only practical line of communications between the two forces. Accordingly, General Rowland Hill successfully accomplished the mission in May 1812. Wellington could then march into Spain without fear of a flank attack.

In control of both routes into Spain, Wellington laboured to develop a strategy that would maximise the impact of his army on the war in Spain. He could strike in Andalucia from Badajoz and possibly force Soult to raise the siege of Cádiz, or he could move from Ciudad Rodrigo and advance on Marmont at Salamanca to threaten French control in Old Castile. After a careful appraisal of each project, he decided to advance on Salamanca. By June the allied army was marching to confront Marmont; simultaneously, efforts were made to coordinate the movements of various Spanish armies so that French forces would be engaged and unable to reinforce Marmont.[42]

For several weeks both commanders manoeuvred their armies in the vicinity of Salamanca. On 21 July, after a bitter evening firefight, Wellington decided to withdraw. The following day as Wellington's movement began, Marmont misinterpreted his intentions and attempted to outflank his army. Wellington's massed troops attacked the French divisions and overwhelmed them as they moved toward his flank. Several of Marmont's divisions were cut to pieces and he was seriously wounded. General Bertrand Clauzel, third in command, rallied the army, repulsed several attacks, and initiated a promising counter-attack that was beaten back. Clauzel withdrew his defeated army skilfully, but with the horrific loss of 14,000 men and 20 guns. Wellington had gained a major victory with just over 5,000 casualties.[43]

The French army, reeling after its defeat, retreated in good order toward Burgos, pursued by the allies. Once beyond the Duero, Wellington decided to move directly east in pursuit of King Joseph's Army of the Centre. On 12 August Wellington's army reached Madrid as Joseph abandoned his capital and fled toward Valencia. By this bold strategy, French troops in Andalucia under Soult were forced to raise the siege of Cádiz and retired northward, fearing Wellington would seal off their escape routes. However, Wellington soon realised that his success had created new difficulties. As Soult's army evacuated Andalucia, his troops reinforced the defeated French armies in the north, thereby gaining numerical superiority over Wellington's army.

After the allied army was established safely in Madrid, Wellington, decided upon a strategy that would keep half of his army under Hill in the vicinity of the capital; the remainder would pursue Clauzel's defeated army. When he reached Burgos, Clauzel quickly fell back, leaving a well-defended citadel. Rather than mask the fortress, Wellington made an erroneous decision to invest Burgos on 19 September 1812. Although the fortress appeared to be easy prey, the French defended it with tenacity and ingenuity, inflicting 2,000 casualties. Eight weeks later, when French relief armies totalling over 50,000 men arrived to raise the siege, Wellington had to beat a retreat. Meanwhile, another 60,000 men under Soult and King Joseph advanced on Madrid, threatening Hill's wing of the army. Hill evacuated Madrid and joined Wellington in the retreat to the Portuguese border. On 23 October the French were in full pursuit with elements of three armies. The allied withdrawal was accompanied by disorder and severe hardship; it only ended on the Portuguese frontier with over 20,000 men missing, wounded, or dead.[44]

After arriving in Portugal, Wellington sought to put the best light on what had become a disastrous campaign. Writing to Liverpool, he acknowledged that the public would be 'disappointed at the results of the last campaign'; yet he insisted, 'It is in fact the most successful campaign in all its circumstances, and has produced for the cause more important results than any campaign in which a British army has been engaged for the last century'. An unusual claim for a general who had been hounded back into Portugal under such humiliating circumstances! He complained about the factors responsible for his failure at Burgos, but he ultimately assumed the blame: 'It was entirely my own act'. However, regarding the retreat, he complained, 'The officers lost all command over their men. Irregularities and outrages of all descriptions were committed with impunity.' During the winter months of 1812–13, Wellington remained in Portugal to recoup his losses, reliving the frustrating events that had undone his 1812 campaign which had begun so gloriously.[45]

Supplies poured into the coastal ports of Portugal and Spain as Wellington prepared for the spring campaign of 1813. To facilitate the movement of reinforcements and supplies, the Royal Navy escorted hundreds of transports to advanced depots established along the coast. With the major logistical requirements completed, Wellington sought to develop a more creative and daring strategy for the campaign. Since he had been named commander-in-chief of the Spanish army after his temporary liberation of Madrid the previous year, he decided to include Spanish troops as an integral element in his new operations. With an Anglo-Portuguese army totalling over 81,000 men, supplemented by several Spanish armies, Wellington decided to take advantage of his numerical superiority. Accordingly, he divided his forces, placing 60,000 troops at Braganca under General Thomas Graham; it would form the left wing of the army and advance north of the Duero. Simultaneously, Wellington would march with the right wing of the army, 30,000 men strong, along the main road, almost 100 miles to the south – from Salamanca and Valladolid to Burgos, supported by Spanish forces. While the French armies of King Joseph concentrated on Wellington's advance, Graham would proceed along the northern route to threaten their flank. It was a brilliant strategy that would force the French army to retreat from town to town or risk envelopment.[46]

Before the end of May, Wellington's strategy was put into operation. When the startled French retired before Wellington's advancing army, they soon realised that Wellington could not be brought to battle until all their forces were concentrated at Burgos. However, before this could be accomplished, Wellington's army was at the gates of Burgos. Unable to hold the Ebro River, King Joseph continued his headlong retreat to Vitoria where he collected some 65,000 men for battle; unknown to him Wellington concentrated over 80,000 men for battle. On 21 June 1813 Wellington launched an attack against the remains of three French armies commanded by King Joseph. While Graham attacked the French right to cut their retreat route, Wellington unleashed a concerted attack on the centre and left of King Joseph's position. Capitalising on obvious French errors, Wellington drove the French from the battlefield late in the afternoon. Meanwhile, Graham cut the main route running towards Pamplona, forcing the French to retreat along a secondary road, already clogged with wagons of baggage and loot. Pursued by the victorious allies who captured their wagons, approximately 140 guns, and the army treasury, the French troops retreated to Pamplona and then continued on into France where they took shelter at the city of Bayonne; their casualty list numbered over 6,000 men while allied losses reached 5,000.[47]

With the exception of the fortresses of Pamplona and San Sebastian, the French army had abandoned Spain. Both Portugal and Spain were liberated and Wellington had achieved what many thought was impossible. Although the French had numerical superiority, they were never able to concentrate their forces, thanks to Wellington's campaign strategy and his coordination of the Spanish armies. The French tried unsuccessfully to relieve the fortresses of Pamplona and San Sebastian, but Wellington intercepted and repulsed them. Yet, rather than mask the fortresses and drive directly into France, Wellington made the dubious decision of delaying the invasion until the fortresses had fallen. As a result, the French had four months to raise a series of barriers along the frontier.

Although the peninsula had been liberated, Wellington saw the invasion of France as the normal extension of his peninsular strategy for the defeat of France.[48] If the French were not pursued and destroyed, they might invade Spain again. Moreover, if the pursuit were not continued, Soult might be able to unite with French forces still fighting in Catalonia or march to join Napoleon's forces fighting the allies in eastern France. Therefore, as soon as the two fortresses had surrendered, Wellington invaded France. Despite the formidable defence position erected by the French along the Bidassoa River, it was forded at low tide. A second line behind the Nivelle River was crossed on 10 November, and the third line on the Nive River was overcome on 10 December despite bitter resistance by Soult's troops. Wellington pushed on to Bayonne where he found a weakened French army, thanks to the transfer of forces to the eastern front by Napoleon. When Soult evacuated Bayonne and turned eastward, Wellington followed him, away from the sea and his source of supplies. After a bitter but essential battle at Orthez, Wellington advanced to Toulouse where he found the remains of Soult's army. With an army of 46,000 men which included 14,000 Portuguese and 10,000 Spanish, the last battle of the peninsular campaign was fought on 10 April; French losses reached 3,200 men while Wellington suffered 4,600 casualties – a tragic loss, for, unknown to both commanders, Napoleon had abdicated four days earlier rendering the battle unnecessary.[49]

In evaluating Wellington's success in the peninsular struggle, it is clear that his strategy was brilliantly conceived and executed. At times disaster loomed on the horizon, but he persevered, never losing sight of his basic objectives. Despite the opposition generated by his critics, he confidently remained committed to his strategy. Central to this strategy was Portugal and its people; notwithstanding his frustration with their inability to make economic and political reforms at the pace he expected, they heroically rose to the challenge despite their appalling losses in resources, both human and material. Also of vital importance to Wellington's strategy were the extraordinary sacrifices of the Spanish people. Although impatient with the idiosyncrasies of their politics and the repeated failures of their armies, he realised that their forces had produced the quagmire that sapped the strength of the French armies.

Coupled with his unique military role in the peninsula, Wellington also exercised extraordinary political power which enabled him to pursue his military strategy. There was probably no general in Europe, other than Napoleon, who had more control in determining strategy – coalition, national, and campaign – than Wellington. As commander-in-chief of the Anglo-Portuguese army, unofficial member of the regency council, and chief representative of the British government in Portugal, he exercised supreme military and political power, enabling him to transform the political, social, and ecomomic structure of the country to achieve his military goals. In Spain, although much more limited in his authority, he exercised inordinate political and military influence on the Spanish government and its armies long before he was made commander-in-chief of the Spanish armies in 1812. Even the British cabinet deferred to his recommendations. With the support of his brothers and his many influential friends in the British government, he exercised unusual political influence in England. As victory followed victory his stature as a military commander reached heroic proportions and increased his political power until he was certainly the most powerful man in the Iberian Peninsula.

In addition to the insights and instincts of an astute politician, his personal traits of leadership, courage, perseverance, loyalty, and charisma on the battlefield produced a European commander whose success was eclipsed only by that of Napoleon. In the final analysis, his achievements rested on the effective implementation of a daring strategy that saved Portugal and Spain, prolonged Napoleon's disastrous involvement in a war he could not win, and laid the foundation for the collapse of the Napoleonic empire.

Notes

1   WSD, Memorandum signed Wellesley, 2 November 1806; Memorandum signed Wellesley, 1 June 1807, vi, 35–8, 68–70.

2   WSD, Memorandum signed Wellesley, 1 June 1807; Memorandum, signed Wellesley, June 1807, vi, 68–70, 80–82.

3   WD, Frederick to Wellington, 14 June 1808, iv, 10–12; John W. Croker, *The Croker Papers* (New York, 1967), p. 11; WD, Castlereagh to Wellington, 30 June 1808, iv, 16–21.

4   WD, Castlereagh to Wellington, 15 July 1808; Wellington to Castlereagh, 21, 25 July 1808, iv, 27–8, 36–41, 42–3.

5   *A Copy of the Proceedings upon the Inquiry Relative to the Armistice and Convention, etc., made and concluded in Portugal in August 1808* . . . (1809), pp. 12 ff.

6   WSD, Wellington to Villiers, 9 January 1809; Wellington to Castlereagh, 9 January 1810, v, 524–6; WD, Memorandum signed Wellington, 7 March 1809, iv, 361–3.

7   James C. Moore, *A Narrative of the British Army in Spain, Commanded by His Excellency Lieut. General Sir John Moore, KB, Authenticated by Official Papers and Original Letters* (1809), Moore to Castlereagh, 25 November 1808, Appendix, pp. 31–32; WSD, Castlereagh to Wellington, 2 April 1809, vi, 210–12.

8   WD, Wellington to Frere, 24 April 1809; Wellington to Castlereagh, 27 April 1810, iv, 266–8, 271–3.

9   WD, Wellington to Sherebrooke, 27 April 1809; Wellington to Junta of Estremadura, 28 April 1809, iv, 276–8, 278–9.

10   WD, Wellington to MacKenzie, 21 May 1809; Wellington to Castlereagh, 31 May, 7 June 1809, iv, 349–51, 378–9, 398–9.

11   WD, Wellington to Castlereagh, 29 July 1809, iv, 532–40; Charles Oman, *A History of the Peninsular War* (Oxford, 1903), ii, 507–88.

12   WD, Wellington to Frere, 31 July, 4 August 1809; Wellington to Beresford, 6 August 1809; iv, 547–9, 561–2, 562–3.

13   WD, Wellington to Richard Wellesley, 13 August 1809; Wellington to Castlereagh, 25 August 1809; v, 34–5, 82–90.

14   WD, Wellington to Richard Wellesley, 24 August 1809, iv, 76–82; Wellesley Papers, British Library, Add. MSS 37286, Canning to Richard Wellesley, 12 August 1809; cited in John Severn, *A Wellesley Affair, Richard Marquess Wellesley and the Conduct of Anglo-Spanish Diplomacy, 1809–1812* (Tallahassee, Florida, 1981), p. 67.

15   WD, Wellington to Richard Wellesley, 16, 21 September 1809, v, 159, 168–69; WSD, Richard Wellesley to Wellington, 19, 24 September 1809; Don Martin de Garay to Richard Wellesley, 23 September 1809, vi, 372–3, 376, 377; Severn, *Wellesley Affair,* pp. 84–5.

16   WD, Wellington to Castlereagh, 25 August 1809, v, 82–90.

17   *Ibid.,* Simão José da Luz Soriano, *Historia da Guerra civil e do estabelecimento do governo parlamentar em Portugal* . . . (Lisbon, 1866–1892), 'Memoria militar em que se descrevem as posicoes defensivas do terreno vizinho e ao norte Lisboa', Segunda Epocha, v, Part ii, 11–45.

18   WD, Wellington to Fletcher, 20 October 1809, v, 234–9.

19   John T. Jones, *Memoranda relative to the Lines thrown up to cover Lisbon in 1810* (1829); Donald D. Horward, ed. trans., *The French Campaign in Portugal: An Account by Jean Jacques Pelet, 1810–1811* (Minneapolis, Minnesota, 1973), pp. 222–78.

20   Donald D. Horward, 'British seapower and its influence upon the Peninsular War (1808–1814)', *Naval War College Review,* xxxi, 59–60; A. H. Norris, R. W. Bremner, *The Lines of Torres Vedras* (Lisbon, 1980), pp. 9–20.

21   Horward, 'British seapower', p. 61.

22   Luz Soriano, *Guerra civil,* Segunda Epocha, i, 606–12.

23   John M. Sherwig, *Guineas and Gunpowder, British Foreign Aid in the Wars with France, 1793–1815* (Cambridge, Mass., 1969), p. 198, 43n; WSD, 'Memoranda on British aid to Portugal, 1809 to 1812', March 1913, vii, 593–4.

24   WD, Wellington to Dundas, 7 June 1809, iv, 393–6; William Carr Beresford, *Collecção das Ordens do Dia, Anno 1809* (Lisbon, 1809), Ordem do Dia, 14, 29, 10, 18, etc., July 1809, pp. 66 ff; Samuel E. Vichness, 'Marshall of Portugal: the military career of William Carr Beresford, 1785–1814', (Ph.D Thesis, Tallahassee, Florida State University, 1976), pp. 225–8.

25   WD, Wellington to Villiers, 14 January 1810; Wellington to Liverpool, 4, 15 Jnauary 1810, v, 411, 424–6, 429–30.

26   WD, 'Proclamation to the Portuguese people', signed Wellington, 4 August 1810, vi, 329–30.

27   WD, 'Proclamation to the Portuguese people', signed Wellington, 4 August

1810; Wellington to Cotton, 4 August 1810; Wellington to Henry Wellesley, 20 August 1810, vi, 329–30, 324, 373–5.

28 Claudio de Chaby, *Excerptos Historicos e Collecção de Documentos relativos a Guerra Denominada da Peninsula* (Lisbon, 1882), 'Contribuicão extraordinaria', 7 June 1809, iv, 105–8; Luz Soriano, *Guerra civil*, Segunda Epocha, v, Part ii, 283–302; Sherwig, *Guineas and Gunpowder*, p. 218.

29 Dom João to Government, 17 January 1810, cited un Mildred L. Fryman, 'Charles Stuart and the 'common cause': The Anglo-Portuguese alliance, 1810–1814', (Ph.D Thesis, Florida State University, 1974), 381–83; WD, Wellington to Stuart, 27 December 1810, vii, 79–80.

30 WD, Wellington to Richard Wellesley, 26 January 1811; Wellington to Stuart, 26 March 1811, vii, 191–2, 403–7; WSD, 'Memoranda on British aid to Portugal, 1809–1812', March 1813, vii, 593–4.

31 WSD, Liverpool to Wellington, 20 October 1809, vi, 412–13; WD, Wellington to Liverpool, 14 November 1809; Wellington to Villiers, 14 January 1810, v, 280–82, 424–26.

32 WD, Wellington to Liverpool, 24, 30, 31 January, 21, 28 February 1810, v, 446–9, 470–71, 511–14; 478–82, 532–3.

33 PRO, WO, 6/50, Liverpool to Wellington, 6, 7 March 1810; WD, Wellington to Berkeley, 24 January 1810, v, 442–43; Wellington to Stuart, 6 May 1810; Wellington to Liverpool, 1 May 1810, 93–4, 78–80.

34 WSD, Henry Wellesley to Wellington, 9, 16, 27 March, 23 April 1810, vi, 490–92, 495–6, 500–1, 514; Richard Wellesley to Villiers, 5 January 1810; Henry Wellesley to Richard Wellesley, 18 April 1810, vi, 476–80, 512–13.

35 WSD, Herbert Taylor to Liverpool, 21 April 1810, vi, 515.

36 WD, Wellington to Forjaz, 6 September 1810; Wellington to Stuart, 11 September, 28 October 1810; Wellington to Liverpool, 27 October 1810; Wellington to Stuart, 6 October 1810; Wellington to Stuart 1, 5, January, 6 May 1811, vi, 408–9, 427–30, 556–9, 555–6, 494–5, vii, 96–8, 107–9, 518–19.

37 Donald D. Horward, *The Battle of Bussaco: Masséna vs. Wellington, 1810* (Tallahassee, Florida, 1965), pp. 65–148; Horward, *Pelet*, pp. 157–91.

38 Horward, *Pelet*, pp. 151 ff.; Oman, *Peninsular War*, iv, 1–90, 131–200.

39 WD, Wellington to Stuart, 27 December 1810, vii, 79–80; PRO, WO, 342/23, 342/24, Stuart to Wellington, 29 December 1810, 19 January 1811.

40 WD, Wellington to Liverpool, 7, 22, 23 May, 20 June, 4 July 1811, vii, 521–5, 595–6, 598–600, viii, 37–9; 78–9.

41 WD, Wellington to Liverpool, 20 January, 7 April 1812, viii, 549–56, ix, 36–45.

42 WD, Wellington to Liverpool, 26 May 1812, IX, 170–75.

43 Jean Sarramon, *La Bataille des Arapiles (22 juillet 1812)* (Toulouse, 1978), pp. 195–249; L. P. Longford, Peter Young, *Wellington's Masterpiece, the Battle of Salamanca* (1973), pp. 199–287; WD, Wellington to Bathurst, 24 July 1812, 299–309.

44 WD, Wellington to Bathurst, 26, 28, 31 October, 3 November 1812, ix, 512–17, 519–21, 524–6, 532–3; Michael Glover, *The Peninsular War, 1807–1814, A Concise Military History* (1974), Returns of November 1812, p. 221.

45 WD, Wellington to Liverpool, 23 November 1812; 'To officers commanding

divisions and brigades', 28 November 1812, ix, 570–74, 582–5.

46 WD, Wellington to Bathurst, 7, 11 May 1813, x, 362–4, 371–3; James Wyld, ed., *Memoir annexed to an Atlas* . . . (1841), Murray to Hill, 20, 21, 25, April, 13, 25 May 1812, pp. 83–8.

47 WD, Wellington to Bathurst, 22 June, 1813, x, 446–53; WSD, Dalhousie to Wellington, 22 June 1813; Hill to Wellington, 22 June 1813, Graham to Wellington, 23 June 1813, viii, 4–9: Jean Sarramon, *La bataille de Vitoria* (Paris, 1985), pp. 446–555.

48 WD, Wellington to Bathurst, 7 November 1812, ix, 541–3.

49 Jac Weller, *Wellington in the Peninsula, 1808–1814* (1962), pp. 362–5; Luz Soriano, *Guerra civil*, Segunda Epocha, iv, Part ii, 267.

Norman Gash

6

The duke of Wellington and the prime ministership, *1824–30*

The duke of Wellington is the only professional soldier in modern British history to have become head of the government. Familiarity with the facts of his career should not blind us to the improbable nature of this event. Unlike the Americans, the French and the Germans, the English do not as a rule display much veneration for their successful generals once the fighting stops. Those of them who take up civilian politics are viewed with suspicion. To be a sailor, and if possible to die like Nelson at the moment of victory, is a surer way to the affections of their fellow-countrymen. For Wellington the precedents of previous soldier-politicians – Cromwell, Marlborough, and 'Butcher' Cumberland – were hardly encouraging. The duke enjoyed greater respect and admiration than any of these but even he damaged his reputation by his subsequent incursion into politics.

The anomaly of Wellington's premiership is all the greater since he was actually commander-in-chief of the forces at the time when he was invited by the king to form a civil administration in 1828. He had been appointed to that supreme military office (usually reserved for members of the royal family) on the death of the duke of York in January 1827 and though he gave it up three months later, when Canning became prime minister, he accepted reappointment on Canning's death in August of the same year. It was a mark of the duke's extraordinary self-centredness that when he agreed to become prime minister in January 1828 he could not or would not perceive any constitutional impropriety in occupying that position along with his command of the army. When he discussed the matter with his colleagues it was evident that he felt a strong disinclination to abandon his military office. It took a decision of the whole cabinet, meeting in his absence, to make him accept the sacrifice. He grumbled to his successor at the Horse Guards, General Hill, that he had never envisaged having to give up command of the army when he became prime minister and was sorry that he had not made a condition that he should be allowed to retain it when he formed his administration.[1]

In this way the constitutional niceties were duly restored; but nothing could alter the fact that the prime minister and first lord of the treasury was also the senior field-marshal of the British army. His political opponents would have been less than human had they not been ready over the next three years to insinuate that the government had militarist tendencies. Nor was the duke as careful as he might have been to avoid presenting them with tempting targets. When the Canningites resigned in May 1828, for example, he appointed General Sir George Murray, formerly quartermaster-general and commander-in-chief in Ireland, to succeed Huskisson as colonial secretary and Sir Henry Hardinge, a senior colonel of the Grenadier Guards and a former officer on his staff, to succeed Palmerston as secretary at war. The Whigs promptly talked of military rule and prophesied that the prime minister would soon gather round him a completely military entourage. In much the same vein, when Peel formed his new metropolitan police the following year, they were attacked by the radicals as an unconstitutional force. The eccentric ultra-tory MP Sir Richard Vyvyan, backed by the *Standard* newspaper, took up the cry and denounced Wellington as a would-be military dictator who had forced Catholic emancipation through parliament by sheer executive intimidation. After the July Revolution in France attempts were made to identify the duke's government with the overthrown authoritarian Polignac ministry in Paris. Such charges had an effect. A personal friend of Wellington told him bluntly in November 1830 not only that his cabinet, with the exception of Peel, 'commanded no share whatever of public confidence' but that 'in the revolutionary tendency of today, even your own fame as a soldier is part of the difficulty because the temper is anti-military'.[2]

Wellington was as rigid an upholder of the law and the constitution as any jurist. Nevertheless, beneath the froth of contemporary propaganda there was a sediment of truth. He was always a soldier at heart. After eight years in the cabinet he could still tell Mrs Arbuthnot that he was no politician but a soldier to whom the army looked for protection.[3] Her tart demolition of this piece of self-deception led to one of the angriest scenes that ever took place between these two old and affectionate friends. Of the duke's dislike of politics, however, there can be no doubt. Most soldiers who enter that alien and devious world have the same reactions. In January 1828, immediately after becoming prime minister, he wrote to the prince of Orange that it was an office 'for the performance of the duties of which I am not qualified, and they are very disagreeable to me'.[4] Thirty months' experience only confirmed him in his opinion. Tired, disillusioned, and unwilling to face the changes which seemed necessary to strengthen his adminis-tration he drafted a letter to Peel in June 1830 suggesting that the king's death (which appeared imminent and in fact occurred before the end of the month) would be a suitable occasion for him to hand over his office to Peel. Such sacrificial gestures are rare in the annals of British prime ministers. Though in the end he changed his mind, partly perhaps because of the remonstrances of the Arbuthnots, the mere fact that he had gone so far as to write such a letter was revealing.[5]

It is reasonable to enquire therefore why the duke had entered politics in the first place. It would be more accurate of course to call it re-entering politics. As a young subaltern he had been elected to the Irish House of Commons when still in his twenties and had later served for a couple of years as chief secretary for Ireland in the interlude between his Indian and peninsular campaigns. But in a society where political patronage was almost indispensable for a successful military career, the two worlds overlapped to a far greater extent than later in the century. In any case Wellington after Waterloo needed no patronage even from his grand elder brother Lord Wellesley. To Lord Liverpool and his colleagues in 1818 the advantages of recruiting such an illustrious figure for the administration were obvious. The duke was no ordinary general. As conqueror of Napoleon he had an inter-national reputation. Among the British aristocracy he was already something of a legend; even George IV stood in slight awe of him. As commander-in-chief of the allied forces in occupied France and diplo-matic representative of his country in the councils of Europe he mixed on equal terms with kings and emperors. At home he was the supreme authority on all things military; he was an expert on Ireland and on good terms with the Roman hierarchy in that country, notably Arch-bishop Curtis of Armagh whom he had known in his peninsular days. That such a great public figure could be allowed at the age of fifty to sink back into routine duties when the occupation of France came to an end was unthinkable. If further arguments were needed, they could be found in the political state of Britain. The period from 1818 to 1820 – the years of the general election of 1818, Peterloo, the Six Acts, and the queen's divorce case – saw the Liverpool administration at its lowest ebb. Nothing could have seemed more desirable than to use the duke's prestige in the service of the government.

For Wellington himself the case was different. He evinced at first a distinct unwillingness to enter the cabinet and his reluctance was only overcome by his sense of loyalty to the ministers who had supported him and his little army in the dark days of 1808–12, in particular Castlereagh who had secured his command in the peninsula against strong opposition. Castlereagh in fact seems to have been the means whereby Liverpool was able to persuade the reluctant duke to identify himself with the administration. Wellington told Lady Salisbury many years later that the argument that had prevailed with him was Castlereagh's insistence that if he refused the invitation it would weaken the government and make him a rallying-point for their opponents.[6] It was a clever argument to use with a man of the duke's disciplined outlook. He believed passionately in government: good government if possible, but firm government at all events. He made a mental distinction between the state as an institution and a ministry of fallible politicians temporarily in charge of that institution. When accepting Liverpool's formal invitation to join the cabinet, he stipulated that should the ministry for any reason go out of office, he must be considered free to take any political course he thought proper. What he clearly meant was that he should not be expected automatically to go into opposition against their successors. 'The experience which I have acquired during my long service abroad,' he wrote, 'has convinced me that a factious opposition to the Government is highly injurious to the interests of the country.'[7] As with lesser men, the duke's actual conduct did not always live up to his principles. Nevertheless, it remained true that throughout his life he was never an ordinary party politician. The prime minister expressed his approval of this attitude in terms which probably indicated something more than a mere desire to smooth over any lingering hesitation on the duke's part. In Liverpool's own mind was a clear distinction between Wellington and the ordinary run of professional or aristocratic politicians who made up his administration. His first thought had been to make the duke minister without portfolio. There would have been an air of contrivance about this, however, and a better solution was found when Lord Mulgrave offered to vacate his post of Master-General of the Ordnance in the duke's favour. It was the one technically military post in the cabinet and as such it provided colourable justification for Wellington's appointment. The prime minister continued to regard the duke as being in a different category to the rest of his ministerial colleagues. When the question of a successor to Castlereagh at the Foreign Office was being discussed in the summer of 1822 and the duke's name was floated as a possible candidate, Liverpool wrote to a colleague that: 'I do not think that anything would be more inexpedient, for the sake of the Duke of Wellington and of his public utility, than to put him permanently into any political office'.[8] This was not a specious argument designed merely to protect Canning's claims. When Liverpool and Castlereagh himself had been discussing a year and a half earlier the future composition of the ministry, both men had taken the view that Wellington must not be placed in any situation that might expose him to political attacks.[9]

It is clear that Lord Liverpool, who was responsible for bringing Wellington into high politics, regarded him as primarily a great public servant, not a potential party adherent or political leader. It was a consideration which applied even more forcefully against his appointment as prime minister. In his prolonged exchange of letters with the duke in the spring of 1827 Canning at one point made an uncompromising statement of the constitutional position.

> The union of the whole power of the state, civil and military, in the same hands (for your Grace as Prime Minister could never have effectually divested yourself of your influence over the army) would certainly, in my opinion, have constituted a station too great for *any subject,* however eminent, or however meritorious, and one incompatible with the practice of a free constitution.[10]

Canning no doubt had an interest of his own in putting the case so strongly. But he was by no means alone in his views. Only a few weeks earlier a vaguer but similar warning had been sent by S. R. Lushington, one of the secretaries to the treasury in Liverpool's government, to the king's confidential secretary Sir William Knighton. He was writing under the apprehension that a plot was afoot to put the duke in Downing Street at the head of a an ultra-tory ministry and he was emphatic that nothing could be more damaging to Wellington's honour and happiness. The actions of such a government:

would be watched throughout the country, with all the jealousy of a military despotism, and whose legitimate acts of authority and vigour his Grace would be incapable of sustaining in his own House with the eloquence and force which the dignity and safety of the Crown require in the First Minister.[11]

Since Lushington was a government whip with every opportunity to gauge backbench opinion, and a 'Protestant' who had no reason for favour Canning, his views were important. In any case George IV was as quick as his father to resent any pressure from an aristocratic cabal on his exercise of the royal prerogative.

Nevertheless, even if the factious nature of the support for Wellington in the spring of 1827 is set aside, the constitutional objections remained. Why then did the king offer, and the duke accept, the leadership of the government only nine months later? For the king – and in this matter the king played a decisive role – the answer was simple. The political situation had changed dramatically since March 1827. Canning had died in August, leaving political parties more fragmented than they had been for fifteen years. His successor Goderich was timid and inept; his coalition ministry split by personal quarrels. In the royal mind the whigs were ruled out as an alternative government because of their pro-Catholic policy and George IV's antipathy to Lord Grey. If he reverted to the old safe, central, Liverpool party, the only conceivable leaders were Wellington in the House of Lords and Peel in the House of Commons. George IV did not like Peel; for him the only possible candidate was the duke. Unlike March 1827, when his eventual choice of Canning was made after much anxiety and internal debate, his summons to Wellington in January 1828 was a quick personal decision. His good humour at what he had done was shown by the way in which he treated the duke to a lively mimicry of the different members of Goderich's dismissed cabinet. For the moment possibly he had the illusion of acting as a real monarch.

The duke was less exhilarated but he accepted the commission to form a government. Yet only eight months earlier he had told the House of Lords that he felt disqualified from the post of prime minister and lacked the capacity to fill it. On that occasion he had been defending himself against the charge that he had intrigued to secure the premiership for himself on Liverpool's resignation and he was telling the truth. He had not plotted to displace Canning. Yet in adding impulsively 'My Lords, I should have been worse than mad if I had thought of such a thing' he was allowing his vehemence to carry him too far.[12] That the idea of becoming prime minister had literally never come to him is simply not credible; but there can be little doubt that he did not mean his words to have that sense. It was in fact a possibility which had been taking shape, in his mind and those of others, for several years. It had happened as a consequence of the growing hostility between himself and Canning. The process had been gradual. In his early years in the cabinet Wellington had been relatively inconspicuous. On the death of his friend and patron Lord Castlereagh in 1822 he took his place as British representative at the Congress of Verona and, more importantly, was of material assistance to the prime minister in persuading the king to accept Canning, then about to embark for India as governor-general, as the new secretary of state for foreign affairs. In this he was merely acting the part of a disinterested servant of the administration. The cabinet seemed to think Canning was the best man for the post and Wellington considered it his duty therefore to assist in overcoming the king's reluctance.

Once Canning was back in the cabinet, however, friction began between the two men and as a result Wellington started to take a more positive role in the Liverpool administration than anyone could have envisaged a few years earlier. In the situation which now developed there was a strong element of paradox. Their main differences as far as policy was concerned were on foreign affairs and Catholic relief. Over the first Canning did little more than continue along lines laid down by Castlereagh; but his flamboyant appeals to the liberal press and public opinion in Britain grated on the susceptibilities of the duke who was understandably averse to anything that appeared to threaten the alliance of European monarchies which had brought victory and peace in 1815. On Catholic Emancipation the duke's abstract views went as far as those of Canning himself; but he had no desire to force the issue. He resented Canning's efforts within the cabinet to get the issue taken up as a matter of government policy; he feared the disruptive effects on the administration if this were to happen; and he disliked the appearance of parliamentary cooperation between Canning and the whig opposition whenever the Catholic question was discussed in parliament. It was also a clash of temperament and character. No leading contemporary politician aroused stronger feelings either of loyalty or repulsion than Canning. The duke, like many others in the cabinet, was antipathetic and apt therefore to put the worst construction on all his actions. On foreign policy Wellington was in a minority in his antagonism – to the point where at the end of 1824 he offered his resignation on the grounds that it must be irksome for Liverpool to find him in opposition so often to the prime minister's own views.[13] On Catholic emancipation, however, the duke was only one of a number of influential ministers, headed by Liverpool himself, who formed the 'Protestant' party in the cabinet. On the issue, therefore, where the duke differed in principle from Canning, he was virtually isolated; on the other, where his disagreement was only tactical, he found himself with powerful allies. It was a deceptive situation, though the full extent of the deception was not revealed until 1829.

The last three years of the Liverpool administration therefore saw the emergence of Wellington as the unofficial head of an anti-Canning, anti-Catholic group within the government with a larger number of adherents in and out of parliament who looked to the duke as their champion. It was a development fostered by the king's frequent and embarrassing assertions, to others besides Wellington that he regarded the duke as the one reliable member of the administration and the natural successor to Lord Liverpool. Wellington's own indiscretion in allowing himself to be implicated in the king's 'cottage coterie' of anti-Canningites at court, could only have strengthened this impression. As early as the summer of 1824, when there was considerable concern about Liverpool's health, the possiblity of Wellington's succession occurred to a number of people. Though the duke protested his unfitness, both to the king and to his over-zealous friends the Arbuthnots, it was clear that he was not entirely closing his mind to such an eventually. When he told Princess Lieven about the representations which had been made to him, she suggested (with a certain feline malice) that his lack of practice in parliamentary speaking would be against his becoming prime minister. No, replied the duke promptly, 'to begin with, I can learn; if I want it, it will come back to me. And, even if I can't, the Duke of Portland had no more idea of speaking than I have, and yet he was at the head of the administration'.[14]

After Liverpool had been disabled by a stroke in February 1827, the notion of Wellington as prime minister gathered strength. To the partisan Arbuthnots the duke merely said that his position as commander-in-chief made it impossible and that he would not lift a finger to secure it. He was particularly concerned, as he had been in 1824, not to appear to be angling for Liverpool's post before it was even vacant and not to do anything that might be construed as encroaching on the king's prerogative. He felt a duty to the monarch and to the paralysed prime minister which was part of his soldierly sense of discipline. Yet these honourable scruples clearly did not constitute an objection in principle to becoming prime minister himself if a call was ever made for his services in that capacity.[15] It is impossible otherwise to explain the paradox that while in March 1827 he was telling Knighton, the ultra-tory peers, and anybody else who would listen to him, that he was disqualified from the premiership, in January 1828 his accepted the post without demur and seemed surprised that his colleagues thought it incompatible with his position as commander-in-chief. One is almost driven to the conclusion that in the spring of 1827 the duke was alleging his army command as a convenient excuse to avoid a situation in which he would be seen as a rival to Canning if, as always seemed likely, Canning was bound to be successful. By scratching his name in advance from the list of candidates, he escaped the humiliation of being beaten by a man whom he disliked and despised. A further advantage of this self-proclaimed neutrality was that it enabled him to warn the king in emphatic terms of the disruptive effect on the supporters of Liverpool's ministry if Canning succeeded him. The political events which followed Liverpool's resignation, so far from confirming the duke's ineligibility for the premiership, in fact brought him a stage nearer Downing Street. Canning's brief administration of 1827 demonstrated not only that he lacked the support of nearly half Liverpool's old cabinet, but that Wellington was his most formidable and inveterate opponent. The duke's immediate withdrawal from the command of the army, in addition to his departure from the cabinet, was a public mark of antipathy which was regretted by his more judicious friends.

From Wellington's point of view the death of Canning in August 1827 transformed the political situation. He had some right to consider himself equal in political weight to either Goderich or Lansdowne, the two most obvious successors, and it would have been natural for him to feel that, given the opportunity, he would be able to halt the drift of government towards liberalism and whiggery and bring it back to the central position occupied for so long by Lord Liverpool's administration. The idea of becoming prime minister had been present in his mind for over three years and responsibility was something which never frightened him. Politics was not war but he had immense confidence in his capacity to master the responsibilities of any post which he felt it his duty to accept. It was said of him that he knew so much that he thought he knew everything. There was a good deal of truth in this. 'I feel that I am capable of doing or acquiring anything I choose,' he once remarked to Lady Salisbury; and that was in 1836 when one would have thought that experience had made him a wiser if not a sadder man.[16] He had in fact many of the qualities necessary for success in high political office – courage, common sense, determination and great administrative ability. Colleagues who had not known much of him before were impressed by the impact he made in his first few months as prime minister. 'A most extraordinary man,' commented his new foreign secretary Dudley in March 1828, '. . . quick as lightning, clear, decisive, at the same time simple and good humoured'.[17] His punctuality and attention to detail were legendary. Yet behind these efficient business habits were other qualities more readily perceived by the women of his acquaintance who were less overawed by his professional reputation and more accustomed to judging men as human beings. Mrs Arbuthnot noted his impatience. 'The Duke is a sort of spoiled child,' she wrote in December 1829. 'He wishes to be liked by everybody; he is by nine-tenths, but the opposition of the *one*-tenth irritates him.'[18] Princess Lieven as early as 1821 had remarked on his vanity. 'It is incredible how his pride has a share in everything that he does. It plunges him into despair not to be able to do something, or to do it badly.'[19]

What made the role of prime minister an uneasy one for him was his instinctive authoritarianism, bred by years of unquestioned command and unbroken success. An army commander is habitually surrounded by pleasant young men, whose business it is to see to his personal wishes and comforts, and by senior officers whose business it is to receive his official orders and see that they are carried out. The transition from this rarefied atmosphere to the argumentativeness and equality of cabinet discussion is not an easy one. Wellington as prime minister still tended to judge his ministers as he would staff officers. Lady Salisbury, another observant woman friend, noted in 1838 that when the duke talked of his colleagues of the 1820s – Canning, Peel and Castlereagh – he assessed their qualities 'wholly in reference to their habits of business, common sense, and information on necessary topics. What one should describe as genius or talent seemed to go for nothing with him'.[20] There is an oblique confirmation of this in a conversation which the duke had with Mrs Arbuthnot in January 1829. Talking about his ministerial colleagues, he told her that the two who pleased him most were Aberdeen and Goulburn. It can hardly be accident that the first of these had a notably mild and unassertive personality and the second the self-effacing habits of a good civil servant. Ellenborough indeed described Goulburn as not looking as if he was a member of the cabinet at all but more like an under-secretary.[21] Another consequence of the duke's military upbringing was his intolerance of criticism and opposition. Disagreements over policy he was apt to interpret as a sign of personal hostility, and where he detected hostility he was extremely stiff. He was a martinet even with men whom he might have been expected to find more congenial than his civilian colleagues. Hardings told Arbuthnot in May 1830 that the duke was positively harsh and ill-tempered with his official subordinates; that he was sometimes so offensive to Hardinge himself that it was all he could do to put up with it, despite his real affection for his chief.[22]

Ever since his peninsular days Wellington had been a vehement grumbler; but the evidence suggests that the longer his premiership continued, the more peevish and bad-tempered he became. As early as February 1829 he was assuring Mrs Arbuthnot that if he went out of office, nothing would induce him to return. Towards the end of the same year he was writing to Knighton that if he had known of what he had discovered since he took office, he never would have consented to be the king's minister.[23] As time went by his suspicions and dislikes spread to most of his colleagues. Lady Shelley in old age could remember how he told her after a year or two in power that he was beginning to doubt the attachment even of his best friends and how grieved she had been to see him losing his old buoyancy of spirits.[24] There is plenty of contemporary evidence to confirm her recollection. Talking with Mrs Arbuthnot in May 1830 about his determination to throw up his office, the duke complained bitterly that he did not possess the authority and influence in the cabinet that as head of the government he ought to have, and that its members had no respect or deference for him.[25] Yet it was not so much that the duke was isolated in the cabinet as that many of his colleagues felt isolated from him. He retained their respect as a man but they had lost confidence in him as prime minister. Their general relief at their defeat in November 1830 and Wellington's failure to get support in May 1831 when the king invited him to form a second administration, tell their own story. Greville's verdict, delivered within less than a week of the defeat on the civil list motion, was simple. 'The Duke will probably never take office again, but will be at the head of the army, and his own friends begin to admit that this would be the most desirable post for him'[26]

What can hardly be denied is that the history of the Wellington government was bound up with the idiosyncrasies of the duke himself. He stamped it with the unmistakeable imprint of his character and this was as true of its failures as of its successes. The supreme achievement, of course, was the passage of Catholic emancipation, the issue that had bedevilled an entire generation of British politics. Just as Grey was probably the only minister who could have passed the reform bill in 1832 and Peel the only minister who could have repealed the corn laws in 1846, so Wellington alone was capable of securing Catholic emancipation in 1829. Indeed, there is a certain significance in the fact that it took a soldier to put through a solution of so intractable a problem. It could be argued with considerable justification that the time had come for the deadlock to be broken. It was obvious that the controversy would never go away; that the Protestant party was beginning to grow weary of the unending struggle; and that O'Connell, the Catholic League, and finally the county Clare election, had given a new urgency to an old question. All that was needed was for government to abandon its neutrality and throw its sword into the scales which had remained so evenly balanced throughout the 1820s.

All that might be true; but the obstacles were still formidable. They existed in the law of the constitution, in the Church of England, in the House of Lords, in the mass of English public opinion, above all in the person of the king himself. Of all men in public life Wellington was the best equipped, perhaps the only man well equipped, to overcome the genuine scruples of George IV's wayward and often stubborn mind. Castlereagh might have been able to do so through his calm, concilia-tory diplomacy; Canning might have done so through his personal charm and persuasiveness. It is hard to think of anyone else alive in 1829 who could have succeeded. As far as the duke was concerned, his opinion had been for many years in favour of concession. Once the necessity for intervention was proved, he had no need to reflect what to do. The whole operation, involving the successive capitulation of Peel, George IV, and the House of Lords, resembled a piece of military planning. It was as remarkable as any of the duke's victories in the field. He once compared it with the battle of Waterloo; it was more like the protracted and costly siege of Badajoz. For the heavy casualties on his side – popular Protestantism and the angry, cheated ultra-tories – he had little concern. He once said in later life that 'nobody can do me either good or harm except myself. Therefore I am very careful what I do. But I care little what is said.'[27] This was perhaps just as well. Unlike Grey in 1832 and Peel in 1846, Wellington had no great movement of public opinion in the country to sustain him. It was an autocratic act in an unreformed parliamentary system that was still amenable to executive pressure in time of crisis. The duke won his battle; but only at the cost of accelerating the decline of that system.

For the rest, his leadership of the government was marked by a steady draining away of parliamentary support. Just as he never understood what he regarded as lack of loyalty on the part of his colleagues, so he failed to appreciate that the innate strength of the government in the House of Commons needed constant nourishment if it was to be maintained. What to Lord Liverpool was a constant preoccupation, the duke seemed hardly to consider. His deficiency in this respect was conspicuously shown in his handling of the Huskisson episode in 1828. Huskisson was a gifted but shy, awkward, prickly man who even in Liverpool's administration had on occasion sorely tried the patience of both the prime minister and his friend and patron Canning. Difficult as he was in the cabinet, however, he was a public figure of considerable reputation in liberal circles and the only eminent figure among the small group of Canningites (the others being Grant, Palmerston and Dudley) who had been invited to join the administration as part of the policy of reuniting Lord Liverpool's old ministry. For the secession which occurred in May 1828 Huskisson was at least three-quarters to blame. On the East Retford disfranchisement bill he had allowed his vote to be recorded against the government and in breach of a cabinet agreement to which he had been a consenting party. When reproached by the government whip he impulsively wrote a letter of resignation in the small hours of the morning and sent it to Wellington. As was emphasised to the prime minister over the next few days, he had only intended, in placing his office at the duke's disposal, to apologise, and make amends, for his conduct and that he did not really wish to resign unless Wellington thought it necessary. The duke, however, took the disciplinarian line that if this were so, all Huskisson had to do was to request the return of his letter. The anguished Huskisson, on the other hand, thought that this would be an humiliation to which he should not be expected to submit himself. Well-intended intervention by others proved to no avail. Neither man would shift from his position and after waiting a few days the duke informed Huskisson in a brief though not discourteous note that

arrangements had been made to fill his post. At that the other three
Canningites, as was foreseeable, promptly retired from office also.

On the surface it was a foolish clash of pride and punctilio which a
dash of common sense or good humour on either side would have
resolved. A prime minister such as Pitt or Liverpool would have had
no difficulty in smoothing over the affair. But there were deeper
reasons for Wellington's disinclination to help Huskisson out of the
pit he had needlessly dug for himself. Personally and politically
Huskisson and his three colleagues shared a distrust of the duke which
was a legacy of the Canning–Wellington feud in the Liverpool
cabinet. They had come into the duke's ministry as a group, behaved
there as a group, and went out as a group, as though only in solidarity
could they feel secure. Their two leading figures, Huskisson and
Grant, were given to nervous, hair-trigger reactions over differences
of policy with the prime minister. Huskisson's letter of resignation
was the third such missive to come from the group in the first four
months of the ministry. Yet they did not in reality form an isolated
faction within the cabinet. On many issues their liberal views were
supported by others, including Peel who as leader of the Commons
was the second most powerful figure in the administration.

This was in fact the fundamental cause of Wellington's antipathy to
the Canningites. Over foreign policy, the long-delayed corn bill, the
Penryn and East Retford disfranchisement bills, the duke had found
himself in a minority in his own cabinet; over corn at one stage he had
all his colleagues against him. Irritated and frustrated, it was natural
for him, however unreasonable, to place the blame for the unruliness
of his cabinet on the subversive influence of Huskisson's awkward
squad. The real difficulty was that though his ministry represented a
reunion of the old Liverpool party, it was a reunion of recent
opponents. The reconstituted party had more the air of a coalition.
Time was needed for it to knit together; and time was what
Wellington denied it. That the failure to retain the Canningites in
1828 was a fundamental error is demonstrated by the fact that two
years later there were active negotiations to bring them back again. By
a singular irony Huskisson's accidental death in September 1830 at
the opening of the Manchester–Liverpool railway occurred as the
result of an attempted meeting with the duke intended as a first step
towards a renewal of their political alliance. After that it was too late.
During the closing months of Wellington's administration the
leaderless Canningites held deliberately and tantalisingly aloof. From

the confused signals which rose from their camp it appeared that they were shy of returning to the duke's cabinet without the supporting presence of a few whigs or a promise of parliamentary reform. The talk of new conditions was vague; the old distrust as firm as ever. The final consequence of the duke's needless severity of 1828 was the presence of four Canningites in Grey's successor cabinet of November 1830, three of them in the key positions of secretary of state.

There were other ways in which the administration suffered from Wellington's lack of skill as a politician. In economic policy, which had been the main strength of Liverpool's government, the duke's social conservatism effectively blocked any further progress. He was prepared to enforce rigid economy in government departments, but the more imaginative measures advocated by Peel, Goulburn and Herries foundered on the prime minister's opposition. The proposal for a modified income tax, included in Goulburn's draft budget of 1830 (anticipating Peel's action when he came to power twelve years later), was eventually dropped, though it probably would have been brought forward again in 1831 had the administration survived. Wellington, thinking in historical rather than economic terms, regarded the income tax as a purely emergency device justified only by such conditions as a great European war. To impose it in peace time seemed to him a panic measure. As well as bearing heavily on the landed classes, it would be interpreted abroad as a sign of internal weakness.[28] Essentially therefore the three budgets of his administration were holding operations. They met immediate needs; they afforded no long-term advantage. Though Goulburn, his chancellor of the exchequer, was always able to balance income and expediture, this satisfactory accountancy depended on two factors – minimal demands for state expenditure and buoyant trade figures – which in their nature could hardly be permanent. The underlying financial dilemma was that nothing further could be done to stimulate trade and industry by means of tariff reductions unless a substitute could be found for the initial loss of revenue involved, either by raising internal taxes on consumption, which was politically unacceptable, or by finding some new source of revenue. This in the view of all financial experts, could only be a revived income tax. Wellington never claimed to be an economist; he was content to balance the books. But this was no answer to the universal cry for cheap government and a reduction of the taxes pressing on the mass of the population.

It did nothing either to dispel the widespread though fallacious belief that the central government was still riddled with waste and corruption. Wellington's ministry was singularly honest and economical. It was not brought down by its economic policy; but its conservatism and lack of initiative in fiscal matters did leave it vulnerable to popular criticisms. It should not be forgotten that it was defeat on an opposition motion for an enquiry into the civil list which technically at any rate led to Wellington's resignation. Though the defeat was rightly taken as proof of the government's lack of support in the House of Commons, it was not without some significance that this lack of control was shown up over a financial matter. Economy and purity, the two issues at stake behind the opposition motion, were also popular cries in the constituencies of members on both sides of the house. For dissident tories the civil list motion offered a much more respectable opportunity to express their resentment against Wellington's government than the parliamentary reform debate due for the following day.[29]

Wellington's final suicidal stroke against his own administration was delivered in his notorious declaration against parliamentary reform on 2 November 1830. Its importance lay both in its timing and in its language. It was made on the opening day of the newly-elected parliament in response to a moderate, almost a conciliatory, speech by Lord Grey, the leader of the opposition in the House of Lords – and also in the knowledge that Henry Brougham had given notice of his intention to bring forward a resolution on the subject at the start of the session in the House of Commons. According to the traditional account, when the duke sat down, he asked Aberdeen on the bench beside him, 'I have not said too much, have I?'. There was in fact practically nothing more he could have said. The government, he told the peers, had no plan of reform. He had never known any plan likely to improve the constitution. It answered all the purposes of good government; it had the confidence of the country. If he had to devise a legislature for the country, he would make it his model. Not only was he not prepared to introduce a scheme of parliamentary reform but he would oppose any such measure proposed by others. Thus Hansard; and the accuracy of the reporting has never been seriously questioned, even though the speech seems to have made more impression on the general public than on its immediate audience – perhaps because the peers were more used to the duke's style of oratory.

The emphasis, the exaggeration, the repetition, though they read today a trifle absurdly, were utterly characteristic. The duke, as Lady

Frances Balfour once observed, was addicted to superlatives. When he wished to express strong views, his only means was to use strong language. It did not necessarily convey a deep or considered opinion nor did it mean that he was incapable of changing his mind if circumstances altered. One has only to recall his similarly inflated language in the House of Lords in May 1827 about the premiership. It was just that Wellington was accustomed to speaking his mind dogmatically as a commander expecting instant deference, not as a politician prudently aware of the mutability of events and the wisdom of leaving options open. The real question is not why he spoke as he did but why he chose that particular occasion to make his views known. One plausible and at the time widely-held view was that the duke hoped, by coming out strongly against reform, to regain the support of the ultra-tories whom he had alienated over Catholic emancipation. The autumn negotiations with Palmerston to bring back the Canningites had failed and since Wellington himself had ruled out on personal grounds an alliance with the whigs, a gesture of reconciliation towards the disgrunted ultras seemed only logical.

Whatever his intentions, this might well have seemed a likely result of his speech. Mrs Arbuthnot, who had been delighted at the breakdown of the Palmerston negotiations, reflected that: 'the not making this junction & the hostility that will necessarily ensue, will bring back our Tory party. If it has that effect, I for one shall be quite satisfied'.[30] A few days later she recorded that 'the Tories are delighted'. Nevertheless, she makes no suggestion that Wellington's main or only purpose in making his celebrated declaration was to conciliate right-wing dissidents in his own party. One may doubt also whether it would have been typical of the duke to indulge in such a politic but cynical manoeuvre. Unlike most of his cabinet, he did not think that his ministry lacked numerical parliamentary support, merely a sufficiency of front-bench ministers in the Commons able to hold their own in debate. All the opposition parties, he told Vesey Fitzgerald at the end of November, would gladly join the administration. The difficulties were not over policy and principles but places and personalities. To the Lord Lieutenant of Ireland he wrote in the second week of October that though the public mind was disturbed on many issues such as electoral reform, tithes, slavery, and taxation, he hoped that when the new parliament assembled, it would have a tranquillising effect.[31] His speech of 2 November, therefore, was less likely to have been a long-premeditated act than a reaction to two specific events. The first was the message from the Canningites, delivered through Littleton the previous day, that parliamentary reform was their only condition for joining the ministry. The second was the form of Grey's speech recommending the ministers to undertake a measure of moderate parliamentary reform.

It is true, of course, that opposition to Parliamentary reform was with Wellington a settled principle. In October, for example, he had been asked by Sir James Shaw, a former tory MP for the City and lord mayor of London, whether he could not initiate such a measure as a conciliatory act. The duke's reply was uncompromising. He would oppose it, he wrote, 'at all times and under all circumstances'.[32] Written a fortnight before the formal opening of parliament, this indicated a state of mind rather than a decision. A better clue perhaps is a letter he wrote to Maurice Fitzgerald four days after the debate in the Lords. In a sixteen-page memorandum the knight of Kerry had argued that in spite of the duke's parliamentary declaration the times made it necessary that 'good men shall accommodate themselves to uncontroulable circumstances', and counselled him to take Lord Grey and his friends into the cabinet and pass a moderate measure of reform. In his reply Wellington doubted whether such a measure would get through parliament and said that if it did, he could be no party to it. 'I must add that I feel no strength excepting in my character for plain manly dealing. I could not pretend that I wished sincerely well to the measure, which I should become not merely a party but the principal in recommending'.[33] These surely are the authentic Wellington accents. In his 2 November speech he probably had nothing more in mind than to make his own position utterly clear and to put an end as far as he was concerned to all the talk of parliamentary reform that had been going on inside and outside the administration for several weeks.

Nine days later his government was defeated on the civil list motion and by 22 November he was out of office. For the fall of his ministry Wellington gave two reasons: the success of the duke of Cumberland in organising an ultra-tory opposition to him, and the effect of the 1830 French Revolution in producing a temporary enthusiasm for reform in the British public. What he would not admit was that either Catholic emancipation alone or his anti-reform speech had been a direct cause.[34] Later on, as is the way of politicians when they look back over their careers, he offered other interpretations of his famous words. In October 1832 he told the Austrian diplomat von Neumann that everybody had misunderstood him. He had been asked whether he proposed to do anything about reform and had replied in the negative because he did not think the House of Lords was the proper place in which to originate such a measure; but he would have carefully considered such a proposal coming up from the Commons even though he did not think it was the business of the king's ministers to change the constitution of the country.[35] This singularly mild interpretation is not supported by any other evidence. Later on he reverted to the more logical and popular explanation of a bid for ultra-tory support. He told Lady Salisbury in 1836 that when parliament met in the summer of 1830 it was a question of counting heads. The ultras were getting restive at the talk of reform and he knew that he would lose as many as he would gain on the issue. In making his declaration his purpose was to reassure tory magnates like Lord Lonsdale that they had nothing to fear.[36] Whether this is historically any more accurate than his remarks to von Neumann may be doubted. It is clear that what he said on that evening in the House of Lords was done without consultation with his colleagues. The actual words he used give the impression of unpremeditation. Aberdeen said afterwards that had the duke spoken to him beforehand he might have prevented him from uttering such an undiscriminating eulogy on the unreformed electoral constitution.

Wellington was on firmer ground, however, when he wrote to General Malcolm in June 1831[37] that it was not his remarks on parliamentary reform which had destroyed the government because its influence in the House of Commons had already broken down. To illustrate his point he instanced forty-six MPs who had voted against the ministry at the end of the civil list debate of 15 November but who subsequently voted against the whig reform bill. No doubt these dissident tories also acted without much foresight or calculation. Yet there was more to the fall of the Wellington administration than the momentary defection of a knot of revengeful ultras. Previous ministries had put up with similar reverses and not resigned. Over parliamentary reform, which was to be debated the next day, there was no certainty that Brougham would get a majority. As it turned out even Lord Grey had to get rid of the 1830 House of Commons and find another elected in the excitement of 1831 before he could pass his reform bill. Yet to steer a safe course through the opening weeks of the 1830 session required good nerves, firm leadership, and parliamentary tact. Collectively the government of Wellington lacked all these qualities. By the autumn of 1830, in fact, their morale had gone; over the whole cabinet there was a palpable air of disintegration. Wellington was tired, resentful and bad-tempered; Peel frustrated and withdrawn; many of the others fatalistic or indifferent. To most of them resignation came as a relief; Peel seemed positively delighted.

Writing immediately after the event, Greville attributed the decline and fall of the administration to the egotism and political inexperience of the duke and the folly or timidity of Peel in not insisting, if necessary under threat of resignation, on changes in the conduct of the government. There is much substance in both criticisms. It should be remembered, however, that when Wellington took office he had great difficulties to overcome. They had emerged the previous year when Lord Liverpool had been forced to retire. Only then was the sustaining and unifying role he had played in politics fully revealed. None of the administrations between March 1827 and November 1830 had effective control of the House of Commons. Canning was denied the opportunity to prove his qualities as prime minister; Goderich demonstrated his lack of them only too well. It was Wellington's fate to transform an inherently weak position into a hopeless one. He was not, after all, the man to do anything by halves. He brought disaster on himself not by lack of leadership but by the wrong kind of leadership; one that depended almost entirely on himself. He was a strong man exercising his strength in a role for which he was not suited either by temperament or training. The unnecessary breach with the Canningites lost him support on one side; Catholic emancipation lost him support on the other. Failure to take any new initiative in economic policy left his government with nothing to divert public attention from grievances. In these circumstances his categorical rejection of parliamentary reform in November 1830 stamped him in the eyes of the public as a reactionary from whose administration nothing further was to be expected. His removal from office appeared, therefore, a prerequisite of obtaining any of the reforms which the country had been led to hope for ever since the general election.

In this there was a great deal of injustice. On its record the Wellington administration could claim to be one of the most economical and reforming of the century, given its short duration. Even over parliamentary reform a number of the cabinet, as was shown in the House of Commons on the evening of the duke's famous anti-reform speech, were in favour of moderate changes and others felt it was inevitable. What paralysed their capacity for further innovation was their dread of exposing themselves once more to charges of ratting on previous policies. Just as the reform battle of 1831–2 unnerved the whigs for any future conflicts with the House of Lords, so Catholic Emancipation in 1829 destroyed the ability of the Wellington administration to deal with the issues which took its place. None felt this more than Peel, potentially the most radical reformer in the cabinet. His negative and fatalistic attitude at the opening of the 1830 session left the initiative entirely with the prime minister. There was no real will in the government to grapple with the problem of parliamentary reform. Certainly the whole subject bristled with difficulties. It could hardly be said that it was an issue ripe for settlement, as the Catholic question had been two years earlier. There was no agreement in political circles on either the principle or details of such a measure. The whigs themselves were no better prepared and the long drawn-out struggle which dominated politics for the next eighteen months was proof of the unreadiness of the legislature itself to pass such a fundamental reform. Little wonder that Wellington's ministers had no stomach for a measure which would bring them discredit by its introduction and humiliation by its rejection. It was, as Peel expressed it to his brother even before the defeat on the civil list, 'better for the country and better for ourselves that we should not undertake the question'. From that point of view the division on 15 November was providential. It presented the ministry with a decent excuse for quitting office and left their successors free to deal with the question as they thought fit.

For the fall of the Wellington administration there is perhaps no single identifiable cause. Its weakness was more in the nature of a long progressive decline which nobody was able to arrest. Yet at the heart of the situation was the personality of the prime minister himself. With all his remarkable qualities he had two considerable defects. In a military commander they did not much matter; in a politician they were sinister. He was not a good manager of men and he was indifferent to public opinion. Even in prosperous times these would have been decided handicaps; in critical times they were disastrous. The confidence in his own powers, which served him so well in war, in politics proved fatal. By an irony of fate the man who regarded himself as the champion of the old constitution became its unintended executioner.

Notes

1   Sir Henry Maxwell, *Life of Wellington,* II (1899), p. 214, quoting WND iv, 253.
2   WP, Maurice Fitzgerald to Wellington, 5 November 1830.
3   *Journal of Mrs Arbuthnot 1820–32* (ed. F. Bamford & the Duke of Wellington), ii (1950), p. 137.
4   Maxwell, *Wellington,* ii, p. 210 quoting WND iv, 335.
5   *ibid.,* p. 251, quoting WND vii, 108. c.f. N. Gash, *Mr Secretary Peel* (1961), pp. 634–5.
6   Carola Oman, *Gascoyne Heiress* (1968), p. 257 (August 1837).
7   C. D. Yonge, *Life & Administration of 2nd. Earl of Liverpool,* ii (1868), p. 378.
8   *Ibid.,* iii, p. 197.
9   *Arbuthnot Journal* i, p. 83.
10 *Wellesley Papers* ed. L. Melville, ii (1914), 176–7, 5 May 1827.
11 *Letters of George IV,* ed. A. Aspinall, iii (Cambridge, 1938), p. 208, 26 March 1827.
12 In House of Lords, 2 May 1827.
13 Maxwell, *Wellington,* ii, p. 173, quoting WND ii, 364.
14 *Private Letters of Princess Lieven,* ed. P. Quennell (1937), pp. 318–19.
15 C.f. *Wellesley Papers,* ii, pp. 165, 185.
16 *Gascoyne Heiress,* p. 216.
17 *Letters to Ivy from the Ist. Earl of Dudley* ed. S. H. Romilly, (1905), p. 333; C.f. Lyndhurst's remarks to Greville, *Greville Journal,* 29 June 1828.
18 *Arbuthnot Journal,* ii, p. 321.
19 Quennell, *Lieven,* p. 102.
20 *Gascoyne Heiress,* p. 278.
21 *Political Diary of Lord Ellenborough 1828–30,* ed. Lord Colchester, i (1881), p. 3.
22 *Arbuthnot Journal,* ii, p. 357.
23 *Ibid.,* p. 244; WND vi, p. 293.
24 *Diary of Lady Shelley,* ed. R. Edgcumbe, ii (1913), p. 380.
25 *Arbuthnot Journal,* ii, p. 355.
26 *Greville Journal,* 21 November 1830.
27 *Gascoyne Heiress,* p. 278.
28 *Ellenborough Diary,* ii, pp. 206, 210, 212.
29 M. Brock, *Great Reform Act* (1973), pp. 128–9.
30 *Arbuthnot Journal,* ii, p. 396.
31 WND vii, 240, 295.
32 Quoted by Elizabeth Longford, *Wellington, Pillar of State* (1972), p. 224 from W. MSS. 18 October 1830.
33 WP, M. Fitzgerald to Wellington and his reply, 5, 6 November 1831. See also WND vii, 352.
34 WND, vii, 382.
35 *Diary of Philipp von Neumann,* ed. F. B. Chancellor, i (1928), p. 260.
36 Brock, *Reform Act,* p. 119 quoting from Salisbury MSS. See also pp. 119–23 for an admirable discussion of the duke's speech.
37 WND vii, 459.

Karen A. Noyce

7

The duke of Wellington and the Catholic question

In 1829 the duke of Wellington's Government introduced a bill designed to place Roman Catholics in a position of civil equality with those of the established church. Many of Wellington's friends and parliamentary supporters were shocked by his advocacy of such a measure. They had believed him to be a firm defender of Protestant ascendancy, committed to a continued exclusion of the Catholics from political power, and hence saw his introduction of the bill as a betrayal of his principles. Historians accepted the contemporary view that Wellington was only provoked into taking action on the Catholic question by the events initiated by Daniel O'Connell in Ireland. Several, therefore, referred to Wellington's 'conversion' to the Catholic cause, forced upon him by circumstances in 1828.[1] It has now been clearly shown, however, that Wellington had been prepared to consider relief for the Catholics for some time prior to that date.[2] By early 1825 he had already written a memorandum containing a plan of settlement. In general, little attention has been paid to this paper. Yet it is very interesting to compare its recommendations with the measures propounded in the 1829 Bill. Such a comparison is very revealing of the manner in which Wellington's thoughts on the question developed during this period. It is also illustrative of the ways in which his attitude was modified as a result of the influence of friends and colleagues.

Wellington's 1825 scheme was drawn up against a background of political upheaval. Since 1812 the Liverpool government had held to a policy of neutrality on the Catholic question, with individual members being free to support or oppose concessions in parliament as they saw fit. The success of Sir Francis Burdett's bill for Catholic relief through all its stages in the House of Commons disturbed the precarious equilibrium created by this system. It precipitated a crisis in the cabinet, as first Peel, and then Liverpool, threatened to resign. Wellington played a major role in all the discussions which attempted to avert the government's collapse. It was in this context that he first suggested to a few trusted colleagues that the Liverpool government should settle the Catholic question. He presented a plan which recommended that the Catholic Church in Ireland be placed under governmental control, and that a concordat be negotiated with the Pope to formalise the arrangements.[3]

Wellington's plan reflected his beliefs about the nature of Irish society. He announced to Mrs Arbuthnot his conviction that the Irish Catholics would never be satisfied until their religion was dominant in that country. In his view, this was primarily because the Reformation had been established in Ireland by means of conquest and dispossession. Naturally those thus uprooted desired to reacquire the position they had lost.[4] In the memorandum outlining his plan, Wellington explained that one of the major difficulties in establishing a settlement was that the Catholic leaders were inexorably hostile to the British connection, to the government, and to the Church of England. Should they be given political power, they would, therefore, use that gift to further their plans for domination, unless the status of the Protestants was somehow secured.

For this reason, Wellington believed it to be essential that securities should be provided for the Protestant church establishment in Ireland. His plan was based upon this principle. He believed that the key to the situation lay in the position of the Irish Catholic clergy and hierarchy in society. They wielded great power, and yet had no connection with the state in which they lived. Wellington had commenced his political career as Chief Secretary for Ireland, and had seen at first hand the personal and political power of the Catholic clergy. Since that time he had been conscious of the Catholic Church's independence from the state, referring to it as an *imperium in imperio*, free from any governmental inspection.[5] The clergy's power was still more suspect because they were under the influence of the Papacy, a foreign power. It was this connection which made the Catholics different from other dissenters. Wellington had come to believe that it was essential to any settlement to bring the Catholic church under state control. He wrote:

> our view must be . . . to bring the Roman Catholic religion in [Ireland]
> under the control of the Crown, and in proportion as we shall be
> successful in attaining this object, will the arrangements be good, and
> the security of the Church of England in Ireland be confirmed.

In order to achieve this goal, Wellington recommended two complementary arrangements. Firstly he proposed the introduction of salaries for the lower clergy, anticipating that this would encourage them to look to the government for their support, and persuade them to act as peacemakers, rather than rabble-rousers in the community. His main concern, however, was with the hierarchy. He had privately done all he could to ensure that men loyal to the British government were appointed to the Catholic sees of Ireland.[6] His settlement planned to ensure the selection of such men by involving the government in the electoral process. Those who elected the Catholic bishops would be required to submit a list of nominations to the government, which would have the right to reduce the list to two names, from which the Pope would make his selection. By such a process Wellington aimed to establish the king as head of the Catholic Church.[7]

There might seem little difference between Wellington's scheme and all those suggested since 1808, when the idea of 'securities' was introduced into the forefront of the debates on the Catholic question. Indeed, Catholic opposition to Crown interference in the appointment of their bishops had first been provoked in that year by the use of the exact phrase, 'the King as head of the Catholic Church'. However, the difference was that Wellington maintained that an agreement with Rome must form the basis for any scheme of this type. A Concordat must be negotiated to limit the Pope's involvement in Ireland, and to define exactly his role in the electoral process. Without this, none of the basic questions concerned in the relationship between the government and the Catholic Church would be truly solved.

Wellington knew that there would be difficulties in any such settlement, mainly owing to the episcopal nature of the Church of Ireland. He planned to avoid many of the associated problems by arranging for the status of the Catholic Church in Ireland to be altered from a national to a missionary establishment. While he accepted that such a change would not be welcomed by Rome, he anticipated that arrangements could be made. With the clergy thus officially tied to government, and the Pope's influence restrained, the position of the Protestant Church would be secured, and political power could safely be granted to the Catholics.

It has been contended that, in bringing forward this scheme at such a time of crisis, Wellington's primary aim was not to settle the Catholic question, but to keep the Liverpool government together.[8] His behaviour during a previous discussion of the question, in 1821, could justify such an assertion. On that occasion, when it was anticipated that Plunkett's Catholic relief bill would pass the House of Lords, Wellington had been determined to use that situation for the good of the government. Rather than organising resistance to concessions, he had instead planned a strategy for implementing the bill once it became law, in such a manner as would most benefit the government. He had aimed to use the expected success of the Catholics' supporters to forward negotiations for a coalition with the Buckingham group, by securing the Lord Lieutenancy of Ireland for the pro-Catholic duke of Buckingham once the bill received the royal assent.[9]

There can be no doubt that Wellington's pragmatism, evident in 1821, also directed his conduct in 1825. He certainly did intend to keep the Liverpool government together if this were at all possible. This may, however, have been a means to his own end. He explained to Mrs Arbuthnot in March 1825 that,

> the arrangement [for a settlement] must be made much better by those who were against than for the Catholics, because by them the interests of the Protestant establishment would be best protected, that the King himself would be more easily brought to yield the question by those who were in favour of Protestant ascendancy than by those who were for granting everything, careless of the consequences.[10]

He felt that the composition of the administration would ensure that the Protestant interest had a major share in the making of the settlement, and thus true securities for the establishment would be obtained.

He did not believe that adequate securities could be attained unless they were designed by those of the Protestant interest. Men like Burdett, who consulted with O'Connell, could never make an acceptable settlement for the Church, or gain the confidence of those who feared the consequences of granting political power to the Catholics. Wellington was convinced that the Irish Catholics would never willingly accept any conditions which would truly protect the position of the Protestants of that country. Hence any scheme in which the Catholics were consulted at the outset would provide no real . safeguards. He hoped to bring the Protestant interest to see the need for a settlement, and then to involve them in its formulation, so that the best possible securities would be obtained.

Wellington's concern for a settlement gave him an additional reason for attempting to keep the Liverpool government together. Liverpool implied that, if he resigned, he would advise the king to send for Canning.[11] Canning had, on two previous occasions, brought forward the Catholic question in parliament, in different forms, and there was every reason to expect that, if he became first minister, he would attempt to settle the question. Although Canning had always proclaimed his concern to protect the established church, Wellington distrusted any scheme which he might bring forward because he was publicly recognised as favouring the Catholics. Any arrangements which he might put forward would not, therefore, fulfil Wellington's stipulations for a purely Protestant settlement.

In putting forward his plan at this particular time, Wellington was also influenced by the increasingly difficult situation in Ireland. The country's stability appeared to be endangered by O'Connell's successful scheme to unite the peasantry behind the Catholic Association. The institution of the Catholic Rent had, by 1825, transformed the Association from yet another talking and petitioning society, into a potentially threatening popular movement. Although O'Connell made sure that all the actions of the Association were strictly within the law, there was always the fear that such an immense organisation might be used for illegal or even rebellious purposes.

Wellington had a great dislike of all popular movements, particularly in Ireland where, owing to the divided nature of society, any such organisation tended to produce counter-actions and mobilisations. In November 1824 he warned Peel that there would be civil war in Ireland unless the Catholic Association were suppressed at once, and in January 1825 he used the disturbed state of Ireland as a primary argument in support of his proposition to augment the infantry. The tone of his letters suggests that he saw some kind of crisis in Ireland as inevitable. However, he also saw that neither the suppression of the Catholic Association, nor even the military defeat of Ireland would actually solve the underlying problem. In either of these cases, the potential would still remain for a fresh organisation of the people.[12] Wellington may have concluded that the Irish would be better served by a compromise settlement than by a pointless war.

Wellington was convinced that a period of stability and peace was an essential prerequisite for any settlement to be arranged and put into practice. The suppression of the Catholic Association effected by Goulburn's bill in February 1825 provided the necessary interlude. Moreover, if concessions were granted at the same time as firm measures, represented by this bill, were put into practice, the government would avoid the impression that it was giving in to pressures from that body. It would be showing its strength, while at the same time granting concessions which would end the need for the association to reassert itself.

There can be no doubt that the political situation encouraged Wellington to bring forward his scheme at this time. However, there are clear indications that he also had a real desire to set the question to rest in a manner of which he could approve. In December 1823, Lord Clancarty wrote to the duke concerning the concordat planned for the Netherlands, insisting that England should seize on the precedent to settle the Irish question. Wellington replied: 'I don't believe that you and I differ much about Ireland. The question is, how to bring people's minds to anything on that subject.' He had apparently come to his decision by 1822, for Major Macauley, in a letter to Wellington in 1828, recalled the duke's saying at Verona that, if a concordat were established, he would personally move the Catholic question in the House of Lords. As early as 1808, Wellington had noted the importance of dealing with Rome, when making plans for the Catholic Church in Ireland. Although he did not mention a concordat, he insisted that any negotiations concerning the selection of Catholic bishops must involve the Pope, to whom, according to the laws of the Roman Church, the right of appointment belonged.[13]

Mrs Arbuthnot's diary for 19 February 1825 refers to Wellington's anxiety to settle the question. On that day she referred to his conviction that any arrangements for a settlement must begin with Rome, and his insistence that no step could safely be taken until the king was made head of the Catholic Church in Ireland. The roots of Wellington's plan were already in his mind in a fairly specific form.[14] This was some time before the government's difficulties became apparent, and indicates that Wellington was genuinely anxious to introduce an acceptable settlement of the question, based upon Protestant principles. It may be questioned why, if he were so concerned to set the question to rest, he made no reference to this in Parliament. It may be presumed, however, that he had no wish to publicise his scheme until it was acceptable to those colleagues with whom he hoped to make the settlement.

It had been rumoured that Liverpool would be willing to compromise on the question, if only he knew how. Wellington was thus showing him the way, and also providing an opportunity to solve the government's difficulties. Nevertheless, despite the Irish and political crises, which required urgent solutions, neither Liverpool nor Peel was convinced of the appropriateness of Wellington's scheme. Peel declared it to be 'full of difficulty'.[15] His specific objections are not stated. However, in his speech on Burdett's bill, he had indicated that, if a settlement were ever made, he would prefer a comprehensive arrangement, with the minimum of securities, and which would satisfy both parties. Wellington's scheme, which was almost certain to be unacceptable to the Irish Catholics, would not have fitted these requirements. Faced with this reaction, Wellington laid aside his plan, and, alongside the other cabinet members, waited to see the outcome.

In the event the crisis in the government was averted by other means. Peel was finally convinced by the arguments of those cabinet members who insisted that his resignation would lead to the collapse of the government, and agreed to remain in office. Under these circumstances, Wellington made no further reference to his scheme. In the following months, he turned instead to alternative arrangements for strengthening the government. His advocacy of an early election in 1826, to take advantage of Protestant feelings raised out of doors as a result of the debates over Burdett's bill, was not a sign that he had changed his mind concerning the desirability of a settlement. Rather it showed that he was aware of the political climate. An increase in the number of anti-Catholics in the Commons would encourage Peel, and strengthen Liverpool's resolve. Dr Machin suggests that Wellington's desire was to see a balance of power created in the Commons on the issue. This would provide an opportunity for the situation to calm down, so that the way could again be prepared for a compromise settlement.[16]

Wellington held to the opinion that a settlement upon the lines which he had suggested was desirable. In November 1825 he expressed such a wish to Earl Clancarty. Moreover, in February 1827, he informed the duke of Buckingham that his views on the Catholic question had not changed, although he recognised that it would be more difficult to act upon them. Even in the autumn of that year, he was still expressing a desire to achieve a settlement of the question through the medium of a concordat.[17]

Political developments, however, were to create conditions in which Wellington's basic criteria for a settlement could not be fulfilled. The collapse of the Liverpool government in 1827, and the formation of first the Canning and then the Goderich administrations, with all the machinations and misunderstandings which these involved, split long-standing political alliances. These changes in the political world were coupled with the formation and growth of the New Catholic Association in Ireland. In the upheaval and disturbance which were the result of these developments, the peace and stability which Wellington required before a settlement had never seemed further away. It must also be noted that although both the Canning and Goderich ministries were officially neutral on the Catholic question, the first ministers were both known as advocates of concessions. Both cabinets also contained members of the whig party, who were not necessarily committed to providing visible securities for the established church. In Wellington's view these facts would have excluded either administration from making a settlement with which he could be satisfied.

When Wellington himself became first minister, he had to face the legacy of all these political changes. Under these circumstances his first priority was not to get involved in the controversial issues presented by the Catholic question, but to recreate an atmosphere of political stability. He informed Peel that his aim was to reunite all those parties who had served under Liverpool, in a Government based upon similar principles. Naturally he was not keen to initiate proceedings on the Catholic question, and rather discouraged speculation as to possible solutions. For example, when Palmerston suggested that the new government might take up the question, Wellington rapidly pointed out all the difficulties involved, particularly those created by certain clauses in the Act of Union with Scotland.[18] Wellington willingly accepted the stipulation of the king that his government should continue to treat the subject as an open question.

He was, however, determined to be absolutely fair in his dealings with Ireland, and firmly rejected the possibility of a strictly Protestant government there. He upheld the principles of impartiality in the distribution of government patronage and appointments even when this brought him into collision with the king.[19] Moreover, from the beginning of his ministry, he was involved in correspondence with Henry Phillpotts, rector of Stanhope, and later dean of Chester.

Phillpotts was an influential controversialist, who had for several years been writing pamphlets on issues involved in the Catholic question. He had won for himself a reputation as a defender of the Protestant Church and constitution. He was, however, strongly inclined towards a settlement based upon real securities for the established church, drawn up by those who had its interests at heart.[20] In the correspondence between Wellington and Phillpotts various aspects of the Catholic question were discussed, a particular emphasis being placed upon the topic of securities. It is clear therefore that Wellington remained very interested in the question, although publicly he was more concerned to recreate political stability than to take actions which would shatter the already divided tory party and create turmoil in the existing political system.

As in 1825, however, developments in the Commons were to influence Wellington's approach to the question. In March 1828 the government was compelled to give way to pressure in the Commons, and to accept the repeal of the Test and Corporation Acts. The possibilities of further change were clearly raised and, in May, a motion in the lower house for a final adjustment of the Catholic question gained a majority of six votes. Once again, Peel intimated that his resignation must be expected shortly. However, on this occasion, rather than hamper Wellington's schemes for a settlement, he urged him: 'to take a course in debate which should not preclude him . . . from taking the whole state of Ireland into consideration during the recess, with the view of adjusting the Catholic question'.[21] Similar advice was given by Phillpotts, who, in a letter dated 6 June 1828, indicated the subjects which he felt that Wellington should cover in his speech in the next debate. He recommended that the need for securities be stressed, and also advised Wellington to point out the impolicy of continually discussing the question before proper securities had been devised. He contended that such a speech would: 'give very great gratification to no small . . . portion of the friends of [the] government and would perhaps facilitate their favourable reception of any future plan for the extinction of this . . . dispute'.[22]

The advice of both men was not given in vain. Now convinced of Peel's support, Wellington's speech on 10 June opened the way, indirectly, for a future adjustment of the question. For the first time he declared publicly that he wished to bring the question to 'an amicable conclusion' and that the question to his mind was not one of principle, but of expediency. However, his speech also emphasised the difficulties in reaching a settlement. He stressed the need for securities, contending that as yet no adequate replacement for the existing laws had been found to safeguard the established Church. He dwelt upon the problems created by the nature of the Roman Catholic Church government and the influence of the priests. Echoing Phillpotts, he rejected the perpetual agitation of the question, and ended his speech with a plea for a period of tranquility in Ireland during which he hoped that it would be possible to do something for the Catholics.

The speech was clearly not an overt declaration that the government would take up the Catholic question. Few people who were unaware of Wellington's private views, and the influence of Peel and Phillpotts, would have seen it as such, particularly as the Irish agitators were very unlikely to allow Wellington the period of peace which he saw as an essential preliminary to a settlement. Nevertheless, it was a significant step forward. Palmerston commented that this declaration: 'advanced [the] question immensely, because it [threw] overboard all objections on principle, and [placed] the matter simply upon the stand of comparative arrangements'.[23]

The speech also showed that a great shift had taken place in Wellington's approach to the question since his plan of 1825. Wellington had always been aware that there would be problems in negotiating a concordat, owing to the episcopal nature of the church of Ireland. Correspondence with Phillpotts had confirmed the nature of these difficulties and the improbability of finding a solution acceptable to Rome. However, Phillpotts had also introduced a far more powerful argument against arrangements with the Papal power. In his letter of 6 June, he had announced his conviction that the general principle of a concordat was incompatible with the Oath of Supremacy. The whole aim of this oath, he insisted, was to deny that the Pope possessed any authority in the kingdom. A concordat, however, was 'in it's very nature . . . an express admission . . . that the Pope [had] such jurisdiction'. If he had no authority, then it would not be necessary to consult him over arrangements for the Irish Catholics. Wellington was cearly impressed by this argument, and, in his speech, he drew upon the examples of concordats negotiated by other countries to show that it would be impossible to accept similar arrangements in the United Kingdom within the existing framework of the constitution.

In making this speech, Wellington clearly set aside his previous plans for a settlement. It may be conjectured that he anticipated a long, and hopefully peaceful interlude during which he might formulate a system of securities to replace the concordat. However, this was not to be. In July 1828 Daniel O'Connell was elected as member of parliament for Clare, after a dramatic contest in which the majority of forty-shilling freeholders cast their votes not at the behest of their landlords but rather under the influence of their priests. It became evident to both Peel and Wellington that a solution to the Irish problem was required immediately. As in 1825, although Wellington already favoured a settlement he was urged into action by the political situation, and events in Ireland. On 1 August, he sought the king's permission to discuss the Catholic question with Peel and Lord Chancellor Lyndhurst, who had also come to a conviction that an immediate settlement was necessary.

The king gave his permission reluctantly, and Wellington immediately commenced work on a plan. On 7 August he produced a memorandum for Peel which outlined the method by which he now felt a settlement could best be secured.[24] At the heart of his scheme, as in 1825, still lay the desire to control the Catholic clergy, and to curb their influence. However, in line with his June speech, any form of concordat or influence in the appointment of bishops was entirely rejected. Such arrangements, he insisted:

> would be in fact an acknowledgement on the part of His Majesty that the Pope possessed an influence and power in His Majesty's dominions which it [had] been the object of all [the country's] laws, from the reign of Henry VIII to the present day to impugn and deny.

Instead, Wellington put forward plans which, like the rejection of the concordat, were almost certainly the fruit of Phillpotts's influence. In a letter dated 25 March 1828 Phillpotts had suggested that a settlement should be made not by negotiation with Rome, but by parliamentary legislation. He had also listed various securities which could be attained by this means.[25] Wellington based his scheme upon the same principles. His major security, the introduction of licences from the crown for the Catholic clergy without which they were not to be permitted to exercise ecclesiatical functions, had been recommended in Phillpott's letter. Wellington contended that this, coupled with the provision of stipends, would bring the clergy fully under the government's control while avoiding any connection with the Pope. Furthermore, he carried the denial of Papal authority further than Phillpotts. The latter recommended that it should be an offence to publish Bulls from Rome without the permission of the Secretary of State. Wellington insisted that no cognisance should be taken of these communications, for to recognise their existence in any way was to acknowledge the Pope's authority over some of his majesty's subjects.

In order to curb the clergy's influence, Wellington also planned to alter the Irish franchise. In this early plan he rejected Phillpott's blanket disenfranchisement of all forty-shilling freeholders, preferring to introduce additional qualifications for the franchise. With the clergy thus restricted, civil offices and seats in parliament might be opened to the Catholics, although he also insisted that an oath should be taken by all Catholics entering parliament. Even with these restrictions Wellington was not, however, prepared to offer everything at once. He made the reservation that, if the settlement were not entirely satisfactory to both Protestants and Catholics then the laws excluding Catholics from office and parliament should not be repealed, but merely suspended, in the first instance for a year.

Wellington first mentioned this scheme to his friend Harriet Arbuthnot, at the end of July. She was in favour of a settlement under Wellington, designed to protect the Protestant interest. Her comments were very positive, and she recorded in her diary that Wellington's was 'the only scheme . . . that has appeared . . . the last feasible or to start upon fair and safe grounds'.[26] Peel, however, was less impressed. As in 1825, he saw several difficulties with the plan which had been proposed.[27] In particular he contended that the licences so favoured by Wellington would rapidly become a mere formality, 'giving no real control to the Crown, but investing the person licensed with a sanction and authority derived from the Crown'. He recognised what Wellington had not seen; that the licensing and payment of the Catholic clergy actually involved an acknowledgement of that Papal authority which was essential to the exercise of clerical functions. Such an arrangement might, therefore, be interpreted as going a considerable way towards the establishment of that church in the United Kingdom.

Peel also pointed out specific practical difficulties in the scheme. He reminded Wellington that many Protestants would have violent objections to paying anything towards the support of the Catholic church. Moreover there were additional problems created by the priests's receipt of dues from their parishioners; would they still be permitted to receive such offerings if stipends were granted? When considering the Irish franchise, he stressed the inequality in the valuation of lands in different parts of Ireland, and contended that it would therefore be very difficult to make the possession of the franchise dependent upon the payment of a certain amount to the county rate. As foreshadowed by his 1825 speech, he explained that his ideal settlement would immediately place the Catholics upon an equal footing with others in the competition for offices and parliamentary seats. Hence he was also critical of Wellington's suggestion that the laws be suspended.

These disagreements did not bode well for the formation of a plan of settlement to be placed before parliament. However, little was done at this stage to obviate the difficulties. Nor was any attempt made to involve other members of the cabinet in discussions. This was because Wellington believed it to be his duty to obtain the king's permission before raising the question in cabinet. It has recently been debated whether such permission was in fact necessary as the first step towards concessions.[28] In many ways, however, this is purely an academic question. It is clear from Wellington's writings that he sincerely believed this permission to be necessary. Whether he was mistaken about this is a moot point. The only other logical explanation is that Wellington deliberately delayed taking any action on the question between September 1828 and January 1829, and that he attributed this delay to the king's action. It is surely very unlikely that a man as devoted to the monarchy as Wellington would have used the king's name to prolong a deception, which served no useful purpose. In the face of his belief, therefore, all he could do was wait, while others speculated about the line which the government was to take on the question.

This permission, however, was not to be gained easily. Throughout September the king was ill and unable to do business. On his recovery he immediately suggested that the government should be given a more Protestant character! Throughout this time of waiting the situation in Ireland grew more worrying. The Catholic Association increased in power and numerical strength while, in response, anti-Catholic clubs sprang up with corresponding vigour. There were also problems with the Irish Government. The Lord Lieutenant, Lord Anglesey, favoured Catholic emancipation. He was therefore inclined to take actions which antagonised the Protestants and created difficulties for the English government. Convinced of the need to solve the Catholic question, Anglesey began to think that the government was shying away from any attempt to settle the issue. Wellington however did not believe himself free to discuss his plans with Anglesey. He also feared that the Lord Lieutenant's rash words and actions would make it harder for a proper settlement to be effected. These misunderstandings led to a souring of relations between the two men and finally, in December, Anglesey was recalled. This only served to disrupt further the process of government in Ireland.

Wellington faced similar problems in England. Disturbed by the government's lack of action against the Catholic Association in Ireland, prominent anti-Catholic peers encouraged the formation of Brunswick Clubs to oppose concessions. Large anti-Catholic public meetings were also held. Such was the reaction before the government gave any indication that they would consider altering the existing laws. In addition to these public demonstrations of opposition to concessions, Wellington also faced similar reactions in private. In November, the Archbishop of Canterbury and the Bishop of London had expressed satisfaction with the scheme which Wellington was planning. However, at a further meeting in January it became clear that they were not prepared to support a settlement publicly, lest they appear to compromise the interests of the Church.

As the problems mounted, Wellington did gain one major advantage. Aware that the bishops's stand exacerbated Wellington's difficulties, Peel declared his willingness to remain in office and assist the government with the introduction of the measure. He set out his views on the Irish situation in a memorandum which Wellington sent to the king and, on 17 January announced his decision to the cabinet. He and other cabinet members previously opposed to concessions then had personal interviews with the king, each one announcing that he believed a settlement to be essential. Faced with this united front, George IV finally agreed that the neutrality which had been the watchword for all cabinets since 1812 might be abandoned. Wellington was given permission to discuss the whole state of Ireland, including the Catholic question, in the cabinet, and to draw up bills which might be laid before parliament as government measures. The king did, however, insist that he was not bound to accept their recommendations.

The cabinet had very little time to settle the outlines of the measure which they wished to propose, for parliament was fixed for 5 February. It must have felt somewhat strange to sit around the table and consider a subject which had previously been purposely excluded from all discussions. It was necessary for each member mentally to set aside this individualistic approach, which left more freedom for idealism, and to look for solutions which might practicably be brought forward as government measures, likely to win the support of parliament. They faced a very difficult task, for Wellington intended that they should put together a series of measures which would be supported not only by those already in favour of a settlement, but also by those members of the tory party who had always opposed concessions. He wished to convince his friends in Parliament that the government was taking the only action which would secure the position of the established church in Ireland.

Some aspects of this settlement were concluded surprisingly quickly. The king had stated to Wellington that the cabinet's plan should include the suppression of the Catholic Association, and it was immediately accepted that any concessions must be preceded by such a measure. It was also agreed that the relief bill should open civil offices and seats in parliament to Roman Catholics. Although there were discussions over the details involved in these measures, for example, concerning the oath which Catholics were to take before entering parliament, and the listing of those offices from which Catholics were to be excluded, the principles were agreed unanimously.

There was also general agreement over one of the potentially contentious issues, the payment of stipends to the Catholic clergy. By the time the question was debated in cabinet, Wellington had been persuaded to relinquish his intention of proposing such a measure as an accompaniment to the relief bill, and he announced this decision at the first Cabinet meeting to discuss a settlement. Peel had pointed out the objections which the Protestant public might legitimately raise to such a scheme. It may be presumed that Wellington accepted Peel's arguments that to introduce a proposal for stipends alongside the relief bill might lead to the defeat of the main measure, and would in any case necessitate protracted discussions which would delay the progress of the bill. Other members of the cabinet who had believed with Wellington that stipends were desirable were also brought to recognise these difficulties during the course of discussions. It was therefore agreed that no such scheme would be included in the government's bill.

It was less easy to decide upon the other security measures which should accompany the relief bill. The king had recommended to Wellington that any relief measure should be accompanied by the disenfranchisement of the Irish forty-shilling freeholders. The cabinet were generally agreed that something must be done to lessen the priests' influence during elections in Ireland. They were, however, initially reluctant to introduce a bill which openly disenfranchised so many Irish voters. It was recognised that the whigs would oppose such a measure, which might legitimately be criticised on constitutional grounds. It was also suggested that such a measure would not, in fact, curb the influence of the priests to any significant degree.[29] Wellington continued to advocate the introduction of additional qualifications for the franchise. As well as frequent cabinet discussions on the subject, consultations were held with several of the government's Irish supporters. Many informal meetings were also held. Finally, despite the continued misgivings of several prominent cabinet members, including the duke, it was decided that they must proceed by open disenfranchisement, and the qualification for the county franchise was therefore raised to ten pounds. Professor Gash suggests that the cabinet came to this decision on the advice of those Irishmen consulted, who were not convinced that any system of indirect tests, such as Wellington recommended, would be effective in Ireland.[30]

Greater difficulties were encountered when ecclesiastical securities were discussed. Peel insisted that the introduction of any measures involving an interference in the internal government of the Catholic Church would always create controversy both in and out of doors. In parliament this could only succeed in distracting attention from the central issue of Catholic relief, and thus the settlement would be delayed, without any real gain for the Protestant Church. The Catholics would not willingly accept such measures, and a fresh source of irritation would be created thereby. This would be a contradiction of the cabinet's aim to produce a final and conciliatory adjustment of the question. He also repeated in the cabinet his conviction that no measures should be introduced which could in any way constitute an establishment of the Catholic Church, or a recognition of Papal authority in any form.

Wellington, however, was still keen to introduce licensing or registration for new priests, and he found support for this measure from Lord Ellenborough. He continued to stress the need for an adequate control over the activities of the Catholic priesthood. Other members of the cabinet were however aware of many problems with such a scheme. Peel had explained to Wellington that the granting of licences might rapidly become a mere formality, providing no security, yet giving the priest the sanction of government. He now reiterated this in cabinet, and also pointed out that the same constitutional difficulties were inherent in a system of licences as in any interference in the appointment of Catholic bishops. He stressed that such an attempt to control the clergy would involve a recognition of the Catholic Church, inconsistent with the constitution, to which the public would take great exception. The measure would also have implications for the Catholics. It was noted that any priest refused a licence or removed from the register would remain a priest in the eyes of the Catholic Church. He would therefore be obliged to perform ecclesiastical functions if asked to do so, despite the government's ban. There was danger that a relief bill incorporating such a scheme would remove existing political grievances, but create in their place fresh opportunities for discontent, on religious grounds.

Aware of all these difficulties the cabinet finally agreed that the relief bill should include no measure which in any way involved the recognition of the appointment of the Catholic clergy or hierarchy. Lord Ellenborough's diary makes it clear that Wellington was not pleased with this decision, to which he 'yielded very reluctantly'. Once he had given up his plans for a concordat, licences had become the key to his settlement, and he was naturally unwilling to give them up. Ellenborough noted that Wellington believed licensing to be the only satisfactory security for the Protestant Church.[31] However, in the face of Peel's arguments, which convinced the rest of the cabinet, he was forced to give way.

In place of these contentious ecclesiastical securities, the cabinet agreed upon several measures, each of which was designed, in a small way, to counteract any impression that the Catholic Church was being officially established in the United Kingdom, or that it was in competition with the Protestant Church in either law or society. The Catholic hierarchy were, for example, forbidden to assume ecclesiastical titles used by the established church. It was also made an offence to hold Catholic ceremonies, or to wear ecclesiastical or monastic dress, anywhere except in places designated for Roman Catholic worship, and in private houses. Wellington did not believe that these measures provided real security for the Protestant Church, but accepted that some people would find such legislation helpful. The ecclesiastical titles clause at least provided a further opportunity to disclaim the existence of any Papal authority in the kingdom. In a speech to the Lords, he explained that the title of a diocese legally belonged to the person appointed by the king. 'It was [therefore] desirable that others appointed to it by an assumed authority should be discountenanced.'[32] It may be assumed that Wellington approved of these clauses without thinking that they were vital for the success of the measure.

He was more convinced about the need for another of the small security clauses; that which involved the placing of restrictions upon the existence of monastic orders and convents in the country.[33] Many people had a great fear and distrust of monks, particularly the Jesuits, and the measure included in Wellington's bill was intended to bring about the eventual extinction of the monastic orders, and to prevent any Jesuits from entering the country. It may be speculated that Wellington's belief in the necessity for this measure sprang not only from his recognition that it would gain the support of some members opposed to concessions, but also from his experiences in Spain and Portugal during the Peninsular War. Soldiers serving in the peninsula had commented upon the laziness and greediness of the monks, and had also criticised the control which they possessed over the people.[34] It is very unlikely that Wellington would have remained entirely untouched by the same reactions. He had also been in far closer proximity to monks and nuns than had the majority of members of the House of Lords.

The only other securities introduced in the bill were an oath for those entering parliament, to be taken in conjunction with the Oath of Supremacy, altered to make it acceptable to the Catholics, and the exclusion of Catholics from some of the higher offices of state. As it finally emerged from the cabinet, therefore, the Catholic relief bill was very simple. With the exception of the disenfranchisement measure, it was very generous to the Catholics. O'Connell was delighted with its relief provisions, and commented to his wife, 'who would have expected such a bill from Peel and Wellington'![35] Moreover it contained none of the contentious matter which had been the major focus of all discussions on the subject since 1808. A letter from the Bishop of Winchester shows that the scheme gained some support by its radical approach; he explained to the king that he must have opposed the bill had it contained anything approaching an acknowledgment of Papal authority, but that in its present form it contained nothing inconsistent with the true principles of Protestantism.[36] Others however, believed that the government was placing the Church in danger by failing to insist upon control over the Catholic Church. Lord Salisbury, for example, wished Wellington to settle the question. However, he was critical of the final measure because, in his view, it would not contain adequate securities.[37]

That Wellington himself was prepared to propose such a bill in the House of Lords was evidence of the great changes which had taken place in his thinking. He admitted in his speech introducing the second reading of the bill in the upper house that he had changed his mind on the issue of securities; that he now opposed any measure involving a connection with Rome, and believed that such measures could not provide any additional security for the Church of England. The Wellington of 1825 would have rejected such a statement immediately. The passage of time, the influence of Peel and Phillpotts, and the practicalities of cabinet discussions had combined to bring about a revolution in his approach to the question. Those historians are therefore correct who have maintained that the settlement of 1829 was the result of a conversion of Wellington's views on the subject. This conversion, however, clearly involved not a change in his basic attitude to the Catholic question, but rather a reversal of his previously-held convictions as to the manner in which a settlement should be achieved.

Notes

1   E.g. Philip Guedalla, *The Duke*, 3rd edn (1937), p. 379.
2   G. I. T. Machin, 'The duke of Wellington and Catholic emancipation', *Journal of Ecclesiastical History*, xiv, *passim.*
3   Wellington Memorandum on the Catholic question, 1825, WND, ii, 604.
4   *Parl. Deb.*, first series, xl, 447, 17 May 1819.
5   Wellington to Richmond, 8 June 1808, WSD, v, 448–9.
6   Wellington to Sidmouth, 8 February 1819, WND, i, 28. Wellington to Curtis, WP, 10 April 1821, 1/666/2W.
7   F. Bamford and the Duke of Wellington, *The Diary of Mrs Arbuthnot*, i (1850), p. 378.
8   Machin, 'Wellington and Catholic emancipation', p. 192.
9   Wellington to Buckingham, 2 April 1821, Duke of Buckingham and Chandos, *Memoirs of the Court of George IV*, i (1861), 150.
10   Arbuthnot, *Diary*, i, p. 380.
11   Liverpool to Arbuthnot, 19 May 1825. A. Aspinall (ed.), *The Correspondence of Charles Arbuthnot*, Camden Society, third series, lxv (1941), p. 77.
12   Wellington to Peel, 3 November 1824, WND, ii, 330–31.
13   Clancarty to Wellington, 16 December 1823, WP, 1/778/13; Wellington to Clancarty, n.d. December 1823, 1/780/8. Macauley to Wellington, 31 May 1828, WND, iv, 480. Memorandum on the Catholic Question, 1808, British Library Add. MSS., 38079.
14   Arbuthnot, *Diary*, i, pp. 377–8.

15 Arbuthnot, *Diary*, i, p. 392.
16 Machin, 'Wellington and Catholic emancipation', p. 193.
17 Wellington to Clancarty, 14 November 1825, WND, ii, 564. Wellington to Buckingham, 22 February 1827, WP, 1/857/18. Horace Twiss, *The Public and Private Life of Lord Chancellor Eldon*, ii, 2nd edn (1844), p. 418.
18 Memorandum on the formation of Wellington's Government, 18 January 1828, Palmerston Papers, Southampton University Library, GMC/25.
19 Wellington to the king, 26 February 1828. A. Aspinall (ed.), *The Letters of King George IV, 1812–1830*, iii (Cambridge, 1938), pp. 399–400.
20 G. C. B. Davies, *Henry Phillpotts Bishop of Exeter 1778–1869* (1954), ch. 2.
21 Lord Mahon and E. Cardwell, *Memoirs by the Rt. Hon. Sir Robert Peel*, i (1856), p. 128.
22 Phillpotts to Wellington, 6 June 1828, WND, iv, 484–5.
23 Palmerston to William Temple, 27 June 1828, Palmerston Papers, GC/TE/201.
24 Various drafts of this memorandum may be found in WP 1/983/4. This quotation from 1/983/4/1.
25 Phillpotts to Wellington, 25 March 1828, WND, iv, 324–9.
26 Arbuthnot, *Diary*, ii, pp. 199–200.
27 Peel, *Memoirs*, i, pp. 189–200.
28 R. W. Davies, 'The tories, the whigs and Catholic emancipation, 1825–1829', *English Historical Review*, xcvii, *passim*.
29 Goulburn to Peel, 14 November 1828. Add. Mss. 40,333 ff. 55–9.
30 Norman Gash, *Mr Secretary Peel* (1961), p. 552.
31 Law, Lord Ellenborough, *A Political Diary, 1828–1830*, i (1881), p. 317.
32 *Parl. Deb.*, second series, xxi, 560–61, 8 April 1829.
33 *Parl. Deb.*, second series, xxi, 56, 2 April 1829.
34 For example, Lieutenant Colonel Willoughby Walker (ed.), *A British Rifle Man – Journals and Correspondence during the Peninsular War and the Campaigns of Wellington*, by Major G. Simmons (1986), pp. 14, 49–50, 236–7.
35 Charles C. Trench, *The Great Dan* (1984), p. 167.
36 The Bishop of Winchester to the king, 9 March 1829. Aspinall, *Letters of George IV*, ii, p. 455.
37 M. E. Gleig (ed.), *Personal Reminiscences of the Duke of Wellington, with Sketches of some of his Guests and Contemporaries*, by G. R. Gleig (1904), pp. 243–4.

James J. Sack

8

Wellington and the tory press,
1828–30

Arthur Wellesley, first duke of Wellington, felt exceedingly uncomfortable with three aspects of British political life in the nineteenth century: the party system, popular pressure groups, and the press. His mistrust of party politics antedated his premiership by a generation and combined both the natural wariness of the professional military man for too close an association with ephemeral ministers and the psychological tension produced in juggling a cradle Grenvillite nostalgia, a fraternal Wellesleyite deference, and a mature Pittite obligation. Indeed, Wellington blamed most of the misfortunes of George III's reign, such as the loss of the American colonies and the early successes of the French Revolution, on the 'Spirit of Party in England'.[1] Although Wellington as duke and prime minister learned to be more circumspect, it is doubtful whether he ever changed his mind. Hence, Professor Gash is no doubt correct in his assessment of the duke as 'the least political of any nineteenth-century party leader'.[2]

Wellington's suspicion of popular politics out-of-doors was equally censorious and rarely qualified even if the cause in agitation was favourable to his own sympathies. The duke feared not only O'Connell's Catholic Association and lectured James Stephen on the odious role of public opinion in the anti-slavery cause, but refused also to follow the duke of York into the Orange society and, at the height of the reform bill crisis, declined to sanction a Kent constitutional society to combat a bill he, as well as the proposers of the society, found noxious.[3] As Wellington told Stephen, parliament, not the forces of public opinion, ought to decide weighty matters of state.[4] The duke adhered to a strict constructionist view of the public's role in the constitution which was somewhat dated even in the third decade of the nineteenth-century and which heavily biased him against the advocatory, aggressive, highly ideological British press, whether whig or tory, liberal or conservative. This chapter will examine the duke and the tory press during and after the greatest crisis of Arthur Wellesley's political life, Catholic emanicipation.

Wellington disliked the press and journalists in general, whatever the political complexion of the paper or individual involved. For example, as early as 1811, the secretary for war had to scold the then viscount for his numerous complaints as to newspaper reporting of the Peninsular War and to remind him that due to the very nature of the British form of government, the public expected accurate information. Wellington was not convinced by Liverpool's argument.[5] His retort to a journalist in 1833 that he 'has nothing to say to the newspapers and . . . is desirious of avoiding to have any communication of any description with any of them'[6] and his characterisation of Thomas Barnes of *The Times*, to whose sagacity the conservative party ultimately owed a great deal, as 'an insolent, vulgar fellow',[7] were typical. Yet, beneath this haughty exterior, Wellington may have been more sensitive to press criticism than his public or private persona allowed. In 1830, at the high point of the tory press attack on the Wellington ministry, the rector of Ash, visiting Walmer, noticed that unlike as Peel and Wellington were, they had one custom in common:

> They abused the newspapers, and professed to hold their comments in contempt; yet twice a day copies of all that were published in London arrived in duplicate at the Castle, and twice a day both the Prime Minister and the Home Secretary spend much time in studying them.[8]

For reasons having little to do either with Wellington or with Catholic emancipation, there were fewer prominent, national, tory, ministerial newspapers during the duke's tenure of office than was customary before Castlereagh's death in 1822 or was to be the case after Peel's first ministry in 1835. The *Sun*, long a Pittite organ, and indeed in the late eighteenth and early nineteenth century, the premier government newspaper, had embraced moderately liberal principles around the time of the Caroline case. The well-subscribed *Morning Herald*, once Carlton House-oriented and to emerge by 1834 as a staunch conservative daily, was erratic in politics during the 1820s but more prone to whiggism than to toryism. The *New Times*, Dr

Stoddart's hammer of the radicals, was defunct by 1828. Hence, there were structural problems at the top of the tory propaganda edifice that could not be blamed directly on Wellington and that would not be remedied until well into the 1830s. None the less, and to their subsequent regret, Wellington and his colleagues did neglect the press during the 1828–30 ministry, especially when compared with the caressing ministered by Canning earlier in the decade or by Brougham in the 1830s. And not all of the ill will of the tory press towards the duke was due to ideological considerations regarding its opposition to Catholic relief. Wellington simply failed to appreciate newspapers, journals, or journalists. He refused upon coming into office to hold any communication with the editors of the *Standard*, the new and successful organ of the ultra-tories, who had supported his political line in 1827.[9] He managed to alienate a former supporter, the pro-Catholic editor of the *Quarterly Review*, John Gibson Lockhart, to such an extent that Lockhart professed that "nothing shall induce me to put faith in any Minister's professions again".[10] No doubt Lockhart was accurate when in 1830 he told his father-in-law and another well-wisher to the duke, Sir Walter Scott, that 'Ministers . . . consider literary allies as worse than useless unless they are prepared to shift at every breath.'[11]

Still, when Robert Stewart in *The Foundation of the Conservative Party, 1830–1867*, asserted that no tory paper in 1830 had a direct link with the party, he may have exaggerated somewhat.[12]

Wellington himself in 1830, stung after the dissolution of his government by the defection of both his lackeys at the daily *Courier* and of his more independent pro-Catholic liberal allies at *The Times*, may have over-dramatised a notion that the whole of the press opposed him. He told Mrs Arbuthnot that:

> The truth is that, with a thorough contempt for the Press as far as regarded myself, which I think was perfectly justified, I carried that feeling too far in respect to others. . . . In my time, nothing was done upon the Press by the Government. We ended consequently by having the whole of it against us, and against the solid Institutions of the Country.[13]

Such overstatement on Wellington's part can perhaps be explained by the vicious nature of the mainstream tory press attack upon him, leading him to conclude that he was 'living . . . in an atmosphere of calumny'.[14] Still, even after the introduction of the Catholic relief bill, the duke enjoyed the not inconsiderable support of four tory papers or journals, the *Courier*, the *Morning Post*, *John Bull*, and, in a more qualified sense, the *Quarterly Review* and only the former deserted him after the fall of his government in November of 1830.

The *Courier* for almost a generation had performed as semi-official mouthpiece for successive Pittite ministries. Joseph Planta, secretary for the treasury under Wellington, played a major role in choosing *Courier* editors who, like John Galt, would 'come every morning to the Treasury, and take his tone from them'.[15] But the grand decades when the *Courier* had been the leading daily newspaper in circulation in the United Kingdom were long since over by 1829 and it was in the midst of a decline that would take it by the mid-1830s to the very bottom of daily newspaper circulation.[16] Contemporaries, no doubt correctly, attributed the *Courier's* progressive emaciation to its slavish adherence to the ideological twists and turns of every ministry between Liverpool and Grey. Hence, it lacked much *gravitas* even in the sometimes jaundiced atmosphere of the late 1820s. The genuine commitment of the editors and the proprietors of the paper to the duke of Wellington's principles can best be shown by its newly discovered whig proclivities after November 1830. Such was the proprietorial grovelling before Lord Grey's new government that letters from the old ministers were actually handed over to Brougham. Said Brougham's secretary: 'It taught us how to deal with' them though 'of course I took care to leave [behind] . . . no specimens of my correspondence.'[17] The *Courier* more than deserved its accolades of 'crawling *Courier*' or 'scratching *Courier*' and this semi-official paper did the Wellington ministry little of positive value.[18]

The *Morning Post* was thought by Professor Aspinall, certainly incorrectly given the *Courier's* status, to be the tories' principal newspaper during the Wellington premiership.[19] He may have been mislead by the *Post's* championing of the duke and Peel in 1827, in contrast to the *Courier's* adherence to the liberal tory ministries of Canning and Goderich. The *Courier's* political line in 1827, however, was merely the normal behaviour of a government-sponsored newspaper, and had little resonance by 1828–30, when a different ministry was in place. Under the long editorship and sometime proprietorship of Nicholas Byrne (1803–33), with a small but select circulation, the *Morning Post* catered to the fashionable world, and hard news and decided judgments were not its forte.[20] Despite its previous anti-Catholic stance, the *Post* loyally, if rather unenthusiastically and indeed tardily, followed Wellington over Catholic emancipation by mid-April, 1829.[21]

John Bull, once the *enfant terrible* of the London weekly press, observed its tenth anniversary in 1830 as decidedly more moderate than in its golden days of the Caroline affair. Unfortunately, with temperance had come mediocrity, and its circulation had declined dramatically since 1821.[22] Though the evidence is not entirely clear, *John Bull* may have been under some sort of Croker-managed government patronage during the Wellington ministry;[23] whatever, it always supported the duke, albeit in a sometimes restrained and even jerky fashion which hardly upheld its credibility.[24]

Not quite as oriented towards the Wellington ministry as *John Bull* was the *Quarterly Review*. By far the leading literary or political review in the United Kingdom, far outdistancing its *Edinburgh Review* rival in circulation, the *Quarterly* had a difficult path to hew in 1828–30.[25] Its controversial new editor, J. G. Lockhart, supported Catholic emancipation and had pledged assistance to Wellington's ministry at its inaugural.[26] In addition, the *Quarterly* had traditionally followed a Canningite political line coupled with neutrality on emancipation. But its leading political reviewer, Robert Southey, was firmly anti-Catholic, presumably reflecting the views of the preponderance of his readership, and another long-time political reviewer, J. W. Croker, a pro-Catholic, had momentarily broken his ties with the *Quarterly*. Hence, in 1828, to retain Southey's support, Lockhart permitted the *Quarterly* an anti-Catholic tone.[27] In 1829 and 1830, however, while there was no orgy of support for Wellington's beleaguered government, there was no devastating criticism either, and long before the advent of the Whig's reform bill, the *Quarterly* was pressing for the reunion of the pro- and anti-Catholic factions of the tory party.[28] The remainder of the tory newspapers and periodicals, however, reprobated Wellington and Peel and all their works and pomps.

Two tory dailies, the *Standard*, an evening paper, and the *Morning Journal*, were the banes of Wellington's existence in 1829 and 1830. The *Standard*, part of the Baldwin newspaper empire, and destined to become one of the great nineteenth-century conservative newspapers, printed its first issue in May of 1827, in reaction to the liberalism of the Canning ministry. It was moderately successful in the late 1820s and had a circulation of around 1,500 in 1829.[29] It supported Wellington quite firmly in 1828.[30] After his introduction of the Catholic relief bill, however, the *Standard*, under its Irish and Orange-oriented editor, Stanley Lees Giffard, decidedly changed its tune. By 1830, Mrs Arbuthnot thought it was in some peculiar sense the newspaper of that ultra of ultras, H.R. H. the duke of Cumberland.[31] After the passage of Catholic emancipation, it was the stated goal of the *Standard* to remove Wellington and Peel from power, even if whigs formed the successor government or if it took the fall of Constantinople to a Russian army to accomplish the aim.[32]

The *Morning Journal* was the heir of Dr Stoddart's anti-radical *New Times*, which had taken a surprisingly liberal attitude towards Catholic relief. Not so the *Journal* under its editor Robert Alexander, late of the *Glasgow Sentinel* and the *Liverpool Standard*. Within days of the introduction of the emancipation bill, the *Morning Journal* called for Wellington's impeachment.[33] There was speculation in high political circles that, like the *Standard*, the *Journal* was controlled by the duke of Cumberland.[34] Granted that its parent newspaper, the *New Times*, had fallen upon difficult days by the late 1820s, the child was scarcely more successful.[35] In inevitable competition with its sister ultra newspaper, the *Standard*, and with its slurs and slanders against the ministry the object of successful government prosecution, the last issue of the *Journal* appeared on 13 May 1830.

Aside from the two dailies, five other tory newspapers or periodicals were vehemently against the continuance of the duke of Wellington's ministry after February 1829: a London tri-weekly, the *St James's Chronicle*; a notorious Sunday paper, the *Age*; the successful Scottish monthly, *Blackwood's Edinburgh Magazine*; the ancient *Monthly Magazine*, formerly unitarian and liberal, but after 1826, in a new tory series; and the new London monthly, *Fraser's Magazine*. The *St. James's Chronicle* was the antiquated flag-ship of the Baldwin family. Hazlitt in the mid-1820s thought it the very model of the old school newspaper in its dullness, meanness, and want of style.[36] One critic surmised that since Londoners liked *daily* newspapers, this ultra tri-weekly's respectable circulation was most pronounced in the provinces.[37] It shared an editor, S. L. Giffard, and (often) content with the other ultra Baldwin paper, the *Standard*. The *Age*, edited by the flagrant tory blackmailer, Charles Molloy Westmacott, had a hardy circulation by the early 1830s of between 8,000 and 9,000 per issue.[38] As *John Bull* became more respectable, ceased libelling (at least grossly) its enemies, and, hence, declined in interest, the *Age* may well have picked up its lost audience. *Blackwood's*, over a decade old in

1829, like the *Bull*, had shed some of that early spunk and vigour associated with the now departed J. G. Lockhart and William Maginn, the one to the *Quarterly* and the other to *Fraser's*. Its circulation, once convincingly higher than both the *Quarterly* and the *Edinburgh*, had suffered accordingly, though it still probably surpassed the latter.[39] The *Monthly Magazine* was edited by the Irish Protestant clergyman, George Croly, formerly of the *New Times*, who, according to a critic, desired to make the *Monthly* the *Blackwood*'s of the south. While such an aim proved unrealistic, Croly did succeed in achieving a respectable if hardly spectacular circulation of 600 and in producing one of the most furious tory magazines of the 1820s.[40] *Fraser's Magazine*, commencing under William Maginn in February 1830, and quickly thereafter serving as a receptacle for some of the greatest British literary talent of the nineteenth century, also associated itself with the ultra cause.[41] All five publications called for Wellington's resignation and failing that event, for his defeat at a general election or in parliament.[42] The *Age* viewed 16 November 1830, when the duke gave up the seals of office, as 'a high holiday in our annals, for on that day the basest administration that ever obtruded upon a free people was overthrown'.[43] A *Blackwood*'s reviewer, oddly, saw Grey as more a Pittite than Wellington or Peel, and the whig assumption of power as 'a step towards national salvation'.[44] The *Monthly* in December 1830 rejoiced in the 'ignominious' downfall of the duke and defied 'any Whig in existence to do worse'.[45]

Yet, frustrating as such tory censures were, when the duke wrote of 'living . . . in an atmosphere of calumny', he most probably referred to assaults of a higher order than intemperate resignation requests. It may have been a Dublin Saturday newspaper, sympathetic to Irish Orangeism, the *Star of Brunswick*, which first, on 14 March 1829, applied from a right-wing standpoint the standard liberal criticism of the ministry as led by a 'military desperadoe'.[46] A week later it had refined the argument to the charge, replete with Cromwellian imagery, that Wellington sought the Lord Protectorship of the Realm if George IV or the duke of Clarence were to die.[47] It regularly thereafter simply called Wellington 'the Dictator'.[48] The ultra-English press speedily took up such charges. To the *Monthly*, he was also the 'Dictator'.[49] The *Age* suggested that the duke, whom it termed the United Kingdom's Mayor of the Palace, along with Judas Peel and Iscariot Dawson, sought control over Princess Victoria of Kent, and hence the Crown as well as the Church was in Danger.[50] Both the *Monthly* and, more vigorously, the *Standard* strongly implied, in the words of the latter, that his 'High Highness' intended to 'perpetuate his power by dangerous designs connected with the succession to the crown'. The *Standard* virtually suggested that Wellington and Peel were traitors, with the duke informed in advance of Charles X's designs upon French liberties, carrying the not very subtle inference that Wellington might soon follow the Bourbon's example.[51] The *St James's Chronicle* stated that the duke sought the prime ministership for life, reducing his sovereign's authority accordingly.[52] The tory press also struck out at the duke's personal life. The *Age* and the *Morning Journal* cast aspersions on Wellington's morality and on his special friendship with Mrs Arbuthnot.[53] The *Star of Brunswick* ridiculed not only Mrs Arbuthnot but, rather ungallantly, suggested that the duchess of Wellington was a smallpox-disfigured woman.[54] The *Monthly* derided Wellington's soldiering at Waterloo.[55]

Though Wellington may well have been outraged by slurs on his wife, his friends, and himself, it was for the calumnies on his political reputation that he chose to fight. At one stage, in mid-1829, the duke informed his attorney-general, Sir James Scarlett, that he was prepared to prosecute the *Standard* for its charges on the regency question.[56] However, it was the more helpless and less successful *Morning Journal*, which had potentially libelled not only the duke but Lord Chancellor Lyndhurst as well, that was chosen for governmental retribution. In *Rex v Gutch, Fisher, and Alexander*, decided in December 1829, the editors and proprietors of the *Journal* were found guilty of libel on ministers and parliament, and sentenced to a year in Newgate. They had asserted that 'dragoon officers direct civil affairs. Troops are our law-givers'. Wellington, who had appeared himself at the Old Bailley to give evidence, achieved a measure of personal vindication when they were also found guilty of an indictment, written by the duke of Cumberland's domestic chaplain and published in the *Journal*, accusing the prime minister of treason.[57] If Wellington, Scarlett and Lyndhurst hoped through this successful prosectuion to procure a more docile tory press, they were singularly luckless. Faced with a press alert to an assault on its order, the most they achieved was the demise of the not very well-subscribed *Morning Journal* itself in May 1830.

Confronted with a reform bill more radical than most ultras were able to countenance, the tory press split from the party leadership was generally papered over by 1831. Only Croly's *Monthly Magazine* kept up the fight and, despite its own detestation of the bill, continued to wish Lord Grey well.[58] Yet, the continuing tension between the ultras and the main body of the conservative party during the 1830s and 1840s, from grand political questions to personal petty vindictiveness, can be largely traced to the fissure of 1829–31, most pronounced in a public way in the tory press.

The vicious assaults upon the duke of Wellington were not unique for the contemporary British press. Canning, Huskisson, and Perceval, among others, had to put up with similar manifestations. But Canning and Perceval gave as good as they got while the duke, no politician and no aggressive patroniser of a friendly press, may have been unprepared for the spiteful criticism which his controversial decision on Catholic emancipation would elicit. The 'decus and tutamen' of the kingdom, as Greville called the duke,[59] had never been as exposed to the cut and thrust of party politics in quite the same way as most of his more consciously political contemporaries. What draws attention to the attacks on the duke are the sustained aspect of them (which may have surprised Wellington) and the role they played in the downfall of the post-1784 Pittite regime. Just how important the tory press was in Wellington's political ruin is difficult to determine. Arguably, it played as important a role in the weakening of the Wellington government as Junius did in that of Grafton's sixty years before. Yet, as regards the duke's downfall in 1830, attention has tended to focus on the ultra opposition in parliament, on the fall of the Bourbon monarchy, and on the parliamentary reform issue in the 1830 general election. It is possible at the least that Wellington's lack of much enthusiastic tory press support, even from the papers and journals grudgingly backing his administration, played a major role in that demoralisation of the duke, the cabinet, the tory MPs and peers, and the party in general so evident in 1830. Hence, from a narrow political viewpoint, it may have been a misfortune for the tories to have been led at that fatal juncture in British politics by a non-political statesman and one who failed to appreciate the virtues of the fourth estate. Even with Catholic relief, Wellington might have flattered or cajoled or bought sections of the tory press. Yet even that may not have worked in the highly charged political atmosphere of 1829 and 1830. For the duke's political nonchalance as well as his undervaluation of the growing role of political ideology in the defining of political principles may have been responsible for his erroneous belief in March 1829 that the tory party would reunite as soon as Catholic emancipation passed.[60] In a way, Wellington's failure to understand British political society on 2 November 1830, when he spoke against any reform of parliament, may have been prefigured by a failure to understand the abiding principles of much of his own party a year and a half earlier.

Notes

1   Sir Charles Webster, ed., 'Some letters of the duke of Wellington to his brother William Wellesley-Pole', *Camden Miscellany*, third series, xviii (1948), pp. 26–7.
2   Gash, 'Wellington and Peel, 1832–46', in Donald Southgate, ed., *Conservative Leadership*, 1832–1932 (New York, 1974), p. 36.
3   WND, Wellington to Stockdale, February 1821, i, 155–6; Wellington to Peel, 3 November 1824, ii, 331; Wellington to Stephen, 25 July 1828, iii, 556; Wellington to Gleig, 4 July 1831, vii, 462.
4   *Ibid.*, Wellington to Stephen, 25 July 1828, iii, 556.
5   WSD, vii: Liverpool to Wellington, 7 May 1811, 120; Wellington to Wellesley, 12 March 1812, 303.
6   WPC, i, 5.
7   A. Aspinall, 'Social status of journalists at the beginning of the nineteenth-century', *Review of English Studies*, xxi, (1945), p. 218.
8   G. R. Gleig, *Personal Reminiscences of the First Duke of Wellington* (Edinburgh, 1904), p. 38.
9   L. J. Jennings, ed., *Correspondence and Diaries of John Wilson Croker* (1884), i, pp. 397–8.
10 Mrs Oliphant, *Annals of a Publishing House* (New York, 1897), Lockhart to Blackwood, 28 December 1830, i, pp. 246–7.
11 M. F. Brightfield, *John Wilson Croker* (1940), Lockhart to Scott, 23 February 1830, p. 201.
12 (1978), p. 73.
13 Seventh Duke of Wellington, ed., *Wellington and His Friends* (1965), p. 92.
14 WND, Wellington to Buckingham, 21 April 1829, v, 585–6.
15 W. B. Pope, ed., *Diary of Benjamin Robert Haydon* (Cambridge, Mass., 1963), 28 October 1832, iii, pp. 657–9.
16 'Appendix to chronicle', *Annual Register*, lxiv (1822), 351. A. P. Wadsworth, 'Newspaper circulation, 1800–1954', *Transactions of the Manchester Statistical Society* (March 1955), pp. 7, 37. *Irish University Series of British Parliamentary Papers: NEWSPAPERS* 2 (Shannon, 1971), pp. 84, 104–6.
17 *History of the Times* (New York, 1935), i, p. 460.
18 *Fraser's Magazine*, xiii, (May 1836), p. 626.
19 A. Aspinall, ed., *Three Early Nineteenth Century Diaries* (1952), p. lix.
20 *Westminster Review*, x, (January 1829), pp. 217–8.
21 W. Hindle, *Morning Post*, 1772–1937 (1937), p. 135. *Morning Post*, 13 and 14 April 1829.
22 The circulation of *John Bull* had been 10,000 in 1821. It was 4,500 in the mid-1830s. James Grant, *Great Metropolis* (1836), p. 150.

23   Aspinall, *Three Diaries*, p. lxi.
24   For example, *John Bull*, 21 February 1830.
25   H. J. C. Grierson, ed., *Letters of Sir Walter Scott* (1936), ix: Scott to Peel, 2 May 1828, p. 144; Scott to Knighton, *c.* May 1828, p. 421.
26   Oliphant, *Annals*, i, pp. 246–7.
27   Grierson, *Letters of Scott*, Scott to Lockhart, October 1828, xi, 24n. See Southey's, 'The Roman Catholic Question–Ireland', *Quaterly Review*, xxxviii (October 1828), p. 548 *passim*.
28   *Ibid.*, xliv (February 1831), pp. 595–6.
29   *Westminster Review*, x (April 1829), p. 476.
30   8 July 1828; 12 July 1828; 22 September 1828.
31   Francis Bamford and seventh duke of Wellington, eds, *Journal of Mrs Arbuthnot, 1820–1832* (1950), ii, pp. 324–5.
32   11 June 1829; 28 August 1829; 2 June 1830.
33   26 February 1829.
34   Lord Colchester, ed., *Political Diary, 1828–1830* (1881), ii, p. 172.
35   William H. Wickwar, *Struggle for the Freedom of the Press*, 1819–1832 (1928), p. 285, estimates a journal circulation of around 1,000 in 1829.
36   *Edinburgh Review*, xxxviii (May 1823), p. 360.
37   *Literary Gazette*, 16 June 1821, pp. 380–1.
38   James Grant, *Newspaper Press* (1871), iii, p. 14.
39   Oliphant, *Annals*, Blackwood to his son, ii: 28 June 1828, p. 84; 12 April 1829, p. 88.
40   *History of the Times*, i. p. 170. Grant, *Great Metropolis*, pp. 306–7.
41   See, for example, *Fraser's Magazine*, January 1831, p. 746.
42   *Age*, 6 June and 11 July 1830. *Blackwood's:* xxviii (July 1830), pp. 88–9; xxv, (March 1829), p. 272. *Fraser's:* July 1830, p. 737; October 1831, p. 263. *St James's Chronicle*: pp. 12–14; August 1830.
43   21 November 1830.
44   xxix (February 1831), p. 346.
45   (December 1830), pp. 617, 629.
46   14 March 1829.
47   21 March 1829.
48   29 August 1829.
49   viii, (September 1829), p. 316.
50   29 March 1829; 6 June 1830.
51   *Standard:* 28 March 1829; 20 July 1829; 17 September 1830; 2 August 1830. *Monthly Magazine*, viii (September 1829), p. 241.
52   14–16 April 1829.
53   *Age*, 5 April 1829; 26 December 1830. *Morning Journal*, 5 February 1829.
54   18 April 1829; 25 April 1829; 23 May 1829.
55   viii (September 1829), p. 247.
56   WND, Wellington to Scarlett, 23 July 1829, vi, 38–9.
57   Sir Theodore Martin, *Life of Lord Lyndhurst* (1883), p. 246. Wickwar, *Struggle for the Press*, pp. 285–7. *Morning Journal*, 11 February 1830.
58   xii (September 1831), p. 308.
59   L. Strachey and R. Fulford, eds, *Greville Memoirs*, 1817–1860 (1938), iv, p. 169.
60   Bamford and Wellington, *Journal*, ii, pp. 251, 254.

F. C. Mather

9

Achilles or Nestor? The duke of Wellington in British politics, 1832–46 *

In biographies of the duke of Wellington the years after the great reform bill feature only as an epilogue. The phase was one of misgiving and withdrawal, of *apotheosis*, but of ceding the practical leadership on the Conservative side to Peel. The celebrated French historian of England, Elie Halévy, put this in classic form:

> The old nobleman and old soldier for whom the age of conquests whether in love or war had gone by had determined to retire from public life. He had received too many insults, had been exposed too often to the hoots of the mob in 1831 and 1832 and in spite of the modesty he had shown when he yielded the first place to Peel and withdrew into the background, he had nevertheless been compelled at the close of 1834 to endure more innuendos and further suspicion. He now adopted a new attitude, the attitude of the sage and the counsellor; he would no longer be Achilles but Nestor, would belong in future not to a party but to the entire nation.

The same note is struck, though with appropriate qualifications, by Elizabeth Longford with her arresting phrase 'The Duke on Elba'. It is this assessment which must now be examined.

There is some truth in the hint of despair. Wellington's correspondence during the 1830s embodies many mistaken allegations that the 1832 Reform Act had introduced a form of government by popular assembly, incompatible with the rights of property. Because it was unco-ordinated with the traditional authority of the king and the House of Lords it also appeared unworkable. A typical comment ran:

'No country ever was or ever can be governed by three separate independent authorities; of which one possesses the power over the purse; another has the executive power; and the third the power of correcting to the laws.'[1] He gave this objection as a reason for not taking office, and grounded upon it what seemed on occasion to be abject fatalism. A Durham clergyman who wrote to him in 1839 calling for greater energy by the local authorities against Chartist disturbances, received the reply: 'I regret what is going on; I am concerned that it is not in my power nor I believe now in that of any man to apply a remedy. . . . Nothing can now restore peace and tranquillity and happiness to this once happy and glorious nation excepting a bounteous Providence.'[2] It is tempting to dwell on the contrast with Peel, in whose mind the emotions of hope and fear competed more evenly for allegiance: whose surges of optimism, apparent to his colleagues in the darker days of the middle 1830s pointed the way to ultimate victory.

Nothing could be more dangerous, however, than to extract from Wellington's occasional *obiter dicta* an interpretation of the last twenty years of his public career. The historian learns that a trend of actions furnishes a better guide to motivation than uttered words. No one was more prone than Wellington to talk or write for effect, or in order to relieve his feelings. His closest friend Charles Arbuthnot warned Peel of this when writing to him about the intensity of the duke's opposition to the Conservative party's taking office in the late 1830s:

I know he had had people of his own family with him of extreme opinions. Such men do great harm; & particularly with him. Without ever looking to consequences, they talk wildly and loosely of turning the government out. They provoke him; & this leads him to give extreme contrary opinions. He is ever ready to enter into calm discussion; but he cannot easily controul himself when people talk to him what seems absurd nonsense.[3]

It will be argued here that Wellington's pessimism, though not without influence on his political behaviour, was in part an intellectual conceit forged to vindicate his earlier stand against the Reform Bill. Despite it he continued to exert, in his characteristically old-fashioned way, an influence which lasted as long as his powers and the options open to him did. The appearance of withdrawal was conveyed by his dislike of

being involved in conferences. This was less an abdication of responsibility than a deaf man's defence against meetings, when, as Arbuthnot
explained on his behalf, 'it is not unusual for many to talk at the same
time'.[4] The duke was aware, however, that there were other means of
getting his own way than by attendance on an endless round of
concourses.

It was Arbuthnot who brought out the importance of language, the
language of the reform bill debates, in shaping Wellington's subsequent outlook. Though the duke is renowned for a previous oration
denying the need for any reform of parliament, his first response to the
whig bill when it was announced, was to pose the practical question.
He challenged Earl Grey to explain how the existing system of
monarchical government could be carried on under the conditions
which would result from the bill. Not receiving a satisfactory answer,
he repeated it in an expanded form three weeks later. Arbuthnot
explained in 1839 how the duke fell a victim to his own rhetoric:

> There never was a wiser question than the Duke's to Lord Grey: How is
> the country to be governed? But I must own that I have often regretted
> that the question was ever put. The Duke cannot get it out of his mind;
> &, as Lord Grey could give no answer to it, the Duke considers it as an
> admitted axiom, which no circumstances can ever shake.[5]

In practical effect, however, the conviction that the country was
ungovernable came to mean little more than that it was difficult to
govern. In an argument with Grey over the Irish Church bill in 1833
Wellington admitted as much. Looking back on the reform bill, he
observed: 'The Bill having passed, I considered it my duty to submit to
it, and to endeavour to carry it into execution by every means in my
power.'[6] In the last resort Wellington's sense of duty was more potent
than his doubts.

His continuing activity was apparent first in his participation in
ministry making. When the first reformed parliament met in January
1833, Peel and Wellington were broadly agreed that the Conservatives
should not oppose the whig government unless some vital principle
came under attack. Their reasons differed according to age and
circumstances. The duke at sixty-three could not adapt from long
cabinet experience to opposition. Peel in his middle forties thought
more about the future, when the Conservatives might provide themselves with an independent base in the country, if only they occupied
the middle ground in politics. To both, however, it was axiomatic that

the Whigs must be generally upheld as a fence against the Radicals. For the duke, Lord Grey's government was 'the last prop of the monarchy'. 'After him comes Lord Radnor probably and chaos!'[7]

It was the disintegration of the Whigs in 1834, under the stresses of their own administrative reforms, that called the opposition to a more active role. Disruption on the ministerial benches revived the latent power of the crown to choose the executive. Thus, when Grey's administration crumbled in July, William IV, displaying the customary royal preference for coalition government, commissioned Lord Melbourne to construct a ministry jointly with Wellington and Peel. It was Melbourne who frustrated an initiative which neither he nor the two Conservative leaders desired, and the Whigs returned to office. But not for long. On 14 November the king took advantage of Melbourne's difficulties in the House of Commons, on the removal of Lord Althorp from the lead, to evict his ministers, whose politics and persons he thoroughly disliked. The duke of Wellington then took office as prime minister with a curious skeleton government in which he was home secretary as well as first lord of the treasury, and took provisional charge of the other two secretaryships. The great seal was assigned to Lord Lyndhurst. Wellington's second premiership – one can scarcely call it a ministry – lasted for only three weeks, at the end of which Peel, summoned from his holiday in Italy, returned to form a full and permanent cabinet. Historians, even biographers of the duke, have missed the significance of this interlude. Aldington and Guedalla both treated it with indulgent contempt, praising Wellington's industry in keeping the country running but citing contemporary satires upon his 'one-man' administration. Lady Longford's better-informed account dismisses the episode as 'three weeks and more of waiting for Peel'. In fact, it was a necessary preparation for Peel's first ministry, which is now acknowledged to have been the crucial point in the reconstruction of the Conservative party after the reform bill. Necessity may be claimed on three grounds. Firstly, because we may question whether a Conservative government would have been formed at all in 1834–5 had not the duke of Wellington accepted William IV's offer. According to a memoir in the Peel papers, when news of the king's dismissal of the whigs was brought to Sir Robert Peel in Rome, he disapproved of it. Only in the course of his twelve days' journey back to England did he make up his mind to accept the premiership. Had he been consulted in advance, he admitted in the memoir, he might have dissuaded the monarch from an action which he thought 'premature and impolitic'. What eventually tipped his judgment was partly a desire to avoid humiliating the the king by forcing him to recall the ministers whom he had dismissed; partly a disinclination to break with colleagues who had already committed themselves to the persuasive attempt at conservative rule.[8] The first would have been less compelling three weeks earlier before the new government had been set up; the second would not have obtained at all, for Wellington would not have acted in face of an outright veto by Peel. True, the king had ejected his former ministers without consulting anyone, but previous experience of Peel's obstinacy at the crisis of the reform bill struggle would have rendered him unlikely to inflict on him the blackmail of a *fait accompli* which he successfully tried on the loyal duke in Peel's absence.

Secondly, it was Wellington who played the prime ministership into Peel's hands. Lord Stanley observed correctly that 'the Duke of Wellington is the person, who, . . . received the first mark of his Majesty's confidence.'[9] The duke's own description of his interview with the king leaves no doubt that the commission to form a ministry was given to him. The suggestion of Peel and the proposal of an interim government under himself came from Wellington.[10] There was no shortage of persons who would have accepted, or even preferred, a permanent administration under the duke. These were not only hard-cast tories like the duke of Gordon whose kinsfolk and guests raised bumper glasses to his success when the news of the fall of the Whigs reached Gordon Castle.[11] They also included reformers of various kinds, especially those antagonistic to the new economic liberalism with which Peel was associated. John Marshall, a critic of machinery, the New Poor Law and the monetary system, sent him the prospectus of one of his pamphlets, urging him, on again becoming prime minister, to turn his attention to such matters.[12] Even the popular radicals warmed to the duke. A friend of the late Major Cartwright exhorted him to rally the country with a new reform bill.[13] Cobbett argued in the *Political Register* that, in one respect, the duke would be stronger without Peel, for he was not bound by the currency views of ' "oracle" Ricardo and all that rubbish'.[14] Wellington made no attempt to exploit this feeling to his own advantage. He drew up a confidential circular, to thirty-six Conservative lords and Sir Edward Knatchbull, an ultra-tory leader in the Commons, explaining that the interim arrangement had been proposed by himself.[15] Shoals of applications for places in the administration and the household flooded upon him, but they were reserved for Peel's attention. The furthest he would go towards influencing his successor's choice was to send him a very comprehensive plan of government, classifying candidates for office according to the type of post for which they were suited – ministerial, Privy Council or Household, diplomatic or judicial. A few comments on individuals were intruded, but it was all done by way of suggestion.[16] Direct pressure on the incoming prime minister was resisted. Even the king, encouraged by his success against the whigs to resume his activities in coalition building, had to be restrained by Wellington from inviting Stanley, the whig dissident, to join the government when Peel returned.[17] Having assisted the royal genie to escape from the bottle, the duke contrived to pop him back into it before he damaged the prospect of a genuine Conservative government.

A third essential contribution made by Wellington to the establishment of Peel's 'Hundred Days' administration lay in the resolution of certain tactical problems which stood in the way of a firm transfer of power. There was the initial formality of swearing the duke into office before a Privy Council largely composed of recalcitrant Whigs who wanted nothing to do with the proceedings. Wellington managed this by mustering eight of his friends in advance of the meeting at St James's to act with himself as a Council.[18] A more serious difficulty was to dispose of the former House of Commons, in which the Conservatives had so small a representation. Unless a general election could be held with speed, Peel on his return would face early in the New Year a parliament more intractable, by reason of the intervening hardening of party, than that which Pitt had grappled with in similar circumstances in 1783–4. Hence the importance of Wellington's promptness. It was agreed with the king at the outset that an election would be needed, and that a secretary or secretaries of the treasury might have to be appointed to prepare for it.[19] A new treasury board was, therefore, established, the former commissioners refusing to allow their names to stand; it was also needed for the conduct of general governmental business. King William IV had pressed Wellington to appoint an interim Chancellor of the Exchequer to prevent the Whigs from slipping in the lord chief justice, Lord Denman, on a precedent of 1812.[20] No evidence can be found of such an appointment before Peel's return. The board, however, was gazetted within four days of the duke's becoming premier, and the following day an election committee was active at the Carlton club.[21]

When-Peel set foot in England the arrangements were well advanced. Candidates were already declared, addresses published and expenses incurred. Among contemporaries it was Peel's brother-in-law George Dawson who came nearest to evaluating what Wellington had done. 'I think you cannot but approve of the clearsightedness and the decision of the Duke', he wrote to his kinsman. 'It is a masterpiece to have dispossessed the late ministers of their power in so short and decisive a manner, and it is evident that the Whigs are thrown into complete confusion by the sudden & complete ejectment from office.'[22] The modern democratic mind might have less admiration for what now seems closer to a peaceful *coup d'etat* than to a change of government by parliamentary processes. But if consequences be the test rather than causes, it may be seen that paradoxically Wellington, the firm traditionalist, gave to Peel, the cautious reformer, the opportunity to construct the ministry from which a revived Conservative party, viable in the reformed parliament, mainly dated. 'It was the period from November 1834 to April 1835', writes Professor Gash, 'that is to say, the period of Peel's first ministry, which witnessed the first national mobilisation of Conservative feeling in the provinces.'

Wellington never again played so prominent a part in the shaping of a government, but his practical influence remained considerable. Lord Blake has argued, and most historians have agreed with him, that the duke's advice to the king to send for Peel in November 1834 'settled the leadership of the party for the next eleven years and settled it in favour of the party's greatest and most distinguished statesman'.[23] But contemporaries like Sir James Graham, spoke for years ahead not of Peel alone but of Wellington and Peel as leaders of the party. Besides his prestige as a natural hero and as an ex-prime minister Wellington had two special strengths to sustain his importance. Firstly he enjoyed, more than Peel did, the confidence of the monarch and of the monarch's private advisers during a decade, the 1830s, when the royal factor in government was only gradually receding. This kept him in the stakes for ministry making as late as 1839, when he heard confidentially from Willoughby Gordon that Lord Melbourne had made up his mind, should the whig ministers resign, to advise the young queen to send for Wellington alone.[24] A month later they did resign, and Victoria invited him to form a government. As in 1834 it was the duke who ruled himself out, partly because of his fixed conviction, by no means then a constitutional rule, that the chief minister should be in the House of Commons.

The second basis of his power lay in the control of the House of Lords, where he led the conservative majority, and in his influence over the ultra and high tory elements within it. That influence is at first sight surprising. The ultras had rebelled against his first ministry over Catholic emanicpation, and had tipped the scales against it in the Commons vote of 15 November 1830 which brought it down. But, as B. T. Bradfield has shown, the ultra-tories were never a coherent party. By the early months of 1831 a common opposition to parliamentary reform was beginning to drive some of them – Burghersh, Eldon, Mansfield, Wetherell and others – back into the camp of Wellington and Peel. A letter in the Wellington Papers shows how warmly their approaches were welcomed by the duke.[25] Reconciliation was slow and partial, and a knot of unpredictable extremists in the Lords remained unreconciled in the middle 1830s. But if anyone could control them it was Wellington, who was closer to them on economic policy than was Peel. Peel's 'bullionism' was ever a stumbling block between himself and the agricultural interest, but during the financial stringency of 1837 the duke advised restoring to the Bank of England the power to deal in silver by weight instead of in gold coins, as a method of lubricating the monetary system.[26] Acceptance of the Chancellorship of Oxford University in 1834 enabled him to identify himself with the Anglican religious sentiments of the ultras and to hold the important middle ground of the party. To conservative consciences of the 1830s Oxford and the Church were one. Lord Francis Egerton jocularly referred to Wellington in his Cancellarial role as 'the head of the Church, no offence to His Majesty', and only regretted that he could not be Dean of Christ Church for a few months'.[27]

It was his personal prestige and ability to handle the tory peers as individuals that most strengthened Wellington's grip upon them. This was never more apparent than in 1836, when a polite exchange of letters with the earl of Winchilsea, with whom he had once fought a duel on Battersea Common, took the edge off a revolt against whig attacks on the Orange Order, which might have led to a head-on confrontation of the two houses of parliament. Winchilsea's first intention was to move an address in the Lords, protesting against the king's discouragement of the Order on the representation of the House of Commons alone. Having sent a copy of his proposal considerately to the duke, he responded to Wellington's full and courteous explanation of his objections by abandoning his own design, and by entreating his associate Lord Londonderry to postpone his motion on the subject until Lord Roden, an Orangeman friendly to the duke, could attend and participate. Londonderry did postpone, and the affair evaporated in a pointless debate on the communication of papers from the Commons to the Lords.[28]

Wellington was never completely successful in controlling the activities of the ultras. In May 1835 the duke of Buckingham intrigued with Cumberland and Lord Londonderry to foist upon him a close-knit tory party in the Lords which, had he not scotched their plot with Lyndhurst's help, would have undermined Peel's strategy of governing in opposition.[29] Only he, however, could have done so well. Without him, moreover, dissent from Peel's new liberal Conservatism would have been greater among more moderate tory lords. The second marquess of Salisbury, who had rebelled against Catholic emancipation, but continued to adhere to the mainstream Conservative party, cannot have been alone when he wrote to the duke in 1841: 'I consider you as my political leader, and I do not consider Sir R. Peel in that light'.[30] If, as Dr Ian Newbould has recently argued, Toryism of the old kind constituted a significant limitation on Peel's achievement during the 1830s, Wellington's contribution to the compacting of the Conservative party was more important than it has seemed to be.

A subsidiary asset commanded by Wellington in the House of Lords was his influence over the election of the twenty-eight Irish representative peers chosen by the generality of Irish peers under the terms of the Act of Union. As a member of one of the great Anglo-Irish families, he enjoyed immense prestige with the electors. It was his job to write to them indicating who should be supported. He did not, however, command an unfettered discretion. Supporters of the whig government constituted the largest single party among the voters, and in order to overcome that, the opposition leaders had to fish for the suffrages of two different groups: non-whig peers resident in Ireland and Anglicised absentee landlords likewise opposed to the government. The degree of management needed to be carefully gauged. Too much of it would add to the strength of the whigs by provoking resentment; too little would divide the Conservative interest by allowing rival contenders to emerge. Wellington's strategy was to throw his weight behind the candidate most acceptable to the residents, especially to the ultra-Protestants headed by Lord Roden, while guiding these to a respectable and not too sectarian choice.[31] The result was a loosely controlled system, which reserved some independence to the representatives when chosen.

A notable feature of the duke's authority in his later years was its independence of departmental office. The foreign secretaryship which he held for four months under Peel in 1834–5, was his last great ministerial post. When the conservatives next formed a government in September 1841, he was a member of the cabinet but, at his own request, without portfolio. Eleven months later, when the illness of Lord Hill threw the position of commander-in-chief of the army back into his lap after an interval of fourteen years, he asked to be relieved both of his seat in the cabinet and of his lead in the House of Lords. It was Peel who persuaded him to abandon the thought.[32] Here may seem to be incontrovertible evidence of a wish to step down. The duke was seventy in 1839, and beginning to display the marks of advancing years. He had some kind of fit after hunting late in the year. Nevertheless, these setbacks were relatively minor, and it is arguable that his principal object was to return to the role assigned to him at the height of his career when, fresh from his victories on the European continent, he honoured Lord Liverpool's government by his adhesion. The first idea then was to put him in the cabinet without portfolio.

The years 1828–35, when he filled the highest offices in the state, constitute an exceptional phase in his long political life, engendered by an acute leadership crisis in the tory party. When stability had been restored, he reverted to the consultative role without fixed responsibility which had been his earlier goal. If this was Nestorian, it did nothing to restrain the energies of an Achilles. The duke's offer to withdraw from the cabinet and the leadership in the Lords was chiefly a feint to remove objections to his resuming the non-political office of commander-in-chief which he genuinely coveted. He knew when he made the offer that his colleagues did not want to accept it.[33] Besides, as Peel reminded him, there was still enough meaning in the distinction between the 'ministry' of the day and the 'government of the queen' to warrant a recourse to the eighteenth-century practice of having the service chiefs sitting in the cabinet as members of the latter rather than the former. He begged him to 'give to the administration and to the Government of the Queen, as distinguished from the ministry, the advantage of your name and authority as a member of the Cabinet and again of the Government in the House of Lords.'[34] Being in the cabinet on the other hand without departmental responsibility gave an ideal opportunity to concentrate his attentions on the things which interested him. These were principally questions of high politics. He could shrug off humdrum detail by telling applicants for his patronage what he told a woman seeking a clerkship for her son, that he held no political office himself, and could not therefore 'become the Solicitor General to his colleagues in the Queen's Councils for every body who thinks proper to apply to him.'[35] The role for which he cast himself was that of being 'kept in reserve with my hands clear' to deal with emergencies which he expected to arise in Ireland, in Europe and in the world at large.[36] In areas like these he continued to exert into the 1840s a powerful political influence. He was commissioned by Peel to guide the impetuous Lord Ellenborough on his appointment as Governor General of India. A letter which he wrote to him, advising on the defence of the country against a possible uprising of the Moslems after the reverses of the Afghan War, earned the tribute of the prime minister that 'for comprehensiveness of views, simplicity and clearness of expression, and profound sagacity' it was 'equal to any production of the meridian of his glorious career'.[37] But the duke's detached position also cut him off from the reforming activity in the fiscal and administrative spheres for which Peel's great ministry 1841–6 is principally remembered. This was a new style of government which could scarcely be assumed without departmental support.

At this point therefore we must turn from measuring the extent of Wellington's remaining influence to assess the quality of it. What imprint did he leave on policies pursued in England after the Reform Act? Viewed functionally, the part he played in the reform politics of the middle and later 1830s does not differ essentially from that of Peel. Like him he sheltered the whig governments of the period from the attacks of extremists in his own party. He issued strict instructions to the tory peers for keeping the House of Lords quiet during the 1836 and 1837 sessions. To avoid unnecessary clashes between the two Houses, he advised Conservative peers during 1836, to 'originate nothing' but 'to allow nothing to pass' which was 'inconsistent with principle'.[38] This was a time when what Professor Gash has styled the 'Lords Reform locomotive' in the country was under fullest steam. In the upper house, where the opposition commanded a large majority, he implemented Peel's policy of accepting moderate reforms while resisting proposals of a more radical character.

A close consideration, however, of their respective responses to such measures as corporate reform, the establishment of a government-controlled police force in Manchester, and the union of Canada bill in 1840, reveals a significant difference of approach between the two men. Peel, as he showed in his rectorial speech at Glasgow University, accepted leading tenets of nineteenth-century liberalism: belief in the career open to talents and in the march of mind. Not so Wellington. He yielded ultimately to reforms proposed by others, but he did so reluctantly, and often after fierce initial resistance. His motives for giving way were themselves profoundly conservative: the need to preserve ancient institutions from a worse fate or to avoid splitting his party to the detriment of strong government.[39]

Lady Longford has contested the judgment that the duke was a 'modernizer *malgré lui*' by pointing to the remarkable innovations of his 1828–30 ministry in respect of religious liberty and police. But her revision does not make sufficient allowance for differences in his outlook before and after 1832. The traumatic experience of the Catholic crisis, the pessimism bred of the Reform Bill and the subsequent behaviour of the Whigs and Radicals, stiffened his resistance to change in principle even when augmenting the prompters to concession in practice. Thus, in a letter to Lord Redesdale, written in 1843 and found among the Wellington Papers, the duke confessed that at one time he had favoured a plan for state payment of the Roman Catholic clergy in Ireland. He had been influenced then, he said, by what he had 'heard of & seen abroad' and by the 'examples of Mr. Pitt, Lord Castlereagh & others'. 'But', he added, 'when I came to consider of these schemes . . . at the period of the Roman Catholic Relief Bill, I found that they were one and all absolutely impracticable, consistently with the laws for the establishment of the Reformation in this country, which could not be touched'.[40] He was, in fact, overruled by his colleagues at the time.

Too much of the duke of Wellington's political mentality was rooted in the past to render plausible the thought that he was after all a reformer. His aloofness from the popular face of conservatism was unconcealed. One of the more promising features of the party's recovery in the decade after 1832 was the establishment of conservative associations in the constituencies. The duke offered them little encouragement. In January 1836 he refused an invitation to become an honorary member of an association in Lancaster, as he had no relation with the town. In response to a question from the applicant he gave only a qualified approval to such bodies in general. Admitting that good men were justified in uniting to prevent seditious combinations from spreading into their localities and to promote a loyal spirit, he insisted that their societies must be open to all and free from secrecy.[41] Doubtless he was suspicious of the growth of Orange lodges under the Conservative umbrella, but his tratment of the Salford Operative Conservative Association was insensitive. When requested later that year to present its petition to the House of Lords, he delegated that task to the earl of Wilton, who lived at Heaton Hall near Manchester. Some warrant for this could be found in the semi-feudal principles which still emphasised a nobleman's special obligations to his own locality. The action was turned into a snub when, the petition having been presented, no notification of the fact was given to the association either publicly or privately. Wellington's clients, who had circulated their document as a model to other bodies, were mortified to learn that the duke of Newcastle had presented a copy of it from the operative society of Nottingham, while they suspected that the original had been spurned. His belated explanation and clumsy apology can have done little to remove their annoyance.[42] Except for a short phase after the Reform Act, when Oastler tried to win him for the Ten Hours campaign, Wellington had no connection with the factory reformers. In 1841 he declined to interview a deputation from the West Riding Short Time Committees which had already seen Peel, Graham and Wharncliffe.[43] His attitude to Ashley's mines bill, when it came before the Lords in the following year, was cautious and evasive.

The feature of his conduct which did most to generate a reactionary impression was his sensitivity, amounting at times to an obsession, to law and order questions. He saw conspiracy, national and international, lurking behind the campaign of Daniel O'Connell for the repeal of the union with Ireland in 1843. Papers which he sent to the Home Secretary had convinced him of 'the connection between what is passing in Ireland with what is passing in Canada, and of both with parties in the United States'.[44] His fears were not wholly groundless. As Graham, who had other sources at his command, admitted, there was 'a strong sympathy with the Irish Repealers in the United States', but this was unlikely to be activated unless 'open insurrection' occurred in Ireland, in which event there would be 'a revolutionary movement in England', aided 'secretly if not openly' by French Republicans and Bonapartists and by 'the most violent Democrats in America'.[45] But Wellington exaggerated the danger. In his zeal to procure the arrest of O'Connell he passed on evidence which by no means supported the inferences that he drew from it. Lord Glengall, a Protestant landlord from Tipperary, wrote to him on 19 August, stating his belief that the repeal leader did not intend to hold together the proposed council of three hundred, but would use the election of delegates to raise money for his political fund.[46] Modern authorities do not regard the threat of anti-parliament as more than a futile retaliatory gesture to the pressure of the Irish executive. Wellington, however, used the information from Glengall to alert the Home Secretary to the danger that the convention might proclaim itself the government of Ireland, and envisaged full-scale warfare against it by blockade of the Irish coasts.[47] His harassment of Graham was inexorable. There is evidence to suggest that it furnished the last goad to the banning of the Clontarf demonstration, which led to the prosecution of O'Connell. Having received on 3 October a missive almost accusing him of failing to carry out the decisions of the cabinet, Graham wrote to Peel as the ministers entered their final deliberations: 'I do not see how it is possible to overlook this letter of the Duke's, when considered in connection with the Lord Lieutenant's warning that the excitement produced by these monster meetings is alarming and that these meetings are to be continued.[48] Wellington's excitement was no doubt fanned by Irish peers with whom he was connected in the Lords. Basically, however, it was a matter of temperament, springing from an aversion to agitation of all kinds.

If the post-1832 Wellington cannot justly be described as a reformer, he may without distortion be accorded the title of improver. He was opposed to levelling, a concept which in his view was broad enough to embrace attacks not only on private property but on the privileges of corporate bodies such as municipal corporations and Oxford colleges. He did not resist, and even supported, a discriminating improvement undertaken by such bodies for their own protection. Thus he defended the redistributive policy of the Ecclesiastical Commissioners against criticisms by malcontent clergy like Gleig and Singleton, because it was the work of the archbishop.[49] An Irish clegyman who objected to any alterations in the tithe was told unceremoniously: 'Matters . . . cannot be left as they are.'[50] As Chancellor of Oxford he reminded heads of houses that their statutes were reputed to be obsolete and needed revision. He was untiring in his efforts to persuade the Weekly Board to revise the Thirty-Nine articles test for youths on matriculation. The governing consideration, he told the vice-chancellor, was the need to confront 'the inquisitorial power of this Leviathan House of Commons', which had already shown disposition to call for three or four committees to enquire into every branch of the administration of the universities and their constituent colleges and houses. Such enquiries he conceded were 'inconsistent with justice, and with the independent enjoyment of property'. It was for the universities to decide whether they would submit to them. But a thorough review of their statutes would enable them to determine 'whether they will or not submit . . . upon sure grounds; and with a certainty that determine which way they may, it will be without loss of reputation'.[51] Universities today are purer than in Wellington's time, but it is still the case that thoughtful self-amelioration by those who understand the totality of academic need offers the best defence against unbalanced intervention from outside.

When the duke of Wellington envisaged changes he nearly always saw them in terms of particularities and individual needs. Here he differed from Peel, who has been criticised by Dr Boyd Hilton for being 'theoretical'. Characteristically the abuse at Oxford which most captured his imagination was the plight of undergraduates who were allowed to run up debts with tradesmen which they could not repay. These were not simply for high living. William Stone of Coleshill wrote to the chancellor complaining that on graduation he found himself in arrears to the tune of £100 for books which he had purchased to compete for prizes, hoping eventually to discharge the debt by writing. Instead he was forced to abandon plans of returning to Oxford, and obliged to retire to a village curacy on £60 a year. Wellington took up the issue of debts with the vice-chancellor and, though the latter protested his inability to devise a remedy, there was quite a brush over the matter.[52]

Wellington's part in shaping foreign policy has been harshly judged and, for the post-1832 era, almost ignored. Criticism has been focused upon his throwing away the gains of Canning's diplomacy in Portugal and in the Near East during the later 1820s. Professor Kenneth Bourne, a leading modern authority, speaks of his 'ineptitude', and indicts him of warmongering against France and the United States of America when serving under Peel in the 1840s. Palmerston, he shows, linked him with the forces of European reaction after Waterloo, deeming him 'an apostolical and holy alliance politican'. The Wellington Papers and other contemporary sources suggest the need of a revision at which it is possibly only to hint here. The duke of Wellington's aims, as he defined them, were well within the guidelines which governed British foreign policy in the post-Napoleonic era. In his approach to Iberian questions he was an extravagant upholder of the principle of non-interference with the right of states to determine their own form of government, which Castlereagh had defined and which Canning had applied. He does not appear to have had any long-term strategy for adjusting the balance of power in a rapidly changing world, to set against Palmerston's policy of supporting constitutional *régimes*. None the less, he deserves a credit which has seldom been accorded to him for his efforts to limit war and to preserve the peace of Europe when it was threatened. A largely unrecorded outcome of his foreign secretaryship in 1834–5 was the Eliot convention negotiated with the commanders of the rival armies in the Carlist War in Spain, to put an end to the systematic shooting of prisoners of war and to provide for the periodic exchange of captives. Historians have obscured the connection between this cartel and the duke's activities by observing that it was concluded some time after he had restored the foreign office to Palmerston. But Lord Eliot's published papers show that Eliot and Colonel Gurwood, who accompanied him to Spain, were not only sent by Wellington but acted throughout under his instructions, even after the change of government in London.[53] Unpublished letters of the duke reveal, moreover, that behind his efforts to humanise the conflict lay a broader objective of bringing it to an end, and of thus preventing it from touching off a general European conflagration. He observed to Metternich just before leaving office: 'En évitant d'aigrir les esprits et de souffler et encourager les querelles, j'espère que j'ai fait ce qui était en mon pouvoir pour la conservation de la paix. En général je laisse le monde en meilleur état que je ne l'ai trouvé.[54]

One feature of Wellington's outlook which especially fitted him to act the part of peace-maker was his disinclination to resort to gunboat diplomacy to protect British economic interests outside Europe or to uphold the rights of British citizens abroad. In this he was more pacific not only than Palmerston but even than Peel. Confronted in February 1835 with the grievances of British miners and speculators in Mexico, who had suffered losses in an insurrection and from the corrupt administration of justice in that country, he first proposed to withdraw a despatch prepared by Palmerston his predecessor, threatening the Mexican government with hostilities, and to replace it by a delaying procedure of joint enquiry and charging interest on liabilities. It was Peel who insisted that the treaty rights of British subjects should be upheld, if necessary by force, and Wellington's draft was amended.[55] In the quarrel with the United States just after the formation of Peel's second ministry in 1841, the duke was keen to limit concessions on the frontier between New Brunswick and Maine, where national interest was involved. Lord Ashburton's negotiating brief was amended accordingly.[56] But he was sensitive to American feeling in the review of unofficial acts of retaliation committed by Canadian loyalists against American life and property during the late Canadian rebellion. It was he who persuaded Peel to order a full enquiry into an invasion of United States territory which had resulted in the kidnapping of a Colonel Grogan.[57] When a British subject, McLeod, was seized by the State of New York for intercepting an American vessel carrying arms to the Canadian rebels, he expressed to Lord Aberdeen 'such an objection to these private wars waged by individuals; without warrant from their government' that the perpetrators might be hanged even if their actions had later been upheld by that government.[58] Wellington's opposition to filibustering was a facet of his conservatism: the international counterpart of his concern for order at home.

The active career of the duke of Wellington in British politics continued to the end of Peel's great ministry. His lead in the House of Lords was not seriously threatened by the arrival of Stanley as his second-in-command. The Rupert of debate was raised from the Commons on 4 November 1844, in his father's barony of Bickerstaffe, with the view that he should ultimately succeed Wellington as leader, but fell far behind him in contacts, and had too much wisdom to try to displace him. As it then seemed, he could afford to bide his time. *Fraser's Magazine* observed that it was impossible to 'recognise in the quiet, unobtrusive minister who now sits under the wing of the Duke of Wellington . . . the fierce , fiery leader who was named the Hotspur of the Conservative forces'.[59]

Relations between the duke and the prime minister were never closer than in 1845–6, when the disintegration of the Conservative party was proceeding. Peel consulted him secretly about cabinet and other high ministerial appointments – who should replace Gladstone at the Board of Trade in January 1845 when confidential efforts to persuade him to stay in the cabinet had failed; whether at that time Sydney Herbert should be chief secretary for Ireland.[60] When he was reconstructing his ministry after the ill-fated whig attempt in the following December, Peel said that he would do nothing about the office of President of the Council until he had talked with the duke.[61] Wellington reciprocated by steering close to Peel on the public controversies of the time. His value to the prime minister was enhanced by the fact that the pot was being stirred by the more conservative elements in the party chafing at Peel's liberal leadership. It was with these that he had always held his closest *rapport*, and he conceived his role in terms of damage limitation. He exerted it conspicuously in two successive and interwoven crises. The first was the Protestant revolt against the extension of the Maynooth grant in spring 1845. Among the positive measures to allay discontent in Ireland after the arrest of Daniel O'Connell, Peel and Graham brought forward a bill to increase the existing annual grant to the Roman Catholic seminary in County Kildare from £9,000 to £26,000 and to place the state's provision on a permanent footing. The government's purpose was to improve the accommodation, raise the salaries of professors and the value of scholarships, and enable the college to turn out well-bred and well-affected priests who would exert a civilising influence upon the whole community. Strenuous and often bigoted opposition to this move came from popular Evangelicalism and Dissent. In the House of Lords resistance came from the ultra-tories, Newcastle, Winchilsea, Eldon and Kenyon, veterans of 1828–9, from Irish peers, and from disaffected Anglican bishops, not all of them Evangelical, ready to vent their resentment of the withdrawal of state funds and privileges from the established Church on a scheme to finance the teaching of 'Popish error'. Professor Gash has observed that the Maynooth crisis did little to disturb the 'general passivity' of the House of Lords under a conservative government, citing the comfortable majorities of 157 and 131 by which the bill passed its second and third readings. But twelve of the eighteen bishops present at the former divided against the government, on Lord Roden's delaying motion and three more together with the two English primates gave their proxies to the 'non-Contents' on the main proposal to go forward.[62] With a small minority of peers excitement rose to such a pitch that the duke of Wellington had difficulty in controlling the debates. No sooner had he risen to move the second reading, than the duke of Newcastle inter-rupted him to ask whether he had the Queen's permission to do so. Amid cries of 'hear' and 'order' Brougham interjected that this was 'one of the most disorderly proceedings I ever witnessed in the whole course of my experience'. But it was Wellington's own good humoured response, in taking the blame on his own deafness, that enabled him to pick up the threads. An acrimonious exchange between Lord Normanby and the bishop of Cashel on the second night brought unseemly cheers from the episcopal bench, and

Wellington clashed again with an explosive Newcastle at the third reading.

The huge government majorities in the upper chamber were swollen by sympathetic whig votes, but these were less important than in the Commons, where the Conservatives divided almost equally for and against the bill. Some credit should, therefore, be accorded to the duke's successful management of the tory peers in producing this result. While he adhered to cabinet policies from the beginning, he defended them with arguments which not only represented his own conservative outlook, but were calculated to remove the hesitations of moderate men holding similar views. In his speech on 2 June proposing the second reading, he distinguished between the laws establishing the Reformation, which even the original foundation of the college in 1795 had infringed, and the principles of the Reformation, with which no real inconsistency had ever been discerned. On the practical level he made much of the political danger of allowing Irish priests to be educated in foreign countries so soon after foreigners and foreign countries had shown a threatening interest in repeal. Somewhat inconsistently with this, but with becoming regard to codes of honour, he invoked the Christian duty not to persecute the weak. It cannot be known how many peers were moved by his persuasions. In the politics of the day men were often swayed by patient negotiation not by speeches. The most serious threat to party stability came from Lord Redesdale, the government chief whip in the House of Lords, who had been airing scruples about Peel's Catholic policies since August 1843. He objected not to the principle but to the details of the Maynooth bill. The duke tried to argue him out of his objections, but the more he tried the more he became convinced that they masked doubts about the administration's commitment to the Church of England, especially in Ireland. Fearing the loss of services so crucial to discipline in the upper chamber, he shared the problem with Peel, who tried but ultimately failed to prevent Redesdale's resignation.[63]

In the more serious political crisis which opened in the following November the rift in the Conservative party followed a similar line. From figures cited by Professor Gash it appears that about three quaters of the 147 Conservative MPs who voted against the Maynooth bill at its second reading in the House of Commons, divided against repeal of the corn laws at its third. The consequences were more devastating, not only because agricultural protection was of greater moment to a parliament of landowners than the fate of an

Irish college, but because Peel was resolved to repeal the Corn Laws even if it meant splitting the Conservative party. The duke of Wellington dissented more from his priorities than from his policies. What was at stake for him throughout the long controversy was not the corn law but the survival of Peel's government and the unity of the Conservative party. When the heads of government started to discuss the failure of the Irish potato crop from October 1845 onwards, he denied the value of removal of the corn laws as a remedy, on the reasonable ground that in a subsistence economy peasants did not buy food in the market, and aligned himself with other colleagues in the cabinet against Peel's proposals.[64] However, he did not accept that the question was one worth breaking the government on. In a memorandum of 30 November he gravitated timidly between the prime minister's plan to suspend and then replace the laws and his own preference for retaining them. Of one thing only he was certain: 'A good government is more important than Corn Laws or any other consideration, and as long as Sir R. P. enjoys the confidence of the Queen and the publick, and has strength enough to last & perform the duty, he ought to be supported.'[65] The duke's avowed willingness to surrender his own opinions to Peel's stemmed not only from his sense of constitutional obligation, but from an appreciation of the things which the second ministry had achieved. As explained later to Stanley, these will be found mostly to accord with the judgments of posterity: 'the resolution of the finance of the country; the settlement of the banking system; the revival of commerce; the settlement of this [very Corn] question and his defence of what had been settled; the success in Ireland in putting down the monster [? Munster] meetings, the universal tranquillity prevailing throughout Great Britain'; the 'confidence which I hear was felt in his government abroad, and even in the United States, and 'the confidence in him and respect for him felt in the great manufacturing and commerical towns of the country such as Manchester, Liverpool, Bristol, etc'.[66] In a man of seventy-seven some of the duke's perceptions were remarkably far-sighted and appear to have been becoming increasingly so.

His decision to stand by Peel was taken before the government resigned but the course of events between then and the Conservative return to office on 20 December strengthened his resolve, and provided him with arguments to deter protectionists from breaking ranks. The usual explanation of the inability of the whigs to supply an alternative administration finds a prominent place for Lord Grey's objections to the return of Palmerston to the foreign office. Wellington had heard, however, from Lord Mahon that the difference had turned on the desire of Grey and others to have Cobden in the cabinet, to which Lord Lansdowne had demurred.[67] Whether true or untrue the report encouraged him to write round to the duke of Beaufort, Lord Redesdale and other tory peers, telling them that if the restored government was not upheld, there was no resource 'excepting Lord John and the Whigs' – a possibility excluded from Beaufort's letter, as the attempt had just failed – 'or Cobden and the League and the tail'. He warned them that neither Peel nor his colleagues could, after the late ministerial crisis, return to their old public defence of the corn law, but led them to expect that the prime minister's plans would include measures for the security of agriculture. He did not know what these were. They should wait and see.[68]

Wellington was never busier nor more anxious than during the first six months of 1846 when the corn and tariff bills were going through parliament. He laboured to deploy his dwindling and overworked band of adherents to promote Peel's business in the Lords and to keep the House in motion. When Redesdale resigned on Christmas Day he found himself doing the business of a whip.[69] He offered to move the second reading himself when Ripon hesitated, though he confessed to ignorance of the state of the question, and had to turn to Peel for instruction.[70] What he cared about, however, was the cohesion of the party and the survival of the government, not the corn bill. The fate of the latter depended in the end not on his efforts but on Russell's success in disciplining the whig lords. But he sent back petitions in its favour from Scottish burghs and parishes desiring him to present them in the upper house.[71] His most dramatic gesture was made in the cause of detaching Lord Stanley from the Protectionists before his allegiance hardened to the point of making him their leader. In February 1846 he offered him the leadership in the House of Lords on no condition other than that he should 'endeavour to rally the Conservative party'. Stanley declined, thinking that only a period in opposition would pull it together.[72]

The duke never accepted this conclusion. On 21 June, when the future passage of the corn bill was assured but the government was threatened by a vengeful compact of the Protectionists with the Whigs, he unfolded to Peel a bold plan. The truncated extract of his letter printed by C. S. Parker obscures the thrust of it.[73] He desired the prime minister to forestall defeat on the (Irish) Protection of Life bill by bringing forward a vote on the sugar bill which would divide his opponents, and by making an issue of the Commons' privileges in the treatment of Lord Hardinge's annuity bill. This would win time to appeal to the country not on the Irish measure only but on the queen's needs and Peel's merits.[74] The value of the suggestion was not put to the test. Tired of a party which would not follow its leaders, Peel had no interest in strategems to remain in power. Having carried the corn bill through the Lords on the day he was defeated on the 'assassination' bill in the Commons, he resigned and his government with him. His fall, on 29 June 1846, marked the end of Wellington's official political career, not automatically but because he felt that as commander-in-chief of the army he could not lead the opposition to the incoming whig administration in the House of Lords.[75]

With reference to their respective purposes, he, not Peel, was the loser of the last battle which they fought together. Nevertheless he had a useful role in the politics of the years after the Reform Act. His contribution was active and practical, not just advisory. By seizing the initiative when the opportunity came in November 1834, by careful management of the House of Lords, by an ultimate willingness to compromise with views more advanced than his own, he won a place side by side with Peel as builder and sustainer of the new Conservative party. It was a necessary role, for Peel never succeeded in shaping the whole of his party in the reforming image of the Tamworth Manifesto. The duke had nothing to contribute to the theory of party. There is no reason to doubt the sincerity of his continual professions of a higher loyalty – to the crown and to 'government quasi-government'. He boasted that as leader of the Conservatives in the House of Lords he had supported the ministries of Grey and Melbourne against his own party 'when I thought that it was going too far'.[76] Government by party, as Disraeli understood it, was as foreign to this thinking as it was to Peel's. Nevertheless he sensed more acutely than Peel that a political party united by its own historic purposes was an indispensable asset which could not safety be sacrificed to the current pursuits of the executive. He told Stanley in 1846 that he was:

> most sincerely anxious that the Conservative Party in this country: that is to say the party of property and intelligence of the country, the heads and leaders of the educated orders, of the learned professions, of the mercantile and manufacturing interests, and of the naval and military professions, should understand one another and act together as a political party.

'The existence of such a party', he added, 'gives a strength to the government of the country, whatever may be the course of its action upon particular questions.'[77] In this pragmatic conviction he worked to build it up, recognising that 'in these days of democracy men cannot permanently stand alone in politics'.

To the country Wellington's chief political service in these later years was in removing obstacles to the progress of reform. The role did not come easily to him, for he believed that the task of Conservatism was to conserve. He knew, however, that 'the principle . . . of conservation', on which he professed to manage the House of Lords, meant the ultimate avoidance of collision with the government and the House of Commons. In the 1830s, therefore, when his party was in opposition, and the Whigs held the political initiative, he had to balance his desire to fend off legislation which he regarded as a threat to 'the religious and ancient authorities of the country' against the danger of provoking, by excessive resistance, an explosion which would damage the constitution. He was, therefore, involved in a sequence of abrupt and embarrassing changes of course over the English and Irish corporation bills and the union of Canada bill. From 1841 onwards, with Peel in the saddle, and the limits of innovation being set by a cabinet in which he had himself a seat, the duke's response was more straightforward. He supported the government's reforms, and to a very large extent he learned to approve of them. In a long political testament written for Lord Stanley in February 1846, he argued that during the nineteen years since he inherited the leadership in the House of Lords from Lord Liverpool, he had gradually forfeited his influence over his followers by objecting to 'all violent and extreme measures', that is to say to their die-hard opposition to change.[78] The assessment was distorted by the emotions of the time. He had been tolerably successful in holding his party among the peers until Peel's retreat on the corn laws rendered his task at length impossible. Nevertheless, a balanced assessment of the duke's career after the great Reform Act must stress not only his political longevity but also his moderation. This quality was more pronounced than his utterances would often suggest.

*This is an extended version of a professorial lecture delivered to the University of Southampton on 6 February 1986.

Notes

1 Wellington to Peel, 22 February 1837, WP, 2/44/134–35.
2 Wellington to Joshua Wood, 26 July 1839, *Ibid.*, 2/60/125.
3 Arbuthnot to R. Peel, 19 January 1839, Peel MSS., British Library, Add. MSS. 40, 341, ff. 46–50.
4 Arbuthnot to Peel, 19 November 1840, *ibid.*, ff. 209–12.
5 Arbuthnot to Peel, 19 January 1839. BL Add. MSS., 40, 341, ff. 46–50.
6 *Parl. Deb.*, third series, xix, p. 948, 19 July 1833.
7 Wellington to Aberdeen, 18 January 1833, WPC i, pp. 32–3. C.f. C. S. Parker, *Sir Robert Peel from his Private Papers* (1891–9) ii, pp. 212–14.
8 'Memorandum as to my appointment to the office of First Lord of the Treasury in 1834 and to the administration over which I presided', BL Add. MSS. 40, 431, ff. 19–23.
9 Stanley to Peel, 11 December 1834, BL Add. MSS., 40,405, ff. 61–6.
10 Wellington to Peel, 15 November 1834, WP, 2/16/6–7.
11 The duke expressed to Wellington his desire that an administration would be tried: 'Te duce'. Gordon to Wellington, 17 November 1834. *Ibid.*, 2/16/20.
12 J. Marshall to Wellington, 18 November 1834 and printed enclosure, *Ibid.*, 2/16/36–7.
13 T. Cleary to Wellington, 18 November 1834, *ibid.*, 2/16/35.
14 *Cobbett's Weekly Political Register*, 29 November 1834.
15 Draft Circular to 'Peers and others', private and confidential, WP, 2/16/99–101.
16 Wellington to Peel, 30 November 1834 and enclosed plan of administration, BL Add. MSS., 40, 309, ff. 344–6, 380–81.
17 William IV to Wellington and enclosure to Stanley, 21 November 1834; Wellington to William IV, 21 November 1834, WP, 2/16/71–3; see I. D. C. Newbould, 'Sir Robert Peel and the conservative party; 1832–1841: a study in failure?', *English Historical Review*, xcviii (1983), pp. 529–57; and I.D.C. Newbould. 'William IV and the dismissal of the whigs', *Canadian Journal of History*, xi (1976), pp. 311–30, for new light on William IV's earlier motives and designs.
18 Wellington to Peel, 20 November 1834, WP, 2/16/61; Greville, *Journal of the Reigns of George IV and William IV* (1875), iii, pp. 148–9.
19 Wellington to Peel, 15 November 1834, WP, 2/16/6.
20 William IV to Wellington, 16 November 1834, *Ibid.*, 2/16/15.
21 Wellington to Peel, 20 November 1834, *ibid.*, 2/16/61; *Annual Register*, lxxvi (1834), Chron. p. 200; N. Gash, 'The organisation of the conservative party 1832–1846, Part ii: The electoral organisation', *Parliamentary History*, vol. 2 (1983), p. 132.
22 G. R. Dawson to R. Peel, 22 November 1834, Peel MSS., BL Add. MSS., 40, 404, ff. 245–6.
23 Robert Blake, *The Conservative Party from Peel to Churchill* (1979), pp. 38–9.
24 J. W. Gordon to Wellington, 9 April 1839, WP, 2/58/80.
25 Burghersh to Wellington, 27 February 1831, WP 1/1176. Wellington to Burghersh, 5 March 1836 (1831), *Ibid.*, 2/38/109.
26 Wellington to Peel, 5 March 1837, WP, 2/45/11.

27   Francis Egerton to Wellington, 13 June 1834, *ibid.*, 2/245/82a.
28   See correspondence passing between Wellington, Winchilsea and Rosslyn, 29 February – 9 March 1836, *ibid.*, 2/38/83–84, 97–98, 104, 110, 120; *Journal of the House of Lords,* lxviii, p. 55, 7 March 1836.
29   See correspondence between Wellington and Lyndhurst, 13 May 1835 and rival memoranda issued by Wellington and Buckingham, WP, 2/33/78–81, 92–3.
30   Salisbury to Wellington, 9 September 1841, *ibid.*, 2/78/60.
31   For a full exposition of the problem and principles of management see Wellington to Peel, 4 January 1836, WP, 2/37/51.
32   Wellington to Peel, 10 and 11 August and Peel to Wellington, 11 August 1842, WP, 2/90/112–14, 122–3.
33   Peel to Wellington, 10 August, and Wellington to Peel, 10 August 1842, WP, 2/90/111–12.
34   Peel to Wellington, 11 August 1842, *ibid.*, 2/90/122.
35   Wellington to Rachel White, 18 December 1841, WP, 2/82/64.
36   Wellington to Peel, 17 May 1841, *ibid.*, 2/76/114.
37   Unaddressed and undated letter by Peel referring to the duke's letter to Ellenborough, 31 March 1842, *ibid.*, 2/86/59–64 and 119.
38   Wellington to Lyndhurst, 15 October 1836, *ibid.*, 2/43/10; c.f. Wellington to the Bishop of Exeter, 17 February 1836, *ibid.*, 2/38/47; N. Gash, *Reaction and Reconstruction in English Politics 1832–1852* (Oxford, 1965), p. 46.
39   F. C. Mather, 'Wellington and Peel: conservative statesmen of the 1830s', *Transactions of the Peel Society*, vols v and vi (1985 and 1986), pp. 7–23.
40   Wellington to Redesdale, 19 August 1843, WP, 2/109/63.
41   R. B. Thompson to Wellington, 18 January and Wellington to Thompson, 24 January 1836, WP, 2/37/111–12.
42   P. S. Sowler to Wellington, 18 June and Wellington to Sowler, 20 June 1836, *ibid.*, 2/40/122–3.
43   Buckingham to Wellington, n.d. Saturday, and Wellington to Buckingham 30 October 1841, WP 2/80/112.
44   Wellington to Graham, 19 July 1843, *ibid.*, 2/107/61.
45   Graham to Wellington, Private, 20 July 1843, *ibid.*, 2/107/64.
46   Glengall to Wellington, 19 August 1843, and enclosed report, *ibid.*, 2/109/60–61.
47   Wellington to Graham, 19 August 1843 at night, WP 2/109/67.
48   Graham to Peel, private, 3 October 1843, Graham Papers (Netherby), Bundle 66A.
49   G. R. Gleig to Wellington, 2 January 1835; Wellington to Gleig, 5 January 1835, WP, 2/24/26–29; correspondence between Wellington and Thomas Singleton, Archdeacon of Northumberland, November 1836, *ibid.*, 2/43/35–37, 47–9.
50   Wellington to the Rev. W. T. Beaufort, 8 July 1836, *ibid.*, 2/41/67.
51   Wellington to the Vice-Chancellor of Oxford University, 27 August 1834, *ibid.*, 2/245/121.
52   William Stone to Wellington, 14 July 1834, WP, 2/245/94; correspondence between Wellington and G. Rowley, Vice-Chancellor, concerning the case of Mr Lukin of Magdalen College, 3–14 January 1835, *ibid.*, 2/246/2–6 and 8.
53   E.G. Eliot, Earl of St. Germans, ed., *Papers relating to Lord Eliot's Mission to*

Spain in the Spring of 1835 (1871); C.f. R. W. Seton Watson, *Britain in Europe 1789–1914* (Cambridge, 1945), p. 189; E. M. Spiers, *Radical General. Sir George de Lacy Evans 1787–1870* (Manchester, 1983), p. 63.

54 Wellington to Metternich, 10 April 1835, *ibid.*, 2/32/45.

55 Wellington to Peel, 15 February and Peel to Wellington, 1 March 1835, *ibid.*, 2/28/31 and 2/29/1. C.f. draft despatches, Wellington to R. Pakenham, 17 March 1835, *ibid.*, 2/30/61–5.

56 Aberdeen to Wellington, 8 February and 22 March 1842, *ibid.*, 2/84/75 and 2/86/8; Wellington's memorandum, 8 February 1842, *ibid.*, 2/84/84–7.

57 Wellington to Peel, 19 October and Peel to Wellington, 20 October 1841, *ibid.*, 2/80/29 and 34.

58 Wellington to Aberdeen, 29 December 1841, *ibid.*, 2/82/142.

59 Quoted from Robert Stewart, *The Politics of Protection. Lord Derby and the Protectionist Party 1841–1852* (Cambridge, 1971), p. 53 (November 1845).

60 Peel to Wellington, 22 January 1845 (Secret), WP 2/127/65–7.

61 Peel to Wellington, 22 December 1845, *ibid.*, 2/135/21–2.

62 References to House to Lords proceedings on the Maynooth bill are from *Parl. Deb.*, third series, lxxx and lxxxi.

63 See various letters in WP, especially Wellington to Peel, 4 April 1845 (2/129/11), Peel to Wellington, 10 April 1845 and n.d. (Saturday), (2/129/31 and 63). Gash, *Sir Robert Peel*, p. 477.

64 Neville Thompson, *Wellington After Waterloo* (1986), pp. 199, 203–04, 221

65 Draft memorandum 1845, WP 2/194/15.

66 Wellington to Stanley, 19 February 1846, *ibid.*, 2/138/39–44.

67 Mahon to Wellington, 20 December 1845, *ibid.*, 2/135/10.

68 Wellington to Beaufort, 22 and 25 December 1845, *ibid.*, 2/135/17–20 and 38; to Redesdale, 25 December 1845, *Ibid.*, 2/135/35; to Salisbury, 4 January and to Rutland, 6 January 1846, *ibid.*, 2/135/109–10, 119.

69 Redesdale to Wellington, 25 December 1845, *ibid.*, 2/135/36; Howe to Wellington, 5 February and Wellington to Howe, 6 February 1846, *ibid.*, 2/137/37.

70 Wellington to Peel, 19 May and Peel to Wellington, 20 May 1846. *ibid.*, 2/142/36 and 49.

71 Replies minuted on Kinnear to Wellington, 7 February and on Hector to Wellington, 10 February 1846, WP 2/137/54 and 69–70.

72 Stanley to Wellington, 18 February and Wellington to Stanley, 19 February 1846, *ibid.*, 2/138/15–16 and 39–44.

73 *Op. cit.*, iii, pp. 365–6.

74 Wellington to Peel, 21 June 1846, WP 2/144/32.

75 See the account of the audience which he gave to Lord John Russell on 1 July 1846. Wellington to Peel, 2 July 1846, *ibid.*, 2/144/56. Cf. Wellington to Londonderry, 7 July 1846, *ibid.*, 2/144/76, stating his subsequent position.

76 Memorandum upon the Leadership of the conservative party in the House of Lords, 1846 (? 19 February), copied from documents obtained from Lord Derby, 15 August 1870 WP 2/138/33.

77 *Ibid.*

78 Wellington to Stanley, 19 February 1846, ibid., 2/138/39–44.

Geoffrey Finlayson

10

Wellington, the constitution, and the march of reform

It is said that when Lord John Russell, by then Earl Russell, was on his deathbed in 1878, he heard a noise in the street and asked if the revolution was about to begin. The years of Wellington's life were seldom free of noises in the street, and elsewhere, that seemed to indicate such an event. Indeed, the span of Wellington's life, 1769 to 1852, arguably encompassed a period which was more pregnant with danger and disorder than that of Russell, some twenty-five years his junior. Though in the lifetime of both men Carlyle's famous phrase, the 'Condition of England Question' became a popular expression for the economic and social difficulties of the times, there were other problems which, to many of all political persuasions in the ruling classes, seemed equally menacing and prevalent since they bore on the political and constitutional structures and practices inherited from the past. And to the state of England could well be added the state of Ireland, in which political, economic and social problems were also present, but to which there was the added dimension of religious and ecclesiastical controversy. Such a dimension was not indeed absent from the situation in England; but it was evident to a greater, and more concentrated, degree across the Irish Sea.

It may be that to emphasise such points of tension and conflict in the late-eighteenth and early-nineteenth centuries undervalues the points of harmony and cohesion which may be found in the same period; and that much historical writing has been unduly couched in these terms. This is a point of view to which Wellington himself might well have subscribed, at least in his earlier years and, to some degree also, in his later life; for he was much given to pointing to the benefits and advantages of British principles and practices particularly when set in the context of the situation which prevailed in other countries. Yet, between 1828 and 1846, the duke was well aware of the various forms of 'pressure from without', and of the difficulties and dangers which they presented. In these years, agitation was focused on the Protestant constitution, on the unreformed parliament and corporations, and on the protectionist system: all of which were seen as bulwarks of the old order. These years also, of course, witnessed the four classic episodes of Catholic Emancipation in 1829, parliamentary reform in 1832, municipal reform in 1835, and corn law repeal in 1846. And in these years, Wellington himself either held high office, or was influential in tory circles in the Lords. Thus the period provides a suitable arena for an examination of Wellington's activities in the civilian battleground in which so much of his later career was spent. Indeed the duke himself – as Mrs Arbuthnot records him – described one of the episodes, Catholic Emancipation, as 'a battle like Waterloo'; and that description might, with some justice, be applied to all four.

There were, indeed, varying perspectives from which the 'battle' was viewed by those in command of, or involved in, the political structure – and varying prescriptions were offered for bringing it to a conclusion which did not involve the surrender of too much territory. Some were rather tangential to the point of view of the principal participants. Thus the solution favoured by some lay in the sponsoring in parliament of measures of social amelioration. This was an approach advocated from the early 1830s by tory paternalists such as Lord Ashley. Clearly, there was more to Ashley's paternalism than political calculation; there was a moral and religious dimension. But Ashley and his associates were not unmoved by the consideration that a paternalistic concern shown by the ruling classes for their less fortunate brethren might well remove them from the ranks of the disaffected, and reconcile them to existing constitutional arrangements and social orderings; it was one way of stifling Chartism and making the world safe for aristocracy.

More central, however, to the concerns of most politicians of the day were other prescriptions and solutions. There was the whig solution, which lay in the direction of reforming the institutions of the country and, in so doing, stabilising them and making them better equipped for survival. Here, too, some measure of abstract political principle was involved; but so was the political judgment that measured institutional reform was the best way to contain a potentially dangerous situation. The whigs, then, were the most natural supporters of making breaches in the ecclesiastical and political establishment which would satisfy the demands of the most powerful of those who lay outside, and incorporate them within a newly-reformed structure. Such a solution was most evident in the 1830s, during most of which the whigs held office. There was, however, another approach which lay not in the direction of liberalising institutions, but in liberalising trade. This would assist economic development and prosperity and improve social well-being – and thereby blunt the edge of radical agitation and save the constitution from extreme attack. This, broadly, was the liberal tory, or conservative solution, most evident in the 1820s and early 1840s while liberal tory ministries held power.

Obviously, such an analysis is greatly oversimplified. The tory paternalist Ashley supported the free-trading Peel over repeal of the corn laws in 1846; whigs and tories grew rather closer on political–institutional solutions in the mid-1830s, as the whigs became less ardent reformers and the tories (or conservatives) post-Tamworth, less ardent resisters; there was always a whig belief in free trade, and the repeal of the corn laws in 1846 was carried by whig–Peelite votes. Yet it is sometimes useful to over-simplify; and the three broad areas of tory paternalistic social amelioration, whig political reform and Conservative economic improvement and modernisation may be discerned as recognisable responses to the Condition of England Question.

Where did Wellington stand in relation to these responses? It may be said with reasonable safety that he was not greatly sympathetic to the approach of the paternalists. As a landowner himself, he may, indeed, have displayed paternalistic traits: Elizabeth Longford writes that at Stratfield Saye, the duke 'was known to be a sympathetic landlord, willing to knock off part of the rent for hard-pressed tenants'.[1] But although private individuals might be paternalistic, Wellington was of the view that there was little or nothing that parliament could do in a very positive way in this area. As he wrote in 1831:

> Of grievances to be removed or relieved by the interference of Parliament there are none. There are plenty to be relieved and removed by our own will, and by a reform of ourselves. For instance, if artisans, artificers and every description of workman will work six days in the week instead of passing Saturday, Monday and Tuesday . . . in the public houses in idleness, dissipation, and extravagance, and chattering

and gossiping upon subjects which they do not understand . . . they
would relieve themselves and their families from the evils of poverty,
loss of health, discontent and many others of the grievances of the day.[2]

Such an uncompromisingly robust defence of self-help was by no
means uncommon among the governing classes; but it did distance
Wellington from the rather more sensitive social conscience of Ashley.
Ashley had close dealings with Wellington in the 1820s: he had a
warm personal regard for the duke, springing, in part, from a youthful
admiration of Wellington's military exploits – and he was a regular
visitor at Stratfield Saye. He held office under Wellington between
1828 and 1830. But the two men rather drifted apart; and Ashley's
efforts over factory and mines reform in the 1830s and 1840s elicited
little, if any, support from the duke. Ashley was angry with Wellington
for his lack of support over mines reform in 1842, when, at one point,
he had seemed more favourable; and Wellington did not think well of
Ashley's conduct over factory reform in 1844, and referred to his
'foolish Vanity'. He clearly felt that Ashley was too much in league
with outside agitators – or, at least, was playing their game. In 1844 he
told Lady Wilton: 'It is true that the Chartists and Radicals on the one
hand and Lord Ashley and His followers on the other, are working to
obtain the same object; and that bye and bye these parties will cooperate together and with confederated Colliers and others who have
struck work to receive payment for work but to do none.'[3]

Such a comment misunderstood Ashley's activities, but it was not an
uncommon misunderstanding; it was Lord Melbourne who struck a
somewhat similar note when he told Queen Victoria that Ashley was
the 'greatest Jacobin' in Her Majesty's dominions.

Could it be said that Wellington was any nearer the other responses
to the problems posed by the state of England and Ireland? At first
sight, the answer would seem to be in the negative. He gave every
appearance in public of being a staunch upholder of the Protestant
constitution. In 1828, he told the Lords that 'there was no person in
the House whose feelings and sentiments, after long consideration, are
more decided than mine are with respect to the subject of the Roman
Catholic claims; and I must say, that until I see a very great change in
that question I certainly shall continue to oppose it.'[4]

He vigorously disapproved of the activities of the Catholic Association, which he regarded as a 'combined faction of priests and
demagogues'.[5] It was not, he acknowledged, an illegal organisation;

indeed, its care to keep within the law was one of the problems which it presented. But in February, 1829, in the Lords, he quoted approvingly a description of the association as a body: 'dangerous to the public peace, and inconsistent with the spirit of the Constitution, which keeps alive discord and ill will among His Majesty's subjects and which must, if permitted to continue, effectively obstruct every effort permanently to improve the condition of Ireland'.[6]

Such public sentiments gave Wellington the reputation of being firmly against any alteration of the Protestant constitution. In September, 1828, the earl of Sefton wrote to Creevey that he did not believe that Wellington had the 'slightest intention of doing the smallest thing for the Catholics, or that he ever thinks about them, any more than he does about the Russians, Turks or Greeks. When the time comes, he will send troops to Ireland. I believe he has no other nostrum for that or any other difficulty'.[7]

Equally, Wellington was a staunch supporter of the unreformed parliament. It is scarcely necessary to quote at any great length his famous speech of November 1830, which expressed his conviction that the country possessed 'at the present moment a Legislature which answers all the good purposes of legislation, and this to a greater degree than any Legislature has ever answered in any country whatsoever'. Some months later, in March 1831, when the whig bill was published, he said that the present system might have faults and abuses, but it had 'afforded to the country a government which has justly satisfied the people for a century and a half'. It had 'raised them to the highest pinnacle of glory in war, and of prosperity and happiness in peace'; it had 'made them the envy and object of imitation of all nations'. Wellington also defended the closed corporations within the unreformed electoral system: those who had entered parliament through these boroughs were, he said, 'essentially a part of the Conservative interest of the country' and included in their number 'some of the ablest and wisest men' who had appeared in parliament.[8] When reform of the corporations was proposed by the whigs in 1835, the duke objected to 'a general and sweeping measure'; and he could not agree to the whig bill without 'some very great alterations being inserted in it'.[9]

If one looks finally at protectionism, once again Wellington appeared to be a firm defender of this fourth bulwark of the old system and the interests which it guarded. In 1828, he argued in the Lords that Britain had been 'brought to its present high state of cultivation, and consequent internal wealth' by the practice of protecting agriculture; this had 'induced gentlemen to lay out their capital in redeeming wastelands and bringing them into cultivation.' 'Nothing', he argued, 'would be more unjust than to take from them that protection by which they have been enabled to bring cultivation to the state in which it now is.' Eleven years later in 1839 – the same year in which the Anti-Corn Law League was formed – Wellington said 'that agriculture could not yet go without protection and thus the law must be kept up. The protection of the agricultural interest,' he concluded, 'is essential to the prosperity of the country'. In 1842, he rejected, by implication, the idea put forward by the League that greater business activity would be stimulated by freer trade in corn: 'We have heard of the interference of the Corn Laws with the commerce of the country . . . but I believe that if the Laws were repealed to-morrow not a yard of cloth or a pound more of iron would be sold in any part of Europe or the world over which this country does not exercise control'.[10]

Even in November, 1845 – more or less on the eve of Repeal – he wrote that the continuance of the Corn Laws was 'essential to the agriculture of the country in its existing state and particularly to that of Ireland, and a benefit to the whole community'. He was afraid that 'it would be found that the country would cease to be the desirable and sought-after market of the world if the interests of agriculture should be injured by a premature repeal of the Corn Laws'.[11] Like the unreformed parliament and the unreformed corporations, the system of protection had served the country well – and should not be tampered with wantonly or carelessly.

Thus on all fronts, Protestantism, parliament, corporations, protectionism, Wellington seemed to be well removed from the solutions favoured by mainstream politicians; indeed, he seemed firmly on the side of another possible response to the problems created by the state of England: that of resistance. Far from being sympathetic to the tory paternalist, whig reformer or Peelite conservative improver, Wellington seemed to be in the camp of the ultra-tory resister. And that is how he had often been seen: the soldier turned politician, but a politician out of touch with the world with which he had to deal: one who had fought to save a world which was, in fact, steadily being lost. Sefton's remark – already quoted – to the effect that the only solution known to the duke for any problem was to 'send troops' encapsulates a judgment which is not altogether uncommon.

Such an interpretation, however, could not go without considerable criticism and comment. Wellington as Professor Mather has pointed out, was given to write and talk for effect;[12] and, on the first issue, Catholic Emancipation, there seems little doubt from the work of Dr Machin[13] that many of Wellington's public statements were desgined to conceal his real views on the matter in the interests of keeping the tory party together. Such views, unlike those of Peel, were by no means inflexibly opposed to some settlement of the Catholic question; indeed, as early as 1825 Wellington had put forward a plan for a concordat with Rome which would have allowed emancipation while protecting and safeguarding Protestant interests.[14] Again on parliamentary reform, although there was no secret sympathy here, it should be said that Wellington did not rule out the possibility of some measure of reform being carried – although not the whig reform. In October 1831, he urged the Lords to vote against the whig bill — but added an earnest entreaty that they should avoid pledging themselves against any other measures that might be brought forward. In April, 1832, he was once again on the side of those who wanted to reject the whig bill, but admitted that one day a reform of the kind proposed might, by a gradual process, reach the statute book. And on corporation reform in 1835, Wellington did admit that there was a case for some measure of reform – although again not the whig one.[15] He did not take the extreme line, favoured, for example, by Lyndhurst, of blocking the reform entirely, but sought to amend the whig bill.

Moreover, on protection, Wellington was not an out and out protectionist, but tried to balance the claims of protection and free trade. He argued that the sliding scale on corn imports which his ministry introduced in 1828 represented such a balance. He acknowledged that a variety of opinions existed in the country on the importation of foreign corn: there was the point of view of those who maintained that importation should be prohibited and the contrary view that there should be free importation into the markets of the country. Speaking of the sliding scale, he told the Lords that he had considered it his duty 'to endeavour to steer [a] course between the two extremes, and to propose a measure which shall have the effect of conciliating all parties: which shall be at the same time favourable to the public and which shall be permanent'.[16]

In the 1840s Wellington approved of the general reduction on tariffs on a variety of raw materials and manufactured goods carried out by Peel. He wrote to Lady Wilton that this plan was one for 'having laid the foundation for getting "the country again upon its Legs" '.[17] He defended the introduction of the income tax in 1842 on the grounds that the sum obtained would enable the government to repeal many taxes on articles of general consumption and duties on raw materials. In this way, consumers and manufacturers would be 'considerably benefited'. He hoped, indeed, that the income tax would be repealed as soon as possible; but meantime, it was necessary to 'restore the country to a satisfactory state and to prosperity'. Wellington still placed the Corn Laws in a special category; but he approved of a further adjustment to the sliding scale in 1842 and admitted that 'with our population increasing as it does year by year, and increasing as it also does in wealth, it is impossible to expect that we should at any period have our agriculture in such a state, as to enable us to rely upon it exclusively for the supply of our wants'.[18]

Thus, even if the matter is left at the level of Wellington's statements, one can find evidence to qualify the judgment suggested by the earlier selection; and if one follows Mather's advice further and looks at Wellington's 'trend of actions' and stretches it a little beyond the last twenty years of his career, one comes up against the undeniable facts that Wellington carried Catholic Emancipation in 1829 (having already carried the repeal of the Test and Corporation Acts in 1828); that he would have carried a measure of parliamentary reform in 1832 had he succeeded in forming a ministry; and that he eased the passage of municipal reform in 1835 and the repeal of the corn laws in 1846. Indeed, one might seize on *this* body of evidence to suggest that Wellington was much nearer the main solutions proposed by other politicians, whig and conservative: that, far from being a resister, he was a reformer *and* an improver. And, again, this kind of interpretation has been put forward. After Catholic Emancipation in 1829, a radical wrote to Lord Ashley of his 'admiration of your Duke, who is now my Duke and every man's Duke, who has a mind in him, throughout the World.[19] A. S. Turberville wrote that Wellington 'brought the Tory ship into some strange and alien ports of call'. Writing of the 1828–30 Wellington ministry, Turberville continued: 'that the Ministry . . . would pass down to history as one of the great reforming ministries did not seem conceivable; but the inconceivable happened'.[20] Elizabeth Longford has pointed to the innovations of the ministry of 1828 to 1830; and the duke himself upheld his reforming pedigree. 'It is curious enough,' he wrote in 1831, 'that I who have been the greatest reformer on earth should be held up as an enemy to *all* reform. This assertion is neither more nor less than one of the lying cries to-day.'[21]

Can, then, Wellington be said to have been 'the greatest reformer on earth'? Certainly the ministry of 1828–30 has claims to be regarded in a reforming light, with the repeal of the Test and Corporation Acts, Catholic Emancipation – and to this might be added new initiatives in police matters. But in the very same letter in which he had called himself the 'greatest reformer on earth' – indeed in the very next sentence – Wellington was careful to qualify what he meant by reform.

> If by Reform (he wrote) is meant Parliamentary Reform, or a change in the mode or system of representation, what I have said is that I never heard of a plan that was safe or practicable that would give satisfaction, and that while I was in office I should oppose myself to reform in Parliament . . . I am still of the same opinion. I think that Parliament has done its duty.

The duke went on to say that he had no personal or vested interest in the unreformed system; he had no borough influence to lose. He knew that he would be popular in the country if he changed his opinion and altered his course; he realised that he excluded himself from political power by persevering in the course which he had taken. But, he continued:

> nothing shall induce me to utter a word, either in public or private, that I don't believe to be true. If it is God's will that this great country should be destroyed, and that mankind should be deprived of this last asylum of peace and happiness, be it so. But as long as I can raise my voice, I will do so against the infatuated madness of the day.[22]

These are scarcely the words of a reformer; and certainly after 1830 the term cannot be used of Wellington, if indeed it can be used with any accuracy at any time of his career.

Possibly, indeed, the key to Wellington's role over the whole period from 1828 to 1846 lies less in trying to see him in terms of labels such as 'resister' or 'reformer' – for claims and counter-claims can be put forward for both of these – than in regarding him, above all, as a pragmatist. And here it is important to focus not only the state of England and Ireland, which he increasingly saw to be in the grip of an 'infatuated madness', but also on the constitution, which he held in the greatest respect – and which, at all costs, had to be protected from the extreme harm which those infatuated by madness might inflict upon it in their zeal to promote the 'March of Reform'. Thus on Catholic

Emancipation it is true to say that, before 1829, his position was not inflexible. But it was the impossibility of upholding British government in Ireland without emancipation, accompanied by other measures, which clinched the argument. In his famous speech on emancipation in February, 1829, Wellington told the Lords that: 'no man who has looked at the state of things for the last two years [in Ireland] will venture to affirm that Government can be carried on in the existing condition of Ireland'.

It was the Clare election of 1829 which forced Wellington's hand. That election returned Daniel O'Connell, who, of course, as a Catholic, could not take his seat at Westminster. This event, taken in conjunction with the surrounding activities of the Catholic Association, held out the prospect of total disorder in Ireland, in which the maintenance of British rule would become impossible, and the Union itself might be severed. Wellington told the bishop of Salisbury, one of his persistent critics over emancipation, that he had always considered the Roman Catholic question 'as one of civil policy'; and he entreated the bishop 'to consider the mode of governing Ireland if this question is not settled'. He told the duke of Rutland that he looked 'to realities'; and the repeal of Catholic disabilities, together with other measures – and these included the suppression of the Catholic Association and the raising of the Irish county franchise from forty shillings to ten pounds would 'give strength to the government in Church and State, such as it has not possessed since the Union with Ireland'.[23] A well-known quotation from Mrs Arbuthnot's journal took up points which the duke himself made in the Lords about the effect of the situation in Ireland on the king's prerogatives of dissolving parliament and creating peers:

> The Duke feels that . . . the government of Ireland is *now* in the hands of Mr O'Connell, that the king cannot dissolve Parliament because he would be sure to have the whole representation of Ireland in the hands of the demagogues of the Association; he cannot make an Irish member a Peer or give him an office because the same scenes would recur that took place in Clare; in fact, the king's Govt. is paralysed and his representative brought into contempt by the state of the Catholic body, and, in order to obtain power from Parliament for putting an end to such a state of things, he must devise some scheme by which, with safety to the Constitution, and with due protection to the Protestant Establishment, he can remove the disabilities of the Catholics. It is an arduous task, but if anybody can do it, he will.[24]

The duke of course, did do it; and, as recorded by Earl Stanhope, he said that what he looked to 'as the great advantage of the measure was that it would unite all men of property and character together in one interest against the agitators'.[25] If he could have done this *without* emancipation, he would almost certainly have taken that course. He told Peel that he saw clearly in the light of election results in Ireland, of which Clare was, in fact, simply one, that 'we shall have to suffer from all the consequences of a practical Democratic Reform in Parliament if we do not do something to remedy the evil'. If, he continued, he could believe that the Irish nobility and gentry 'would recover their lost influence, the just influence of property without making these concessions,' he 'would not stir'.[26] But such was the temper of Parliament that recovery of this influence without emancipation was not an option open to him. It was, then, much less the merits of the case which made the duke 'stir' on this occasion than the need to meet the threat to the Constitution.

It might be thought that, having recognised that the only way to quieten the agitation in Ireland and save the constitution was to grant emancipation, Wellington would have come to a similar conclusion about the agitation for parliamentary reform in Britain – and granted parliamentary reform. And there were strong rumours that Wellington would follow this course, if only to recoup his political fortunes, so badly affected by Emancipation. But such rumours and expectations were wide of the mark. Wellington was not, in fact, convinced that there *was* widespread and dangerous agitation in the country for parliamentary reform. He felt that it was manipulated and managed – and whipped up by the Whigs: a mere 'rage for Reform', which, given time, would subside. Far from it being expedient to introduce reform, there was a need to 'stem the tide as long as possible'.[27] Thus, unlike Ireland, government *could* be carried on in England; and, indeed, adoption of parliamentary reform would be the very means of making government impossible. This was a constant theme in the duke's pronouncements on the matter. 'I have always considered the Reform Bill as fatal to the constitution of the country' he told Eldon in May 1832; and this had, indeed, been his belief from the first. How, he asked time and again, could a government carry any measure once the good understanding between king and parliament had been destroyed – as it would inevitably be by the whig bill. 'To conduct the government will be impossible,' he wrote, 'if by Reform the House of Commons should be brought to a greater degree under popular influence.' The duke told Wharncliffe, to whose efforts to secure a negotiated compromise he did not lend his support, that he did not see how the government of the country was to be carried on under any scheme of reform 'if the King and his government are expected still to protect establishments, institutions, rights, interests and property as now existing in England'.[28]

Nevertheless, once again, Wellington had to look 'to realities': and the constitutional realities were that the king was on the side of reform – if increasingly doubtful about it as matters progressed – and that, after the general election of 1831, there was a strong pro-whig majority in the House of Commons. In these circumstances, it would not, as Wellington admitted to Wharncliffe in November 1831, 'be easy to govern in [the king's] name without Reform'. 'But', he continued, 'the more gentle and more gradual the reform, the better for the country and the more satisfactory will it prove to all who know its interests and feel for its greatness and prosperity.'[29] It was very much in this context that he felt it unwise to commit himself against all reform and urged the Lords to keep themselves 'free to adopt any measure upon this subject which shall secure to this country the blessings of a government'.[30] It was very much in this context that he felt it necessary to give his weight to amending the bill: 'as the proposal of anything else [i.e. opposition] would certainly fail', he told Bathurst in April 1832, 'the next best thing is to form, out of this bill, something as nearly similar as possible to what we have'.[31] And it was very much in these circumstances that he professed his willingness to come into office in May 1832 when the king refused to accede to the request of the whigs that he should create peers to push the bill through the Lords. Lords.

Here two constitutional issues were at stake. The first was that the king's ministers were, in effect, dictating to the king and the tories must attempt to save the king from this indignity. Thus Wellington wrote to Lyndhurst:

> I shall be very much concerned indeed if we cannot at least make an effort to enable the King to shake off the trammels of his tyrannical Minister. I am perfectly willing to do whatever his Majesty may command me. I am as averse to the Reform as ever I was. No embarrass-ment of that kind, no private consideration shall prevent me from making every effort to serve the King.[32]

If the king's position should be upheld, so too should that of the Lords;

for to Wellington it was an intolerable violation of the constitution to interfere with the authority of the upper house by a creation of peers such as that demanded by the whigs. There was, of course, the problem that the only way in which Wellington could uphold the prerogatives of the crown and those of the Lords was by doing the very thing which he had always said would subvert the whole constitution – reforming parliament; for, in accepting the king's invitation to attempt to form a ministry, he knew that the main task of that ministry would be to pass a reform of parliament. There was, in fact, a certain constitutional inconsistency in Wellington's attitude in May 1832 compared with his earlier views, in addition to the obvious political inconsistency; for in January, 1832 he had told Lord Exeter that it was better to force the whigs to create peers – and so destroy the constitution – than 'for us, the peers of England, to vote for that which we must know will have that effect.'[33] But in May, he had somewhat revised his opinion – not of the whig bill, for, as he told the Lords, 'no part of the Bill is safe'. But a tory ministry would modify the bill; and, as he continued, 'undoubtedly a part of the Bill is better, that is to say less injurious, than the whole Bill, and, certainly, it must at least be admitted that it is better than the whole Bill, accompanied by the destruction of the Constitution of the country by the destruction of the independence of this House'. Once again, then, Wellington adopted an entirely pragmatic view; if reform had to come it was better for it to come with the least possible damage to the constitution.

Reform did, of course, come – but not under the aegis of a Wellington or any other tory ministry, for no such ministry could be formed. A tory ministry was indeed formed after William IV – fearful that the whigs would proceed to further reform – dismissed Melbourne in 1834 and called the tories to office. Once again, Wellington rallied to the support of the crown and held things together until Peel returned from Italy. But, of course, the tory ministry was short-lived and, after defeat in the Commons was forced to resign in April 1835. With the return of the whigs, there was little that Wellington could do to keep reform at bay, the more so since Peel in the Tamworth Manifesto of 1834 had accepted the principle of moderate reform – and carried this out by his support for the main provisions of the whig bill for municipal reform in 1835. Constitutional considerations dictated that Wellington must do likewise, whatever his own sentiments. As has been seen, the duke did not like many aspects of the municipal corporations bill, and said as much in the Lords; but he used his influence to rein in the more extreme peers like Lyndhurst from a course which would bring about a worse result: a collision between Lords and Commons and a split in the tory party. Again, he rallied to the support of the Crown. Sir Herbert Taylor, the king's secretary, wrote to Wellington urging him to check 'any Ebullition of feeling which should produce the Risk of a serious Collision between the two Houses of Parliament and increase the Embarassment of His Majesty'. The king, already embarrassed by having to take the Whigs back, did not want to make things worse by having a Lords and Commons clash on his hands – which would not be to the benefit of the Lords – and weakening the tory party. Wellington was forced – with some reluctance – to agree with this analysis.

Finally, Wellington saw corn law repeal in 1846 in similar governmental, constitutional terms. He remained unconvinced by the economic arguments for repeal rather than adjustment, even in the emergencies of the Irish famine; but the political and constitutional arguments became overwhelming. The Anti-Corn Law League was active in its agitation; Russell in his *Edinburgh Letter* of November 1845 announced his conversion to Corn Law repeal and urged the nation to throw its weight behind the campaign; and Peel was convinced that repeal was desirable and necessary. Wellington read the signs. In November, 1845 his memorandum spelled out his continuing belief in the Corn Laws: 'my own judgment', he wrote 'would lead me to maintain the Corn Laws'. But if Peel thought differently, then the cabinet should support him and Wellington announced his own intention to do so.

> In respect to my own course, my only object in public life is to support Sir Robert Peel's administration of the Goverment for the Queen.
>
> A good Government for the country is more important than Corn Laws or any other consideration, and as long as Sir Robert Peel possesses the confidence of the Queen and of the public, and he has strength to perform the duties, his administration of the Government must be supported.[34]

Such considerations became even more pressing in 1846, when Peel returned to office, after his resignation and the failure of the whigs to form a government. Wellington had been appalled at the prospect of a whig government, backed by Cobden: 'you can have no notion how much the Duke suffered, when he thought we were to be cursed with a Whig–Radical Government', Arbuthnot told Peel. Once the whigs had failed to form a government, the prospect seemed to reduce itself to something even worse: either Cobden or Peel. Wellington put it in these terms to Redesdale: 'The Question of forming a Ministry now rests between Sir Robert Peel and Cobden! There is no chance of any other Conservative coming forward! and the Whigs have decalred themselves not able to form an Administration. We are very sick! God send us a good deliverance'.

Wellington's role in cooperating with the Almighty in obtaining deliverance lay in smoothing Peel's path in the Lords. Again, this was in accordance with royal wishes. Prince Albert told the duke that he had such an influence over the House of Lords that he would be able to keep them straight: to which Wellington replied: 'I'll do anything: I am now beginning to write to them and to convince them singly of what their duty is.' He stressed to Beaufort the desire of Peel to reach a 'just and fair' settlement: after all, Peel himself was a great landed proprietor with 'social habits of intercourse with the Landed Interest'. And larger issues were at stake. The corn laws were 'not the only interest of the country and it was worth some sacrifice to preserve good government'; and even if it were possible to form a protectionist ministry what, he asked, would 'become of the other Questions of external and internal Policy, commercial, financial, Colonial, Irish which press upon the consideration of the Govt every day?'.[35]

It was not an easy task; and Wellington had to withstand entreaties, such as that made by Croker, that he should resign and not submit to be dragged 'through the mire' of Peel's 'changes of opinion'. The duke told Croker in reply that he was 'the *retained* servant of the Sovereign of this empire':

> Nobody can entertain a doubt of this truth as supplied to my professional character. I have invariably, up to the latest moment, acted accordingly. When required, and the Sovereign has been in difficulties, I have gone further . . .

> Happen what may about the Corn Laws, I will not take a course which may have a tendency to reduce the Sovereign to a necessity of requiring such men as Mr Cobden to be her Ministers . . . [nor] be instrumental in placing the Government in the hands of the League and the Radicals.[36]

Wellington thus kept to the task. In May, 1846 he told Peel that the course which he could take in the Lords and in which he could 'really be of service to the Government' was 'in urging the House to avoid to separate itself from the House of Commons and the Crown': a course which, as he said, he had 'successfully taken on former occasions'. His speeches in the Lords simply reflected the constitutional points which he had already stressed in individual correspondence: that he was in Her Majesty's service and 'bound to Her Majesty and to the Sovereigns of the country by considerations of gratitude' on which he did not need to elaborate; that the Lords must not by rejecting a measure which had been recommended in a speech from the throne and had passed the Commons, place themselves in a lone position: 'Now that, my Lords,' he said 'is a situation in which . . . you ought not to stand; it is a position in which you cannot stand, because you are entirely powerless: without the House of Commons and the Crown the House of Lords can do nothing.' There is no doubt that such entreaties, coming from one so eminent as the duke, played their part in securing the Lords' acquiescence in repeal.

When Croker had urged Wellington to resign rather than support Peel over Corn Law repeal, he had stated his belief that 'the only trust of the country is in your Grace's consistency and firmness'. Here, Croker clearly looked to Wellington for a kind of consistency: that of resistance. But, as has been seen, the duke cannot be regarded in this light; he was not an out-and-out resister. Equally, as has also been seen, it is mistaken to go to the other extreme and call him a reformer; he was, as Professor Mather has said, 'ill at ease with the values of the age of Reform'. Wellington did, indeed, accept many of Peel's measures of improvement and modernisation; but it is tempting to accept the phrase used – if somewhat disputed – by Elizabeth Longford of him: 'a moderniser *malgré lui*'. For, unlike Peel, Wellington did not initiate; he responded to circumstances and initiatives which were not of his making. And the line of consistency which runs through such responses was the need to protect the constitution as far as circumstances allowed and to uphold the sovereign's government. Wellington was essentially a servant of the Crown and man of government and administration; and that involved a willingness to submerge his own opinions in the interests of keeping government going. In the midst of the corn law crisis, he told Lady Wilton that he did not know what Peel would propose, still less what he would be able to bring the 'great Landed Proprietors to consent to'. 'But', he continued, 'I am endeavouring to keep things together.'[37] And that, in many ways, encapsulated what Wellington had done since 1828: he had reacted pragmatically to the circumstances created by the State of England and Ireland and to other people's initiatives to solve them; and, amidst all, he had endeavoured 'to keep things together'. By so doing, one might argue, he helped to ensure that what Russell may have heard on his deathbed was no more than a noise in the street.

Notes

1　Elizabeth Longford, *Wellington, Pillar of State* (1972), p. 206.
2　WND, viii, p. 7.
3　Seventh Duke of Wellington, *Wellington and His Friends. Letters of the First Duke of Wellington to the Rt. Hon. Charles and Mrs Arbuthnot, the Earl and Countess of Wilton, Princess Lieven, and Miss Burdett-Coutts* (1965), pp. 195–6.
4　*The Speeches of the Duke of Wellington in Parliament* ed. Colonel Gurwood (1854), i, pp. 166–7.
5　WND, v, p. 43.
6　*Speeches*, i, p. 229.
7　*The Creevey Papers*, ed. Sir Herbert Maxwell (1904), ii, p. 170.
8　WND, viii, pp. 15–16.
9　*Speeches*, ii, pp. 21, 28.
10　*Ibid.*, i, pp. 151–2, 266, 485.
11　*Memoirs by the Rt. Hon. Sir Robert Peel* ed. Lord Mahon and E. Cardwell (1857), ii p. 198.
12　F. C. Mather, *Achilles or Nestor? The Duke of Wellington in British Politics after the Great Reform Act* (public lecture delivered at the University of Southampton, 6 February 1986), p. 2.
13　G. I. T. Machin, 'The Duke of Wellington and Catholic Emancipation', *Journal of Ecclesiastical History*, xiv, 1963, pp. 190–208.
14　*Ibid.*, p. 192 fn. 2. See also WND, ii, pp. 598–607.
15　*Speeches*, i, pp. 474, 532; ii, p. 25.
16　*Speeches*, i, p. 150.
17　*Wellington and His Friends*, p. 181.
18　*Speeches of Wellington*, ii, pp. 487, 492, 497.
19　Quoted in Elizabeth Longford, *op. cit.*, p. 240.
20　A. S. Turberville, *The House of Lords in the Age of Reform, 1784–1837* (1958), p. 228.
21　WND, viii, p. 20.
22　*Ibid.*, pp. 20–21.
23　WND, v, pp. 491, 514.
24　*Journal of Mrs Arbuthnot*, ed. F. Bamford and the Duke of Wellington (1950), ii, p. 198.
25　Earl Stanhope, *Notes of Conversations with the Duke of Wellington, 1831–1851* (1886), p. 60.
26　WND, v, 43.
27　*Arbuthnot Journal*, ii, p. 399.
28　WND, viii, pp. 20, 89, 341.

29 *Ibid.*, p. 98–9.
30 *Speeches*, i, p. 474.
31 WND, viii, p. 286.
32 *Ibid.*, p. 304.
33 WND, viii, p. 162.
34 *Peel Memoirs*, ii, p. 200.
35 Neville Thompson, *Wellington after Waterloo* (1986) pp. 224–7.
36 Bernard Pool, *The Croker Papers, 1808–1857* (1967), p. 201.
37 *Wellington and His Friends*, p. 202.

11

Wellington and local government

It is only recently that Wellington has started to be taken seriously as a politician and statesman, but a true understanding of the degree and nature of his activity in other affairs after 1815 remains obscure. No aspect of his later life has been so neglected as that of his interest and involvement in local government. To some extent this is understandable: Wellington was not primarily a local government man, and in any case the churchwardens and overseers of the poor of Stratfield Saye parish excite less interest than Napoleon and *La Grande Armée*. Yet the complete neglect of the subject is also surprising. The duke's celebrated facility of attending to detail well fitted him to master the minutiae of local affairs and the contents of his postbag demanded that he did. The truth is that local government excited his very real and deep concern and an analysis of this concern throws considerable light on his general political philosophy in the decades after Waterloo.

Wellington's involvement in local government can most obviously be demonstrated by the fact that several of the many offices which he held were local government ones. They included those of constable of the Tower of London and lord warden of the cinque ports. The precise detail of his activity in these two positions still lies unexplored in his correspondence, but in volume alone their affairs were deemed important enough to merit separate categorisation. It is nevertheless possible to provide a brief outline sketch.[1]

The most esoteric of Wellington's local government offices was the constableship of the Tower, which he held from 1827. The initial attraction of the position probably lay in the Tower's continuing role in the early nineteenth century, in theory at least, as a royal fortress. For somebody who was entering manhood when the Parisian mob stormed the Bastille, exploiting the Tower's potential as a tourist attraction was very much a secondary consideration: the gentleman who innocently requested the duke to act as his guide received understandably short shrift. In the event, most of Wellington's time as constable was consumed by his attempt to eliminate the petty corruptions practised by a number of the Tower's near thousand inhabitants, who, living within its ancient liberties, were beyond the jurisdiction of bailiffs, and in particular in attempting to reduce the number of sinecurists who enjoyed offices in the Tower itself. The duke also addressed himself to the threat to public health which literally emanated from the Tower's moat being used as a communal rubbish tip.

More attractive to Wellington, since it brought with it what proved to be his delightful summer marine retreat of Walmer Castle, was the lord wardenship of the cinque ports, the office in which he succeeded Lord Liverpool in January 1829. Like the constableship of the Tower, the lord wardenship was traditionally associated with national security, but in practice its burdens proved to be equally mundane. These included being responsible for harbour works, lifeboats and salvage, the safe piloting of vessels into the Thames estuary, the appointment of officials to Dover Castle prison and the recommendation of names for the magistracy. The duke's tenure of the post seems to have been characterised by the successful elimination of some of the patronage and concomitant incompetence which had previously bedevilled appointments to positions which, he rightly emphasised, were in some cases vital to human safety.

Easily the most important and onerous of Wellington's local government offices – he once complained that he needed a pair of eyes exclusively to deal with its affairs – was that of lord-lieutenant of his adopted county of Hampshire.[2] This he occupied for some thirty-two years from the end of 1820. The lord-lieutenancy, the highest administrative office in an English county, was traditionally filled by one of the county's leading magnates, and as such it provided Wellington with his most representative insights into the workings of English local government.

As lord-lieutenant, his most important task was to recommend to the lord chancellor, when he deemed it necessary, the names of suitably qualified gentlemen to be appointed as county magistrates. Thus, over time, Wellington's prejudices came to be reflected in the composition of the Hampshire bench. His personal idiosyncrasies, by no means untypical, included, unless they had retired from their profession, the exclusion of attorneys, manufacturers and traders, and particularly brewers, for fear that the magistrates' control over the licensing laws would lead inevitably to corruption. Less typically, he entertained no objection against recommending members of the armed forces. He also shared with reformers like Brougham the belief that clergymen, because of the incompatibility of spiritual and judicial functions, should not be recommended unless there was no alternative, and even then only if the clergyman possessed the requisite property qualification for the magistracy (landed property worth £100 per annum or £300 per annum in reversion) independently of his benefice. Beyond this, Wellington denied any political or religious bias in making his recommendations and in part proved as much through his willingness to recommend the names of deserving Catholic gentlemen in Hampshire as soon as propriety admitted after 1829.[3] They no less than anybody else could meet his general criteria for recommendation of being gentlemen 'of wealth, worth, consideration and education . . . and that above all they should be associated with, and be respected by, the gentry of the country'.[4] If problems or discord did arise, he offered advice to, and if necessary arbitrated between his magistrates. In the event of major unrest, such as the county witnessed with the agricultural labourers' disturbances of 1830, he attempted to encourage and co-ordinate the efforts of his magistrates in suppressing them.

Although of lesser importance, Wellington's other responsibilities as lord-lieutenant could be equally time-consuming. It was he who co-ordinated, through the various troop commanders and the government, the training, exercise periods and inspection days for the county's yeomanry cavalry force. He was personally instrumental in rejuvenating that institution – most yeomanry troops in the country, and all of those in Hampshire, had been disbanded in 1828 – in the wake of the 1830 agricultural labourers' disturbances. He paid no less attention to the county's other para-military police institution, the militia. He attended whenever possible the meetings of his deputy lieutenants. These were similar in constitution to the magistracy – that is to say composed of country gentlemen with landed property worth at least £200 per annum, recommended by the lord-lieutenant and appointed by the crown – and were the body responsible for raising and organising the country's two militia regiments. Admittedly, the militia was in decline well before 1815 and had fallen largely into abeyance by the end of the 1820s, but the duke responded with characteristic zest when it was revived in face of invasion scares in the 1840s. Barely a month before he died, he was to be seen in Winchester encouraging his deputies, as they set about implementing the new Milita Act of 1851.[5]

It might be objected that this survey of Wellington's involvement in local government does not so much demonstrate his interest in it as confirm the familiar theme that he was a slave of duty. It is true that somebody of Wellington's outlook could hardly refuse the offer of the lord lieutenancy of his adopted county. It might further be argued that there was little altruism in the duke's accepting such posts as the constableship of the Tower and the lord wardenship of the cinque ports, since they were basically sinecures. Yet to do so is unduly cynical, for the fact remains that he did not, as so many of his contemporaries did, choose to remain inactive. Rather, he sometimes went beyond established routine. One of his first initiatives on becoming lord lieutenant of Hampshire was to revive the practice, whenever he was at home, of entertaining the assize judges at Stratfield Saye. Why too, if Wellington was basically uninterested in local government, did he feel it necessary to contribute fairly frequently to parliamentary debates on local government subjects, particularly those which concerned the magistracy, yeomanry and militia, the latter two being subjects on which even his political opponents acknowledged him as an expert?

To fully understand Wellington's interest in local government however, one needs to be reminded of its structure and his response to the changes made in it during his lifetime. Wellington was born at a time when the local government system was one of bewildering complexity and, before 1832, becoming ever more so. Reduced to its fundamentals, there were three basic units of administration: the parishes with their open or closed vestries; the corporate boroughs, administered usually by an oligarchic corporation; and, most importantly, the counties governed by country gentlemen acting together as justices of the peace either singly or together in petty and quarter sessions. In practice the system was less symmetrical, for there existed some places that were extra-parochial, corporations with jurisdiction over only part of a town, towns administered by counties (as most were), and even a few towns, which for administrative purposes, were technically counties in themselves – quite apart from a plethora of other and lesser administrative units and qualifications too numerous to mention. By 1852, the reform of this system, if still incomplete, was well advanced. The parish, eclipsed in particular by the poor law union, was becoming increasingly outmoded as an administrative unit, and the parish constable was being slowly but surely superseded by officers of a new professional police. Meanwhile the government of municipal boroughs was overhauled in 1835. Thereafter, the incorporation of new boroughs and the proliferation of improvement acts literally changed the face of urban life.

The impact of such changes can be illustrated by reference to Wellington's own county.[6] By the end of 1834, 367 of the 408 Hampshire and Isle of Wight parishes had been arranged into 27 poor law unions, the significant exceptions being Southampton and the Isle of Wight where unionisation had already taken place under Gilbert's Act. In the following year, the government of the county's eight boroughs with active corporations – Andover, Basingstoke, Lymington, Newport, Portsmouth, Romsey, Southampton and Winchester – was reformed under the provisions of the Municipal Corporations Act. Four years later in 1839 the magistrates in quarter sessions adopted the Rural Police Act and by 1846 the force numbered 165. Its constables and superintendents were responsible not only for preventing and detecting crime, but also for performing administrative functions previously discharged by others, such as acting as inspectors for weights and measures; and new ones, such as acting as assistant relieving officers in poor law unions. If these changes together amounted to something less than a complete administrative revolution, they constituted at least an unprecedented administrative reorganisation. Only the constitution of county government really withstood the tide of reform before 1852, although with several attempts to establish ratepayer-elected county boards already having been made, it was perhaps more a question of *when* the oligarchic county quarter sessions would be reformed, not *if*. It is against this background that one should consider Wellington's response to the three areas which did most to effect the changes just described, namely poor law, municipal and police reform.

The governing class was in broad agreement by 1832 that the existing poor law needed alteration. The complex laws of settlement impeded the free movement of labour, thus contributing to an uneven distribution of population. The bastardy clauses, which bore unfairly on the accused man, appeared to encourage illegitimacy. Above all, the hybrid Speenhamland system which granted wage supplements to the low paid according to scales fixed by the magistrates, was believed to encourage early marriage and large families, and thus create rather than relieve poverty. This made the system both morally and economically indefensible, for it conspired to penalise the industrious with spiralling poor rates, whilst rewarding the potentially profligate, and consequently demoralised the honest labourer by encouraging him to become indigent and idle.

Structural unemployment, it is now appreciated, was the underlying problem, but contemporaries believed their diagnosis to be confirmed by the agricultural labourers' disturbances of 1830 which seemed to signal the final bankruptcy of the existing paternal policy and high-light the necessity for a harsh and radical response. The 1834 Poor Law Amendment Act thus adopted in large part the recommendations contained in the Benthamite-influenced report issued by the 1832–4 royal commission on the poor laws. Relief was to be granted only if the recipient agreed to enter the workhouse, the regime of which was to be so draconian as to deter all but the genuinely destitute. Comple-menting this principle of less eligibility, the responsibility for adminis-tering relief was transferred from individual parishes to groups of parishes in poor law unions, run by ratepayer-elected boards of guardians who would appoint salaried officials. The whole structure was to be overseen by a board of three government-appointed com-missioners in a scheme which involved an unprecedented level of centralisation and bureaucratisation.

This palpably Benthamite-inspired piece of legislation provoked some opposition on a mixture of moral and constitutional grounds across a spectrum ranging from popular radicals such as William Cobbett to uncompromising tories such as Lord Eldon. Wellington too had his reservations. He advocated a mitigation of the bastardy clauses which placed the burden for maintaining illegitimate children squarely on the mother's shoulders. He was also wary of the amount of power to be vested in the three central commissioners and insisted that they be made to keep very full records in order that government could maintain tight surveillance over their activities. Subsequently, he complained that the new regime was being implemented too harshly in some places and doubted whether purpose-built workhouses had been necessary, an extension of an earlier criticism that the allowance system should be phased out gradually rather than immediately. Ironically enough, in supporting an amendment to this effect, which vested a discretionary power in the commissioners to continue relief outside the workhouse where and when they deemed necessary, he succeeded in adding further to their powers.[7]

But these were relatively minor criticisms. Although Wellington remained largely aloof from the debates on the measure as it went through parliament, he was not just, as mainstream conservative opinion was, in favour of the Act, but unquestionably one of its warmest supporters. In the first place, it was not rigidly Benthamite: relief was not to be administered, as doctrinaire Benthamites advocated, in the form of a loan. Neither was the representative principle fully established, for alongside the poor law guardians, elected on a franchise with provision for plural voting, the traditional governors of the English countryside, the county magistrates, were empowered to sit as *ex officio* members of the board. In some respects indeed, the Act was hardly radical at all. Unionisation, as he was well aware from his Hampshire experience, had already in part taken place under Gilbert's Act of 1782, while the idea of less eligibility was not so much novel as restorative, having 'the effect of causing the poor laws to be administered in compliance with the original [i.e. Elizabethan] intention'.[8]

Above all, Wellington supported the Act because he had become almost obsessed with the prevailing popular notion that the Speenhamland system bred demoralisation. At least as early as 1826 he was writing that poor law abuses 'require the serious attention of the government and parliament'.[9] No subject in his Hampshire correspondence was so likely to elicit a protracted response as the suggestion to the contrary. Thus to his most regular Hampshire correspondent, the Tory county MP John Fleming, who was bold enough to complain about the extent and severity of distress in 1829, which he attributed to the economic liberalism of the 1820s, Wellington thundered in reply that such little distress as existed was due to 'the faulty administration of the Poor Laws'.[10]

Wellington's obsession was based upon a misconception. Fleming, armed with greater local knowledge, responded to the above exchange, with a good deal of historical accuracy, for it is now agreed that poor rates fell as political replaced 'moral' economy during the 1820s, that 'of late, the difficulties of the landowners have forced their attention on the subject, & I believe in almost every district, parochial relief is now administered as sparingly as the necessities of the people will admit'.[11] Yet if Wellington's misunderstanding of the evils of the old poor law was even more exaggerated than that of most contemporaries, one is prompted to ask why, as prime minister, Wellington had done nothing to reform it himself. Quite simply, he seems almost to have despaired of being able to find an effective remedy. Able reformers of the previous generation had tried, but failed, to cure the abuses about which he complained. When therefore the radical solution of 1834 was proposed, he lent it his support in the belief that it is 'unquestionably the best which has ever been devised', however much he might have disliked the political philosophy of some of those who had influenced it. If such a solution as he desired could only be found in the establishment of a central board, then so be it. He saw little in the early history of the Act to make him change his mind. On the contrary, on the basis of attending guardians' meetings in Hampshire and having seen the management in several workhouses, he confessed that the Act 'has surpassed any expectation which I had formed of the benefits likely to result from it'.[12] Throughout the late 1830s, at a time when anti-poor law propaganda provided an important focus for resurgent toryism, Wellington almost invariably persisted in defending it.

The Municipal Corporations bill, like the Poor Law Amendment Act, was preceded by, and predicated upon, the recommendations of a royal commission. The bill proposed replacing the existing 183 predominantly tory-anglican oligarchic corporations which administered property and patronage to their own advantage, with ratepayer-elected borough councils. Councillors would sit for three years, one-third being elected annually, and the institution of freeman would be abolished. Amongst other powers, the new councils would obtain the right to appoint the borough magistracy. Peel and the Conservative Party in the Commons did not like the detail of the bill, but they did accept the principle of reform, and Peel voiced the hope that Wellington would cooperate with him to see it safely enshrined in statute.

Wellington did not deny that some degree of municipal reform might prove beneficial. Corporation finances, for example, might be improved, and the magistracy made more effective. Even so, he at first rejected Peel's overtures, for in general he deprecated the government's method of proceeding. The royal commission, he complained with some reason, had been dominated by Benthamites. Its work, he believed, represented an incomplete inquiry into the existing corporations, and was less an objective investigation than an exercise in seeking out 'political scandal & gossip', thus enabling selected evidence to be fitted to predetermined conclusions. Such conclusions were, as a consequence, 'of no more value than so much waste paper' except that in so far as 'we may be certain therefore that we have before us everything that can be laid against these corporations; which is after all a trifle' there was no justification for the sweeping reform measure which was being proposed. Each corporation should at least be considered individually on its own merits. So far as the specific detail of the proposals was concerned, he objected that the ratepayer franchise was too broad, and insisted that there should be a property qualification for councillors, that freemen should be retained, and that the right of appointing magistrates should remain with the crown.[13] There is no doubt that could he have treated the bill as he wished, he would have advocated its rejection.

But Wellington was denied this luxury, for there was an important political dimension to the question. Peel let it be known that he would refuse to form a government if the whigs resigned on the issue and Wellington appreciated that no obvious alternative conservative prime minister was to be found. More seriously, he recognised that the House of Lords needed to exercise restraint if its opponents were not to use the question of municipal reform as the pretext for its abolition. The combination of these two factors convinced him, that though for one he sympathised with the ultras, he must use his influence to stop wrecking amendments. Buttressed by the knowledge that he had the king's support in his chosen course, Wellington duly persuaded Lyndhurst and his associates to temper their opposition. One might be forgiven for thinking, therefore, that Wellington would have taken some comfort from the facts that the final Act included amendments laying down a three-year residence qualification for electors, a property qualification for councillors, a provision that the council elect one-third of their number to be aldermen for six years, that freemen retain their parliamentary franchise and that borough magistrates should continue to be appointed by the crown. But he did not. It remained instead 'the worst measure of these bad times', tending 'to compleat the destruction of the ancient system of Representation, as far as the Reform Bill had left the work undone'.[14]

Thus far it is an ambivalent Wellington who emerges, one who warmly welcomed local government reform in 1834, but who accepted it only through political necessity in 1835. According to Elizabeth Longford, it is the latter which we should see as the exception, for she argues that the duke took considerable interest in police reform. After all, had he not sent his famous memorandum of 1819 to Lord Liverpool, urging upon him the necessity of establishing some form of constabulary force to maintain public order in the event of disaffection in the army? Had he not also, as prime minister, sanctioned Peel's 1829 Metropolitan Police Act and, in admitting the necessity of some form of improved borough policing, welcomed the clauses in the Municipal Corporations Act compelling town councils to establish watch committees? Certainly amongst contemporaries Wellington was presumed to be a progressive on policing, for Charles Shaw-Lefevre, Wellington's Hampshire neighbour and chairman of 1836–9 royal commission on rural policing, sent him an early copy of the completed report on the grounds that he had always envinced a keen interest in the question.[15] Yet it will not do to deduce from the above isolated pieces of evidence that Wellington was in the vanguard of police reform. The 1819 memorandum was penned at a time of acute concern for public order. A decade later, although Wellington endorsed Peel's police initiative, there is no evidence that he took much personal interest in the question, whilst borough policing was hardly a major issue against the other principles which he perceived to be at stake in 1835.

More importantly, Wellington's perception of police reform, particularly in the later 1830s, was broader than most have interpreted it. For him it was a question not just whether a professional constabulary should supersede the existing high and petty constables, but what would happen to those other police institutions, the militia and the yeomanry. So far as the former was concerned, he did not 'think it safe that the Country should be entirely deprived of the means of using the militia', despite its having been progressively run down since 1804. His own administration, he believed, had reduced it to a miminum strength consonant with efficiency. When Lord John Russell therefore sought his opinion in 1835 concerning the government's proposals to halve its permanent staff, he responded with a long memorandum detailing his objections. He reiterated, but did not press them, in parliament.[16]

Wellington was even more alarmed at the government's plans for the volunteer yeomanry cavalry. Although they had originated in the 1790s in response to fears of French invasion, their rejuvenation in 1830 in the wake of the rural disturbances unequivocally placed them, as the earl of Malmesbury put it, 'in the light of a *constabularly police*

for the district in which they are raised'.[17] The institution had its
weaknesses, in particular the problems of maintaining a full complement of men, the petty jealousies to which rival troops were prone, and
the fact that as each troop was allowed to determine its own rules
subject only to Home Office confirmation, they were not subject to
true military discipline. But the institution's advantages outweighed
these shortcomings. A mounted force was ideal for rural policing; its
mere existence served as a deterrent to the potentially disaffected.
There was also the constitution of the force. The rank-and-file
comprised 'the most desirable kind of farmers and tradesmen of a
superior description' whilst their officers were drawn from the ranks
of the country gentry. In Wellington's view this made it the ideal
means for rural community policing:

> It unites the Nobility and Gentry of the Country with the middling and
> lower classes in the service of the Govt. in the way the least offensive to
> the feelings of others, and the least dangerous to the Govt and the
> Constitution of the Country, at the same time that it preserves the peace
> and prevents outrage and riot . . . and in case of their occurrence affords
> to Govt the readiest means of suppression.[18]

When therefore in 1838 the government announced that because fears
of public unrest were receding, the yeomanry was to be reduced from
18,303 to 13,594, Wellington was prominent in a series of parliamentary debates opposing the proposal. On the contrary, he insisted,
the threat to public order was still very real: the army was preoccupied
with Canada, the rail network which would facilitate its movement to
trouble spots as yet in its infancy. There was also the still vivid memory
of the 1830 rioting in the rural districts, the perennial sore of the game
laws, the perceived evil effects of the 1830 Beer Act, the agitation
surrounding the implementation of the new poor law, and a statistical,
if not real, rise in the crime rate.[19] The reductions went ahead,
nevertheless.

Although Wellington did not deny the existence of defects in the
established police institutions, and in particular believed the constabulary system to be capable of improvement, the balance of evidence suggests that he opposed wholesale police reform. The point is
in part confirmed by his response to the government's decision to
improve the police of Manchester, Bolton and Birmingham in the
wake of the Chartist disturbances of the summer of 1839. Following
Peel's recommendation, the government appointed commissioners

answerable to the Home Office to control the newly created forces. Taking as his criterion, his anxiety 'to see the best possible means taken to give the security of an effective police', Wellington endorsed the Birmingham bill, questioned the efficacy of the Bolton one, and at first recommended opposing the Manchester one on the grounds that the force to be created would be less well funded than the existing one.[20]

The great police measure of 1839 however, was the Rural Police Act. Some have seen this too as a rushed response to the Chartist disturbances of that year. Others have emphasised Benthamite influence, for the mind of Edwin Chadwick undoubtedly lay behind much of the report from the 1836–9 royal commission on rural policing. Wellington, for one, presumed that a rural police bill would follow Benthamite lines, that is to say that a professional, salaried and centrally controlled force would be created. This he would strenuously have opposed, for it could only in his view have been created at the expense of the militia, and even more, the yeomanry. In 1838 he privately believed that the real reason for the yeomanry reductions was to clear the way for such a body. The notion may not have been entirely fanciful. The 1839 report did recommend the creation of a centrally controlled institution and the home secretary, Russell, a self-confessed critic of the yeomanry, left little to the imagination when he declared in 1838 that he hoped soon to introduce 'a more available and efficient force for the country'. Since at least 1836 he seems to have been determined upon a sweeping measure of police reform.[21]

In the event, neither Wellington's fears nor Russell's hopes were realised, for concessions had to be made to a Commons dominated by the landed interest, as a result of which the final act was permissive in nature, and vested control of such new constabularies as were created in the county magistrates in quarter sessions, subject to the ultimate control of the Home Office. Although it was still opposed by some parliamentary radicals and by sections of the whig and tory press on the grounds that the new police would be expensive and unconstitutional, Wellington supported it. He welcomed its permissive character and recognised that although the new constabularies were to be theoretically controlled by the Home Office, the county magistrates would have virtual autonomy in practice. He therefore recommended to the Hampshire quarter sessions that they adopt the act – the only occasion on which he broke with his self-imposed rule not to attempt to influence their deliberations – and they became only the second county authority to do so. Even so, Wellington's support remained qualified, for he was appalled to learn that the implementation of the act would cost the Hampshire ratepayers some £7,000; so much so in fact that less than two months after he recommended quarter sessions to adopt the act, he urged that the decision be reconsidered.[22]

This survey of Wellington's attitude to local government and its reform reveals a number of contradictions. As constable of the Tower, lord warden of the cinque ports and lord lieutenant of Hampshire, one can fairly describe Wellington as a competent executor, even to some extent a reformer in local government, whether it be in dismissing drunken pilots at Dover harbour, improving the salubrity of the Tower or encouraging the Hampshire magistrates to improve the county's policing. At national level too, he acknowledged the need for police and some municipal reform, and he was conspicuous in his support of poor law reform. This suggests that Wellington was less rigidly attached to the constitution in local government than he was in national government. He doubted the efficacy of the parish as a unit of poor law administration and he was quite prepared to see the old constabulary system superseded. Yet it must also be admitted that Wellington's attitude towards police reform sometimes gave the appearance of ambivalence, whilst to wholesale municipal reform he was emphatically opposed.

Perhaps it is a mistake to look for any rigid consistency in Wellington's views on local government. He was inclined to support straightforward improvements such as the permissive Rural Police Act and usually opposed radical reforms such as the Municipal Corporations Act, but he was nevertheless prepared to endorse the far-reaching changes effected by the Poor Law Amendment Act. Similarly, although Wellington was no Benthamite and particularly feared the possibility that the rural police might be constituted along Benthamite lines, he was prepared to support most of the recommendations in the Benthamite-inspired poor law report. Such examples can be multiplied. As the tenants of his Stratfield Saye estate who received generous rent reductions during times of economic depression, or had patent heating stoves installed in their cottages at the duke's expense could have testified, Wellington was a paternalist, but not to the extent that he opposed a punitive poor law regime. In voicing support for the latter he was being to some extent Malthusian, yet neither did he favour the total abolition of the old poor law, for he did not deny that the sick and aged were entitled to relief and proved the point with his amendment that the poor law commissioners be vested with the discretion to continue outdoor relief. The ambiguity persists even in what was arguably the most important principle established in the local government reforms of the 1830s, that of democratisation. Not surprisingly, it was not a principle for which the duke had much sympathy; he would have viewed with anathema any attempt to place the police under a popularly constituted body. Yet he did not deny during one debate on the Municipal Corporations Act that the people had a right to share in the administration of their localities, and he positively welcomed the democratisation of poor law administration.[23]

One is tempted to suggest therefore that Wellington's response to local government reform was simply pragmatic. His reluctant support of the Municipal Corporations Act was certainly so, for it seemed the one means by which a more serious constitutional clash between Commons and Lords might be avoided. So too, his support of the Rural Police Act had an element of pragmatism about it, for in view of the yeomanry reductions which preceded it, it seemed to him that 'Proprietors should be too happy to have an opportunity of raising a police to protect themselves! They are now without protection of any kind.'[24] The best example however, is provided by the willingness with which he accepted the necessity for centralisation in poor law administration. Since previous reform schemes had floundered on the point, 'it has become absolutely necessary that such an appointment as a central Board of Commissioners should be made, with powers to control the whole of the parishes in the land, and to adopt such remedies as will secure a sound administration of the poor law throughout the country'.[25]

It is nevertheless possible to identify certain consistent threads in Wellington's thinking on local government. First, he believed in cheap government. Hence part of the explanation for his drive against patronage at the Tower and his support of the Poor Law Amendment Act as poor rates spiralled in the wake of rural unrest. Hence also his admission that some financial improvement in borough affairs might be accomplished through municipal reform. On policing too, part of his argument that the militia and yeomanry be retained was his belief that they were cost-effective, whilst his decision to qualify his initial recommendation that the Rural Police Act be adopted in Hampshire was based squarely on the fact that he feared that the expense would cause needless discontent among ratepayers.[26]

Economy went hand in hand with efficiency. Thus Wellington attempted to end petty corruptions at the Tower and improve the standard of pilots at Dover harbour, and exhorted the Hampshire yeomanry troop commanders to maintain a full complement of men and magistrates to be active. His support for the Poor Law Amendment Act was grounded upon the belief that it would produce administrative order out of the prevailing chaos and he saw improved efficiency as one of the few justifications for municipal reform. The Rural Police Act too, he presumed, would improve both preventive and detective policing. But if improved efficiency was not guaranteed, reform was pointless. Hence Wellington's initial opposition to the Manchester Police bill on the grounds that the new force was likely to be less well funded and manned than the existing one.[27]

One concern above all others, however, dominated Wellington's thinking on local government: the magistracy. His greatest concern over the Municipal Corporations Act, once it had become a *fait accompli*, was what was to become of the borough magistracy. Although the act retained the right of appointing magistrates with the crown rather than the town councils, as had been originally proposed, Russell defiantly declared that he would always take account of council recommendations when making appointments.[28] This incensed Wellington on a number of grounds. Most obviously, Russell was not acting in the spirit of a statutory provision. Second, since Wellington considered the magistrate's work as being primarily judicial in character, the proper officer to scrutinise appointments was not the home secretary but the lord chancellor. Finally, council involvement might cause the magistracy, an impartial judicial institution, to become a party political one for which, in the event of controversy, the council being collectively responsible for appointments, no single individual would be answerable.[29]

Wellington found himself unable to remain silent on this question. Since the first municipal elections had produced a reformer landslide, he believed the borough magistracy, because of Russell's declaration, to have become politicised and filled with improper persons. A flow of correspondence, complaining that radicals, nonconformists, anti-corn law leaguers and even Chartists had been made borough magistrates, seemed to confirm him in his diagnosis. He even attributed the 1839 Chartist disturbances to this fact. Mob intimidation, he complained to William Napier:

has been universal I believe for the last four or five years, and the improper selection of Men to be Justices of the Peace because they were the Associates and in some instances parties, and in others even the Abettors of these dangerous Combinations of which it ought to have been the duty of the Justices of the Peace to get the better, has tended to their increase, and materially to the state in which we find ourselves now.[30]

It was the same intensity of feeling which explains what to contemporaries and historians was his inexplicable outburst following the July 1839 Birmingham Bull Ring riots. One should pay less attention to his colourfully exaggerated description of the town as one that had been gutted, 'an outrage such as never happened, to my knowledge, in any siege that I have been present at', than to the underlying source of his anger that the disorder had taken place 'under the eyes of those magistrates appointed – not by the proper authority, not by the Crown, not by the noble and learned lord on the Woolsack, but – by the Secretary of State for the Home Department'.[31] It was with understandable alacrity that Wellington responded to Sir James Graham's invitation to assist him in revising the list of borough magistrates when the Conservatives returned to office in 1841.[32]

Wellington's fears for the borough magistracy were complemented and reinforced by his fears for the county magistracy. These were not without foundation. Joseph Parkes, for one, enthused in the wake of municipal reform that 'the unincorporated towns will lust after and soon accomplish the destruction of their Self-Elect, and the County Magisterial and Fiscal Self-Elect will be next and be early mowed down by the scythe of Reform'.[33] The royal commission on the poor laws had already recommended that ratepayers should have some sort of representation in county government, and in 1836 the royal commission on county rates recommended that the oligarchic county quarter sessions should be superseded for administrative purposes by county boards, whose members would be drawn half from the elected boards of poor law guardians, half *ex officio* from the county magistrates. The same year Joseph Hume introduced a bill to establish county boards for administrative purposes on a ratepayer franchise. Although it did not survive a first reading, its principle was accepted by Russell when a second abortive attempt was made in 1837. Consequently, Wellington's thinking in the months before the details of the Rural Police bill became known, was dominated by his conviction that it would herald a final attack on the county governors. He wrote:

The Govt will not make use of the Magistrates and the existing Civil Authority of the country to regulate and direct the newly formed Police Force. . . . The Justices of the Peace and all their machinery connected with the land will be thrown aside altogether. They will at first be rendered useless and contemptible and then the institution will be abolished altogether.[34]

Wellington was of course wrong: county government remained unreformed up to 1888. Even so, there was, according to Halèvy, 'a silent revolution . . . in the appointment of the men entrusted with the local government'. This theme has been curiously overlooked by subsequent historians but it is evident that the Whigs were attempting to change the composition of the county benches during the 1830s. The process started, not as Halèvy supposed, with Russell but with Brougham. As lord chancellor, he was writing to Grey at least as early as December 1832 advocating 'a transition from the present strict and absurd rule which really subjects the Government to its own deputies – the Lieutenants'.[35] Specifically, he wished to end the convention that the lord chancellor appointed as county magistrates all and only those recommended to him by the lords-lieutenant, since he believed that it left him exposed to a narrow source of patronage and that too many abused their position as the supposed impartial head of the county bench and recommended names on the basis of narrow, social, religious and political prejudices. In an attempt to end at least the latter, he proposed that when in future, lords-lieutenant recommended names, he would respond by suggesting the same number of names of the opposite political persuasion, asking why they too should not be appointed. Russell used the fact of the great seal's being in commission in 1835–6 to extend the initiative, both in writing to lords-lieutenant with his recommendations for the bench without waiting, like Brougham, for their recommendations; and in persuading Melbourne that an attempt should be made to broaden the social composition of the bench by appointing traders, manufacturers and industrialists. From 1836 he continued these initiatives alongside the new lord chancellor, Cottenham. Wellington, refusing to concede Russell's point that lords-lieutenant were as prone to make partisan recommendations as the councils about which the duke so vociferously complained, was outraged at what was happening. He was in the forefront of several debates on the question which came to a head in 1838.[36] Not only, in Wellington's opinion, was Russell again improperly involving himself in judicial affairs and casting aspersions on his own integrity as lord lieutenant, but he was undermining the traditional responsibility of the lords lieutenant for ensuring the unity and harmony of the bench. It was also ungentlemanly to place lords lieutenant in the position of 'general accusers' in asking whether they entertained objections towards making specified individuals magistrates, individuals moreover whose names Wellington believed to have been obtained from 'persons of the lowest description.' So untenable did he believe that his own position as lord-lieutenant of Hampshire had become, he more than once threatened resignation.[37]

As with Wellington's fears about the whigs' ultimate intentions towards the magistracy however, so his fears surrounding their method of appointment during the 1830s were exaggerated. Contrary to what he believed, the whigs always sought a lord lieutenant's approval before making appointments and if the lord lieutenant's objections were substantial, they did not overrule them. Neither did they seek recommendations from 'persons of the lowest description'. In Hampshire, for example, their channels of communication were Palmerston and the whig county MP, Charles Shaw-Lefevre. The very practice of writing to lords-lieutenant was probably more irritating than common. As home secretary, Russell wrote over eighty letters to lords-lieutenant or Cottenham with recommendations for the county bench; but there were some 18,000 names in the commissions of the peace in 1851.[38] Halèvy's 'silent revolution' never therefore took place. Parliamentary returns suggest that of all new magistrates appointed between 1836 and 1842, some 8.4% were drawn from the aristocracy, 13.4% from the clergy, a massive 77.1% from the squirearchy and only 1.2% from other backgrounds.[39] The existing system of appointment was simply too engrained to admit of any rapid change. To effect a noticeable change in the political composition of the benches, the Whigs really needed to dismiss the predominantly tory lords lieutenant but they were not prepared to do this. Even if they had been, it would not have overcome the powerful prejudice which existed against admitting those from a non-landed background to the bench, a prejudice epitomised by Melbourne when he   wrote that 'country gentlemen have held, and do hold, a higher character than Master Manufacturers'.[40] If the social composition of a bench was transformed during the 1830s, as it was in Lancashire where cotton masters found their way into the commission of the peace in large numbers, it was the consequence of rapid industrialisation, which, in creating a shortage of resident country gentlemen, made their inclusion a necessity.[41]

Ironically enough, it also seems to have been the case that, for all his protestations to the contrary, Wellington was guilty of entertaining political bias in his recommendations for the Hampshire bench. Whenever Wellington wanted or received them, he had them vetted by the fiercely partisan tory county MP, John Fleming. Fleming, as his correspondence with Wellington makes obvious, did not share the duke's lofty ideals about the apolitical nature of the magistracy. Hence he inclined to endorse applications from tories, but often created objections to those from reformers. One example must suffice. In 1830 and again in 1833, a Mr William Hughes asked Wellington to recommend him for the commission for the Isle of Wight. On both occasions, Fleming was asked for an opinion and replied that no magistrate was required but that – rather contradicting himself – if one was, then there were more suitable persons than Hughes. It is clear that Fleming's basic objection to Hughes was that he was a nonconformist and a reformer. This much is proved by the fact that when Hughes applied for a third time in 1836, Fleming warmly endorsed the application, adding that prejudice had previously existed against Hughes on the grounds of his politics, but that 'these are now wholly changed, as he has now become a *most zealous conservative*'[42] Wellington professed irritation, but nevertheless recommended Hughes to the lord chancellor. How far Wellington was actually aware that Fleming was manipulating him like this is unclear. Other affairs pressed more heavily upon his time, and so he is unlikely to have remembered previous applications such as those made by Mr Hughes. He also periodically threatened that if the Hampshire tories wanted to politicise the bench that 'I must resign, for I cannot be a party to the execution of such a system'. But the facts remain that Wellington did not resign, that he continued to take advice only from Fleming, and that he hardly ever failed to follow that advice. Perhaps he squared it with his conscience that, since Fleming was a gentleman, his word could and must be trusted, but if so it was a degree of self-deception which was tantamount to hypocrisy. The outcome however was unequivocal. During the 1820s, Wellington recommended, where political affiliations are ascertainable, the names of 41 tories and 20 whigs. During the 1830s, the corresponding figures were 86 Tories and 24 Whigs.[43] Whig pressure, applied in an attempt to redress a political imbalance, succeeded perhaps only in stimulating interest in the question in the localities, as a result of which the county bench became more and not less tory dominated.

If Wellington's partisanship on the magistracy is indefensible, his motives are understandable, and allow one to see his concern for local government in something more than pragmatic terms. Wellington viewed local government less as a matter of providing services than as a question of providing order, not in the narrow police sense of the word, but in the broader sense of maintaining the existing social hierarchy of the country through institutions such as the corporations, and above all, the magistracy. He told parliament in August 1839:

> We must put an end to this system of employing men as magistrates, for the maintenance of the peace, who have been concerned in its violation. When we shall have taken this necessary step we may then trust to the old constituted forms which exist in this country, and call on the people themselves to preserve the public peace, without having policemen under our noses to whatever quarter we turn.[55]

Although he sometimes misunderstood the detail and realities of local government, and tended to attribute to his political opponents schemes for the destruction of local government which existed only in his own mind, he never lost sight of what was for him this essential point. The magistracy, properly constituted, was a vital precondition of social order. It was after all, along with the aristocracy, clergy, great merchants and bankers, one of the constituent elements of the famous *parti conservateur* which he defined to Mrs Arbuthnot in 1827.[45]

Seen against this perspective, Wellington's response to the local government reforms of the 1830s becomes comprehensible. A thorough reform of the poor law could be supported because he was convinced that the existing system of relief, in breeding demoralisation, actually constituted a threat to the established social order. In putting an end to this system, the new poor law would help preserve the social order. Poor rates too would fall, easing a potential source of friction between landlord and tenant and thus help to place them 'upon a true and friendly feeling of confidence'. Moreover, the act infringed no important property interests and may have strengthened the traditional landed interest since county magistrates were to be *ex officio* members of the boards of guardians. It has even been suggested that as a consequence they both dictated the constitution of the new poor law unions and dominated relief policy after 1834 far more so than they had done under the old poor law.[46] This perhaps is to go too far, for all the correspondence which Wellington received on the subject agreed that the new poor law had 'very much reduced the labours of the magistracy'. Even so, the point is not without some force, since Wellington welcomed the socially unifying tendency of reformed poor law administration which 'has connected the man of property, the man of the highest rank in his county, with the lowest class, with the labouring class, by admitting such to the board of guardians'.[47]

Wellington could not view municipal reform with such equanimity, for in his view the proposed elimination of the old corporations and in particular the extinction of freemen, their privileges and the right of the crown to appoint borough magistrates, constituted an attack upon the traditional guardians of property and order. Thus although he finally accepted municipal reform, he attached great importance to securing amendments – at the risk of a constitutional clash between Commons and Lords – which mitigated the democratic tendencies of the measure, in particular by introducing qualifications for councillors and electors, the creation of aldermen and the retention of the right to appoint magistrates by the crown. These offered some hope, albeit in his view slight, that the propertied, wealthy and respectable would continue to exercise some sway in borough government and its policing.

As far as police reform was concerned, Wellington was inclined to support any genuinely ameliorative proposals. His first preference for rural policing, however, since he did not consider the parochially-based constabulary system to be beyond redemption, would have been for a rejuvenation of that institution together with a reorganisation of the country's militia and yeomanry forces, the latter after all, being little more than landed society in a paramilitary guise, administered by country gentlemen in their capacities as deputy lieutenants and county magistrates. Hence his grave fears for a proposal which might supersede the existing police institutions and presage the abolition of the county magistracy. He entertained no such fear of course for the final act which, in vesting effective control of the new constabularies in quarter sessions, strengthened not weakened the country gentleman's hold in local affairs. As a recent examination of the act's origins has confirmed, foremost amongst the concerns which fashioned it 'was the maintenance of order in the countryside under the leadership of England's traditional ruling *elite*'.[48]

From her brief survey of the subject, Elizabeth Longford has concluded that Wellington viewed his connections with local government as being 'congenial sidelines'. This assessment is erroneous on two counts. First, there was nothing congenial about time-consuming correspondence on routine affairs, or worse still, having to arbitrate in local disputes. Second, and more important, local government was no sideline. Particularly in the years after 1832, Wellington believed the country's institutions to be under attack.[49] Any reform which furthered that attack had, if possible, to be prevented, and one means of preventing the wholesale reform which Wellington dreaded was to strengthen existing institutions by improving them. In local government this meant making its institutions cheap and efficient and exhorting the *élite* in the existing social order to discharge the duties of magistrates, yeomanry and militia officers which their social standing conferred upon them.

Wellington did not, therefore, as is common today, make a distinction between primary national and subordinate local affairs. The tendency to see Westminster as the apex of a government pyramid dictating to, and served by, its base of local government, is not one that he would have shared. Wellington's conception of government was of a one and indivisible whole. True, he was also imbued with a strong sense of hierarchy, but in his hierarchy it is important to recognise that it was local government and its institutions, not central government, that was the more vital, because it was England's system of local government by the landed gentry as willing, unpaid amateurs which bred deference to, and acquiescence in, leadership by social superiors, and thus made possible the continued aristocratic domination of national affairs. In Wellington's view, without the foundations of support which such a system of local government afforded, the monarchy itself would soon crumble. Local government, which Wellington's biographers have dismissed as peripheral, if indeed they have considered it all, was in fact one of the duke's central concerns. To appreciate this is to come closer to a true understanding both of the man and his political philosophy.

Notes

1   The following two paragraphs are based on Elizabeth Longford, *Wellington. Pillar of State*, 1972, pp. 246–50.
2   See my book, *The Politics of County Power. Wellington and the Hampshire*

Gentlemen 1820–1852, Hemel Hempstead, (1989), *passim*.

3   WP, 4/2/8, Wellington to Cottenham, 3 December 1837; *ibid.*, 4/1/1/43, Wellington to Fleming, 13 September 1829.

4   *Parl. Deb.*, third series, xliii, 1278–81, 17 July 1838.

5   *Hampshire Chronicle*, 14 August 1852; R. E. Foster, 'Leadership, politics and government in the county of Hampshire during the lord lieutenancy of the first duke of Wellington, 1820–1852', unpublished Ph.D. thesis, Southampton University, 1986, ch. 7, *passim* and appendix D.

6   William White, *History, Gazetteer, and Directory of Hampshire and the Isle of Wight*, 1859, *passim*.

7   *Parl. Deb.*, third series, xxv, 268–70, 21 July 1834; *ibid.*, third series, xxxvii, 851–2, 7 April 1837; E. Halèvy, *The Triumph of Reform 1830–1841*, 1950 edn, p. 128, note 1.

8   *Parl. Deb.*, third series, xxv, 447–8, 24 July 1834.

9   WP, 1/864, Wellington to Robinson, 20 October 1826.

10   *Ibid.*, 4/1/1/60, Wellington to Fleming, 20 December 1829.

11   *Ibid.*, 4/1/1/61, Fleming to Wellington, 26 December 1829.

12   *Parl. Deb.*, third series, xxxvii, 851–2, 7 April 1837.

13   *Ibid.*, third series, xxx, 356–61, 12 August 1835; WP, 2/33, memorandum of 23 May 1835.

14   *Ibid.*, 2/33, memorandum of 23 May 1835; *ibid.*, 4/1/7/1/2, Wellington to Fleming, 2 January 1836. For a slightly different emphasis, see Neville Thompson, *Wellington after Waterloo*, 1985, pp. 158–62.

15   WP, 4/1/10/9, Shaw-Lefevre to Wellington, 30 March 1839.

16   *Ibid.*, 2/34, Wellington to Russell, 1 October 1835.

17   *Ibid.*, 4/2/6, Malmesbury to Wellington, 1 December 1830.

18   *Ibid.*, 4/2/6, Wellington to Melbourne, 27 November 1830.

19   *Parl. Deb.*, third series, xlii, 349–50, 3 April 1838.

20   Thompson, *op. cit.*, p. 184; WP, 2/61, Wellington to Lord Francis Egerton, 19 August 1839.

21   *Ibid.*, 4/1/9/6, Wellington to T. A. Smith, 7 March 1838; *Parl. Deb.*, third series, xlii, 653–4, 26 April 1838; Chadwick MSS., University College London, Howick to Shaw-Lefevre, 25 November 1836.

22   WP, 4/1/10/43, Wellington to Fleming, 24 October 1838; *ibid.*, 4/1/10/52, Wellington to Fleming, 12 December 1839.

23   *Parl. Deb.*, third series, xxx, 356–61, 12 August 1835; *ibid.*, third series, xxxvii, 851–2, 7 April 1837.

24   WP, 4/1/10/43, Wellington to Fleming, 24 October 1839.

25   *Parl. Deb.*, third series, xxv, 268–70, 21 July 1834.

26   4/1/10/52, Wellington to Fleming, 12 December 1839.

27   *Ibid.*, 2/61, Wellington to Lord Francis Egerton, 19 August 1839.

28   Halèvy, *op. cit.*, p. 216, note 1.

29   *Parl. Deb.*, third series, xxx, 356–61, 12 August 1835.

30   WP, 2/61, Wellington to W. Napier, 23 August 1839.

31   *Parl. Deb.*, third series, xlix, 373–5, 16 July 1839.

32   WP, 2/91, Wellington to Graham, 19 August 1842.

33   Cited in G.B.A.M. Finlayson, 'The politics of municipal reform, 1835', *English*

Historical Review, lxxxi (1966), pp. 690–1.

34 WP, 4/2/8, Wellington to Sturges-Bourne, 16 November 1837.

35 Henry Brougham, *The Life and Times of Henry Brougham Written by Himself*, iii, Edinburgh, 1871, pp. 258–9, Brougham to Grey, 30 December 1832.

36 For example *Parl. Deb.*, third series, xliii, 1268–82, 17 July 1838. See also Foster, thesis, ch. 5, *passim*.

37 WP, 4/1/7/2/39, Wellington to Fleming, 22 October 1836.

38 'Returns of the number of justices . . . .', *Parliamentary Papers*, 1851 (662) xlvii, p. 418.

39 Carl Zangerl, 'The social composition of the county magistracy in England and Wales, 1831–1887', *Journal of British Studies*, xi (1971), p. 115, table 1.

40 Cited in Halèvy, *op. cit.*, pp. 216–7, note 2.

41 David Foster, 'Class and county government in early nineteenth-century Lancashire', *Northern History*, ix (1974), pp. 48–61.

42 WP, 4/1/7/1/10, Fleming to Wellington, 3 February 1836.

43 Foster, thesis, pp. 150–1.

44 *Parl. Deb.*, third series, L, 432–3, 20 August 1839.

45 The seventh duke of Wellington, ed., *Wellington and His Friends*, 1965, p. 74, Wellington to Mrs Arbuthnot, 20 April 1827.

46 Anthony Brundage, *The Making of the New Poor Law: The Politics of Inquiry, Enactment and Implementation, 1832–39*, 1978, *passim*.

47 *Parl. Deb.*, third series, xxxvii, 851–2, 7 April 1837.

48 Anthony Brundage, 'Ministers, magistrates and reformers: the genesis of the Rural Constabulary Act of 1839', *Parliamentary History*, v (1986), p. 62 although it will be obvious that I cannot support the author's interpretation of the role of Russell.

49 WP, 4/1/7/2/46, Wellington to Fleming, 27 October 1836.

Michael Partridge

12

Wellington and the defence of the realm, 1819–52

When Wellington returned to England in December 1818, after three years commanding the allied army of occupation in France, his days as an active officer commanding troops in the field were over. The duke did not know this: to the very end of his life, thirty-four years later, he was convinced that at any moment he might be required to undertake active service. In the event he was not called upon to do so, but he still served his country in a military capacity. Between December 1818 and January 1827 he was master-general of the ordnance, and he then, on three separate occasions, served as commander-in-chief of the army, between January and April 1827, between August 1827 and January 1828, and between August 1842 and his death ten years later, in September 1852.

Wellington was not the only military adviser successive British governments had at their disposal in this period, but he was the most influential, and his views were sought by governments of all political persuasions. As the years went by, the duke became increasingly concerned at the apparently defenceless state of Great Britain: 'I am bordering upon 77 years of age passed in honour', concludes his famous letter to General Sir John Fox Burgoyne in January 1847, 'I hope the Almighty may protect me from being the witness of the tragedy which I cannot persuade my contemporaries to take measures to avert'.[1]

If this is Wellington at his most pessimistic, it is in many ways a reflection of his state of mind respecting the national defences in the mid-1840s. The duke had strong views on the dangers facing the country and the steps needed to counter them. These views will be examined, and an attempt made to assess the impact of his ideas on British defence policy. It may then be possible to reach some conclusions as to whether criticisms levelled at the duke, both at the time and by historians since, as to his ineffectiveness in office, can be justified.

The period from 1818 down to Wellington's death witnessed profound changes in the strategic position of the United Kingdom, as technological advances helped to increase the uncertainty felt by British strategic planners. Wellington fully shared these anxieties. He was well aware that changes in technology could lead to changes in military strategy, and he did his best to ensure that the country was guarded against them.

The duke's tenure of office as master-general of the ordnance was at a relatively quiet period in British defence planning, although he did preside over some investigations into Britain's strategic position in these years. The same may be said of his first and second, but certainly not of his third, term of office as commander-in-chief.

Wellington was appointed to the post of master-general of the ordnance for political reasons; as master-general he had a seat in the cabinet. Command of the army remained in the hands of the king's second son, Frederick, duke of York. The master-general of the ordnance, nevertheless, had considerable power. He was in command of the engineer and artillery forces of the country, and he was responsible for the construction of all barracks, fortifications and other military buildings in the British Isles. He therefore played an important role in British defence planning, and, despite being called off to other duties – attending the Congress of Verona in 1822, for example, or the funeral of Tsar Alexander I early in 1826 – Wellington worked hard in his time as master-general.

The duke's appointment as commander-in-chief of the army did not, officially, increase his authority in matters of defence planning. Indeed, he often stressed the limitations of his power. He told one correspondent in May 1846:

> You are not aware of the constitution of the office which I fill, that of C[ommander] in Chief of the Army.
>
> You would naturally assume that that officer has some relation, if not control over the military defences and communications of the country. The fact is directly the contrary. He has nothing to say to them. These matters are exclusively under the cognisance of the M[aster] G[eneral]

of the Ordnance, as far as any military authority has cognisance or control over them.[2]

This, of course, was an attempt to put off a pertinacious petitioner, but Wellington was not always any more open to senior political figures. In September 1845, for example, he returned some papers on naval defences to the earl of Haddington, the first lord of the admiralty, declaring that these were matters 'on which I have nothing and I desire to have nothing to say'.[3] In August 1846 he informed Lord John Russell that he would give his opinion on some papers concerning the national defences which Lord John had submitted to him, even though 'these subjects are not exactly my official business', while he told Prince Albert in 1848 that:

> in truth the Commander-in-Chief of the Army has no legal Power or Authority excepting over his troops; and that only what is conceded to him by the Mutiny Act, Articles of War and Her Majesty's Regulations. ... Nor can he carry into execution the pleasure of the Sovereign excepting under such authority.[4]

On his resignation as prime minister in 1830 Wellington was out of both political and military office, except for a short break in 1834–5, until 1841. Politically, of course, he was an ally of Peel, but this did not prevent the whigs seeking his advice on a variety of military matters during the 1830s. When, however, in 1840, Lord Hill, the officer commanding in chief, approached the duke for his opinions respecting the defences of Dover, he gave them willingly, but warned Hill that 'I have no communication with the Government and I will have none.' Later he relented sufficiently to allow Hill to show his letter to the prime minister, Lord Melbourne.[5]

Back as commander-in-chief on Hill's retirement in 1842, Wellington found much to do. As a cabinet minister without office in Sir Robert Peel's second ministry and with both his prestige and fears about Britain's insecurity reaching new heights, and despite his denials, the duke became deeply involved in British defence planning. When Peel's ministry was replaced by that of Lord John Russell, Wellington told Russell how he had worked with Peel, and promised to continue similar work for the whigs, even though, as he told the queen, 'it is impossible for Field Marshal the Duke of Wellington to form a political connection' with Lord John.[6]

In some areas of defence planning, Wellington fully deserves the criticism levelled at him for diehard opposition to change. Despite growing evidence of inefficiency in the administration of the army, for example, he saw no need for reform. Some of Melbourne's cabinet, who had seen the great reform bill safely through parliament and who were anxious to keep up the good work, thought differently. Changes in military administration were first suggested in 1834 by the duke of Richmond, who had taken office solely with this aim in view. Three years later Lord Howick proposed a radical revision of the administrative machinery, with the aim of 'consolidating' the ordnance department with the commander-in-chief's office. By doing this, he meant to end the independent existence of the ordnance department, placing it under the authority of the commander-in-chief and hence, indirectly, under the control of the secretary of state for war.

Wellington would not have this. 'I do not think any consolidation is practicable', he told a Royal Commission in 1837. 'I believe the Board of Ordnance is going on very well.' This helped bury the scheme for the time being. When Howick tried again later in 1837 to revive it, Wellington came out strongly in opposition. The more the ordnance was attacked, the more extreme the duke's defence of it became. When in 1849 a parliamentary report criticised the administration of the ordnance, Wellington claimed it was a 'model' department, and should be left alone.[7] He was equally opposed to the creation of a chief of staff for the army: 'The Commander in Chief stands at this moment in the situation and performs all the functions of a Chief of the Staff in one of the foreign armies'[8] — although he believed that if Prince Albert became commander-in-chief he would need an effective chief of staff. Wellington's firm defence of the *status quo* in these matters shows his conservatism at its most damaging. The ordnance was far from the 'model' department he claimed. It became notorious as a slow-moving and cumbersome organisation, which, with its poor store-keeping procedures, became grossly overstocked with supplies. Clearly it made little sense for the army to be dependent on an outside body for supplies of heavy guns and other materiel, and a degree of streamlining would undoubtedly have been beneficial. Wellington's opposition, however, ensured that such a change did not come about until the weaknesses of the system were revealed by the Crimean War. The consequences of administrative confusion and lack of planning on Britain's Crimean army is well remembered, but administrative divisions had serious effects on British home defence policy too. There was too little cooperation between the ordnance department, the commander-in-chief's office and the admiralty, and no coordinated defence strategy ever emerged. It is not to the duke's credit that he defended such a system.

Nevertheless, Wellington put in considerable efforts to make the administrative machinery work, and to devise an effective scheme for national defence. As the years passed the matter became more and more urgent. The duke believed Britain's most likely enemy in any future war was France, a country he regarded as Britain's 'restless and ambitious neighbour and . . . implacable enemy'. He was always ready to see 'symptoms of deadly hostility' in France, and warned Peel in September 1845:

> Whatever may be the chances of war during the lifetime of Louis Philippe, that misfortune will become more and more certain, and is to be expected immediately, in case of his death. It is so because in truth the prevailing sentiment in the minds of Frenchmen is implacable hostility. We cannot change their feelings.

The duke was painfully aware of the size of the French army, so much larger than the number of British troops available in the United Kingdom: 'the King of the French has in his service an army of 350,000 of regular troops and national guards. At least 50,000 . . . could attack us. We have no more than 5,000 disposable men'.[10]

There was, however, nothing especially new in this: the British army always had been outnumbered by that of France, but since the French were trapped on the other side of the Channel, that fact did not necessarily cause panic in Britain. In the mid-nineteenth century, however, it did since the development of steam power at sea appeared to change the character of naval warfare and – so it appeared – suddenly made the British Isles vulnerable to attack. Contemporaries rivalled each other in their efforts to portray the deleterious effects of steam power on the strategic position of the British Isles. Wellington fully shared the fears engendered by the new developments; he appreciated earlier than most that steam would effect great changes in naval warfare.

As early as August 1824 Wellington wrote that steam power made it impossible to predict when an attack would be mounted, since an enemy could now launch one 'at any given moment of departure and arrival without our having any previous knowledge of such intention'. In that year, too, the ordnance department spent some time investigating the defences of the naval arsenals (dockyards) 'in reference to the Improvement of navigation by the application of steam'.[11] In time the duke became more alarmed over the possible effects of steam power. In 1830 he remarked that steam 'had made a great alteration in Maritime warfare'. Fourteen years later he was more positive: steam power would 'revolutionise naval warfare'.[12]

The development of steam navigation reinforced Wellington's view that the Royal Navy was the country's first line of defence, especially as the land defences had been allowed to decay so badly. He told Peel in October 1845: 'We are certainly not now in a situation to defend ourselves against a moderate outbreak in France, excepting by means of our fleet,' while he remarked to Sir George Murray, the master – general of the ordnance, a month later, that 'we have no defence at present, excepting our fleet at sea'.[13] There were problems, however: 'I have the highest opinion of, and the firmest reliance upon the exertion and gallantry of the British navy', Wellington wrote to Peel in January 1845, 'but . . . we have no fleet.'[14] There was a measure of truth in this, as the Royal Navy could deploy only six sail of the line in 1844 and there was no fleet in the English Channel. The duke reiterated constantly that 'we must be in strength everywhere, or something unfortunate will happen'. 'I am convinced', he told Peel in August 1844 'that we must immediately revise our establishments, and take care to have a superiority of force in every station on which it is necessary to maintain any naval force'.[15]

But not only was the Royal Navy too small: the other problem was that steam power did, indeed, 'revolutionise' naval warfare, to the detriment of Britain's strategic position. In 1830 Wellington pointed out that steam 'can be applied to attack and not to defence'.[16] Because the endurance of the early steam vessels was limited they could only stay at sea under steam for short periods – hence blockade would have to be undertaken by ships under sail. But this might mean an enemy fleet could choose its moment to steam out of port, leaving the blockaders far behind. For this reason, Wellington was 'convinced', as he wrote to the marquess of Anglesey, Murray's successor as master-general of the ordnance, in 1847, 'that steam navigation makes blockades of the enemy's ports out of the question',[17] and that Britain's traditional naval strategy would have to be changed.

One favourite scheme to counter this development was proposed in the early 1840s, namely, the adaptation of merchant steamers for purposes of war. It was argued that such ships could operate as a coastal patrol from small 'harbours of refuge' on the coast of England,

and it was hoped they would be available in such numbers that constant patrols would be possible. Wellington, although he hoped such a scheme would work, doubted whether the number of ships required existed. He insisted, before any great hopes were placed on this means of defending the country, that detailed knowledge of the number and type of steamers available had to be obtained. He also wanted to know how long it would take to arm the vessels for military duty, and was very sceptical when forty-eight hours was quoted as the time needed.[18] In the event, the duke's scepticism proved correct: an investigation of likely commercial steamers in 1844 proved that very few could be adapted to take heavy guns, and the proposal was dropped.

Lacking clear professional guidance in the matter from the Royal Navy, Wellington's increasing alarm at the effects of steam power is not, perhaps, surprising. But it was exaggerated, and it had serious consequences. If Wellington believed French steamers could evade a British blockading squadron then others did too. In fact, he over-estimated the effect of this development; steam ships were not as fast or powerful as was believed, nor could they manoeuvre with the kind of precision the duke expected. But it was overestimation of the power of steamships that lay at the root of Britain's defence strategy as it developed in the middle years of the nineteenth century.

The development of steam navigation and the weakness of the royal navy reinforced Wellington's view that it was essential that Britain's land defences be improved. By the mid-1840s this had become a matter of urgency, but the duke had long been alarmed by the desire of successive governments to cut down on expenditure in this area. There were, so Wellington believed, four separate regions of the British Isles that particularly needed land defences: the naval arsenals, the Channel Islands, Ireland, and the south coast of England.

If the fleet were to proceed to sea and defend the country as it ought, it needed bases to operate from, and these bases needed to be secure. Wellington was very anxious that the naval arsenals should receive an adequate degree of protection, and had been since the 1820s. As master-general of the ordnance, despite other calls on his time, he took a keen interest in their defences. In August 1824 he wrote a long memorandum on 'Our undefended naval & military arsenals'[19] pointing out that:

in the first three or even six months after the breaking out of war it would be absolutely impossible to find ten thousand or even I will say two thousand men to oppose . . . invasion. The Defence of our Arsenals then must depend upon Guard Ships and upon works.

Wellington thought four arsenals needed protection: Portsmouth, Plymouth, Sheerness and Pembroke. The two former, being the country's principal naval bases, at least had plenty of ships to guard them:

and are not liable to surprise, at least till the Fleet & Armies of the country shall be employed in foreign and distant enterprises. In regard to Sheerness it is my opinion that it ought to be strengthened upon this principle: vizt to keep the Enemy at such a distance from the Dockyard as that he could not bombard it with facility.

The duke then outlined where he thought land defences were required at Sheerness and paid some attention to Pembroke, although he felt he needed more information before reaching any conclusions with regard to the Welsh arsenal.

Even though the years down to the mid-1830s witnessed drastic reductions in defence expenditure – and Wellington himself made many such cuts – the duke hoped some work could still be undertaken at the naval arsenals. In November and December 1824, for example, a committee of engineer officers was detailed to investigate the defences of Sheerness. When their report was completed Wellington sent it to the prime minister, Lord Liverpool, 'to obtain the decision of HM Gov't whether the measures . . . shall be proposed to Parl't in this session; and if so in what manner they shall be brought forward'.[20] The duke's hopes were disappointed: lack of money meant that nothing was done that year or, indeed, for many years afterwards.

In the meantime, Wellington's anxiety at the state of the dockyard defences increased. In 1827 he informed the duke of York's private secretary, Sir Herbert Taylor, that steam power had made a surprise attack on the naval arsenals somewhat more likely, and therefore more precautions were needed. By the 1840s his alarm was profound: the defence of the naval arsenals, he wrote in December 1844, 'is a subject of the utmost importance, not only to the influence and Power and greatness of this country; but to its very existence as an independent state'.[21]

As commander-in-chief Wellington did not generally trouble himself with the details of works required at the various dockyards – that was the duty of the master-general of the ordnance and the inspector-general of fortifications – but he kept progress on the defences there in mind. In December 1844, for example, he was sent copies of a series of reports on the subject by the first lord of the admiralty, Lord Haddington, and responded with a long memorandum. A year later he was passed some reports on the defences of Portsmouth for his perusal.[22]

Wellington's views on the defence of the naval arsenals were eminently sensible. He thought their defence was an important matter, and steps ought to be taken to protect them. But he believed they only needed to be protected from attack from the sea: he did not consider the question of the landward defence of the dockyards very important. Moreover, he never placed the naval arsenals at the centre of his defence strategy; they remained only one of many places requiring protection. In this he was out of sympathy with the later trend of British defence planning. The growing enthusiasm for permanent fortifications was concentrated around the naval dockyards, and in 1860 the Royal Commission on National Defences recommended the expenditure of over ten million pounds on works to defend them on both the land and sea sides, but did not make any recommendations on defences elsewhere. This was far from Wellington's views; he believed what money was available should be spread more widely.

Wellington also paid considerable attention to the construction of the so-called 'harbours of refuge' in the 1840s. In June 1845 estimates were presented to parliament for the construction of such harbours at Dover, Portland and Harwich, as well as in the Channel Islands of Jersey, Guernsey and Alderney. Wellington wanted a harbour at Dungeness, and pressed for the rapid completion of the large works begun at Dover.[23] Overall, however, he devoted far more attention to the harbours in the Channel Islands than he did to those on the mainland. As early as 1831 he remarked that 'there is no one more impressed than I am with a sense of the importance of the Channel Islands.' Harbours on Jersey, Guernsey and Alderney, he told James Walker, the civil engineer in charge of the building works, in September 1847, 'are forty times more important than a harbour in Dover Bay'.

> I think that some of those who consider of these Harbours of Refuge in the Channel Islands and object to the sites selected are not sensible of all the objects in view in forming these works.

It is not for the mere defence of the Islands. That object could be facilitated at a moderate expense. But the object is to augment the maritime means of defence of the country: to give to the Gov't facilities for a greater development of its Navy force, by hastening to form a great naval station in the seas surrounding those islands.[24]

Consequently, the duke pressed for the construction of harbours of refuge on all three of the main islands: he declared this would be *'true economy'*, despite the high cost involved. Throughout 1845 he was in close contact with Sir James Graham, the home secretary, and therefore responsible for Channel Islands' affairs, and constantly reiterated the need for haste in finishing the harbours.[25]

Even with the duke's strong support, however, construction did not proceed smoothly. The difficulties involved meant costs rose dramatically, and as a result work on the harbour at Guernsey was abandoned in 1848. The harbour on Jersey was similarly left incomplete in 1855 and not even that on Alderney was finished, although work on it carried on until 1870.

Thus, despite the efforts made, Britain's security was not enhanced by the harbours of refuge. Indeed, the whole concept was gravely flawed, since after the failure of the merchant steamer scheme there were no vessels to place in the harbours anyway, and they might well have served as refuges for the French invasion fleet. Wellington's enthusiasm for Channel Islands harbours of refuge, in particular, helped lead Britain's defence planners into a *cul-de-sac*.

This trend was reinforced by considerations relating to the general defence of the Channel Islands. Wellington insisted that large-scale fortifications were needed on Jersey, Guernsey and Alderney. There had always been land defences on the Channel Islands, but they were more than ever necessary now: as the duke declared in 1831, the development of steam navigation had served simply 'to deprive the islands of all the advantages which the inhabitants have hitherto enjoyed in their defences'.[26] Wellington believed steam power made navigation less hazardous, and the rocks and shoals which had helped to protect the Islands in the past were no longer obstacles. From the late 1840s, down to the Crimean War, vast sums of money were spent on land defences in the Channel Islands, particularly on the island of Alderney, but they really appeared no more secure in 1856 than they had in 1840, since few men were available to garrison the large works constructed.

Walker was very impressed with Wellington's agitation about the Channel Islands: 'I never before saw his Grace as energetic on any subject, nor anyone more energetic than he was.'[27] In the interview, Wellington claimed that he thought of 'nothing else' save their defences, but this was not, in fact, true: the duke also worried about Ireland. In 1807 he had declared that Ireland was an 'enemy's country', and the only way to defend it was by 'fortified places' in Dublin, Ulster, Munster, Connaught, Leinster and along the river Shannon.[28] He had no illusions that the Irish people would help the British in case of a foreign invasion: indeed, he believed quite the reverse. Consequently, Wellington argued that the main aim of British defence strategy in Ireland should be to defend Dublin, and keep up communications with England from where a relief force could be sent, if and when it was available. The duke never varied in his belief that, in the event of an invasion of Ireland, it would be impossible for the British to distinguish between the dangers posed by internal insurrection and by those emanating from an invading army.

As a result of this conviction, he told Graham in October 1844 that he would like to see in Ireland:

> a local force organised and in the hands of the government, of strength to put down the insurrection, while the troops should be employed to resist the foreign invader. I have some experience in war [he pointed out] and know what military operations are.[29]

Graham replied that such a force would be either Protestant, and loyal but tyrannical and likely to lead to civil war in Ireland, or Catholic, and therefore disloyal, and Peel's government refused to sanction the scheme.

In time, therefore, Wellington became increasingly pessimistic about the chances of British rule surviving an invasion of Ireland. In 1849 he was in correspondence with Russell over the defence of Ireland in the case of insurrection or foreign invasion and in 1850 he again stressed the importance of Dublin to British rule there: 'it is the great point of communication with England and must be preserved if every other point be given up to ensure it'.[30] But he did not believe his efforts had achieved very much. He told Croker in 1848 that: 'I perfectly recollect my views for the defence and security of Ireland, but one might as well propose to recommence to build the Tower of Babel as to act on such a system.'[31]

Despite the hyperbole of this statement there was a large measure of truth in it: British defence planning for Ireland was not effective while it relied primarily on land defences. The real defence for Ireland, from the British point of view, was to try to prevent a foreign enemy reaching it. But Wellington's strategy helped encourage the belief that an enemy could reach Ireland in force without undue difficulty. If this belief were correct, then Ireland was, as the duke said, liable to be overrun and to need reconquest.

However, Ireland was no more at the centre of Wellington's thoughts on home defence than the Channel Islands. The duke never let his attention be diverted away from the position the British had to defend if they were to survive an invasion: the south coast of England. In the 1820s Wellington did not believe Britain could be successfully invaded:

> I confess that I am one of those who do not much apprehend invasion . . . I think the solid invasion of the country, with a view even to the plunder of the Capital or of Woolwich, or even to take possession of, or to do more than bombard one of our arsenals, is out of the question.[32]

But he became more concerned over the years.

When asked by a dinner guest in the late 1840s whether invasion was possible, the duke retorted:

> Possible! is anything impossible? Read the newspapers. The French would have an immense advantage over us. . . . They start at midnight and arrive off our coast just before sunrise. The dawn, which renders everything clear to them will not enable us to observe what they are about. They will have a full hour of light before we shall be able to . . . observe boats in motion. And let me tell you, in calm weather, with preparations well settled beforehand, a great deal may be done towards throwing troops on an open beach in half an hour.[33]

In September 1845 he believed the blow could fall 'at any point or all points, between the North and South Foreland'. He was at his most alarmist in his letter to Burgoyne of January 1847:

> except under the guns of Dover Castle there is not a spot on the coast on which infantry might not be thrown ashore, at any time of the tide, with any wind and in any weather, and from which such body of infantry . . . would not find within the distance of five miles a road into the interior through the cliffs practicable for the march of a body of troops.[34]

The duke believed an invasion of Britain would be made 'in very commanding force', and if the enemy could get ashore they would detach enough men from their main body to mask the naval arsenals, and then march on London. To prevent the enemy reaching the capital became, therefore, the centre of his defence strategy. He did not believe London could be surrounded by a ring of fortresses: such works, he thought, would cost far too much and require far too many men in garrisons to be effective. As befitted a master of the defensive battle Wellington turned his attention to likely points between London and the coast where a decisive engagement could be fought with the invaders. He believed the most eligible sites were round Reigate or Croydon, both important route centres. But, as he pointed out in 1845, the defence of London by a battle in the field was probably beyond the capacity of the British army. The reason was simple: 'We have not now one disposable man' who could form an army to fight it.[35]

As a result of this conviction, Wellington concluded that the most effective way of defending England from invasion was by the construction of coastal fortifications at threatened points, to prevent an enemy getting a foothold ashore. The great problem was how to defend the long stretch of threatened coastline with the limited resources available. In the 1830s the duke believed that 'there is no better way of defending a coast than by Martello towers. They require no expense to keep them up when built'.[36] But such towers could, and did, decay (one or two were washed into the sea) and naval ordnance grew larger over the years, so that ships in the 1840s carried guns heavier than those the Martello towers had been built to resist. By this time, therefore, those that were left were of doubtful value, and Wellington consequently pressed for a fresh start to be made, with the construction of new fortifications along the whole south-east coast of England.

To see exactly what needed to be done the duke, in his seventy-seventh year, began, in September 1845, a personal survey of the south coast. He was not reassured by it. On 5 October he sent Sir George Murray a detailed report on the coast between the North Foreland and Seaford.[37] Between the North Foreland and Brighton, he declared, the only effective defensive work was at Brighton, and that could be outflanked. Heavy guns could be landed in numerous small harbours or along undefended small rivers which, he said, 'abound' in this area. To counter this Wellington wanted heavy batteries placed to overlook the Downs with, in addition, defensive works around Sandgate. These ideas were reiterated in long letters sent to Murray. On 13 October, for example, he warned Sir George that the Essex coast, too, was open to attack, and he again stressed the strategic importance of Brighton, which he saw as a vital point on the route to London. On 16 November he drew Murray's attention to defences around Rye, and later to those around Newhaven. To ensure these letters were read in the right quarter, copies were sent to the prime minister, Peel, and after Murray's retirement, to his successor, the marquess of Anglesey.[38]

Wellington's views on coast defence were, on the whole, judicious. He certainly overestimated the ease with which troops could be put ashore on the open coast, but to defend likely landing places was undoubtedly the best response. But he was also fully aware that coast defences alone were not sufficient. A chain of fortifications, once pierced, becomes useless. Wellington believed he had found a way of supporting the coast defences: to do this, he proposed to utilise the new form of motive power which was causing him so much anxiety, steam.

Notwithstanding his well-known conservatism, Wellington was greatly impressed by the strategic possibilities of the new 'railroads', even though he disliked travelling on them. By 1842 there were 2,000 miles of railway operational in Britain, and Wellington placed greater reliance on them than many of his contemporaries. In the event of impending invasion he proposed placing most of his available troops close to London and deploying them by rail to the threatened points on the coast. In December 1844 he pointed out that it was a weakness in Britain's defence strategy that no railway line existed to transfer 5,000 troops from London to the south coast – even if that number of men were available.[39]

As always, however, the duke took care to look at the practical details involved. In 1847 he was in correspondence with Prince Albert on the subject, suggesting arrangements should be made to 'embark' 10,000 men in London, Edinburgh and Dublin, as an experiment, although this idea did not come to fruition. He also sent the prince plans of the London and South Western and South Eastern Railways for linking London with the south coast of England.[40] Unfortunately, no detailed plans for the use of railways were drawn up in the duke's lifetime, and the strategic value of the system only became fully apparent with Prussia's successful mobilisation in 1870.

Wellington's thoughts on the defence of southern England were very advanced for his day. Given that the British army was not strong enough to guard the whole of the vulnerable south coast – and the assumption that the Royal Navy would not be able to do so either – the concentration of the army in one place and its deployment from a central point was, in effect, the only possible strategy. Wellington never allowed himself to fall in completely with extravagant claims for permanent land defences concentrated on particular points.

Even so, the duke's plans had brought him face to face with perhaps the greatest weakness in Britain's defences at this time: the shortage of trained manpower in the British Isles. Wellington placed great reliance upon the regular army in his defence plans, and throughout his later career he strenuously opposed cuts in the size of the army.

As early as 1827 he was 'in despair' at proposed reductions in the army which, reported Charles Arbuthnot, he believed would be 'diasastrous in the extreme.'[41] Reductions were nevertheless made. The size of the army, standing at over 130,000 men in 1816, was reduced to a low of just over 71,000 in 1822, and did not again exceed 100,000 until 1842. It was cut again to below that figure in 1851.[42]

But the figure for the overall size of the army was not the only reason Wellington believed the number of regular troops available in Britain was too small. Another reason lay in the duties the army was called upon to perform. The British army in this period was deployed across the world, not just in Britain. In 1844, for example, the number of men in the service stood at just under 114,000: only 50,000 of these were stationed in the United Kingdom. In 1847 the army numbered over 120,000 men, of whom nearly 59,000 were stationed in the United Kingdom. In 1851, of the 109 battalions of infantry, only thirty-nine were at home.[43]

In Wellington's opinion 'the continued and increasing demands of the permanent service of troops to Garrison the New Colonies' was the principal reason for the numerical weakness of the British army.[44] It emphasised – if any emphasis were needed – the limited number of regular troops available to undertake the defence of the United Kingdom.

In the 1840s, therefore, Wellington fought hard to increase the military forces of the country, especially the regular army. In August 1845 he sent a memorandum to Peel which pointed out that the danger facing Britain was 'certain . . . and imminent'. At the same time, because Peel's views were 'inconsistant with those which I entertain', he sent a personal letter to Lord Stanley, the secretary of state for war and the colonies, warning that, should the French land and attack a naval arsenal, 'we have no military force; not a man to relieve it or to oppose the enemy'. He received little comfort in return: the army estimates were not increased.[45]

Wellington repeatedly stressed the need for more regular troops, over and above all other defence preparations. It was *'most essential'* to increase the size of the army, he told Prince Albert in November 1847. A year later he informed Russell: 'that the existing military establishments are founded upon what is absolutely required for peace . . . this country has not a man not necessary for its service in time of peace'.[46] Every year between 1847 and 1851 Wellington pressed for increased army estimates. In 1847, for example, he informed Earl Grey, the secretary of state for war, of 'the urgent necessity of making a considerable augmentation to the present Military Force of the Country', adding hopefully, 'to effect which the present composition of the army appears to me to afford every facility'. Unfortunately, neither this nor succeeding appeals were successful, and the duke's last public pronouncement on the state of the national defences, in June 1852, reflects this: 'We have never, up to this moment, maintained a proper peace establishment', he declared.[47]

Because the regular army was so small Wellington strongly opposed any attempts to change the military system of the country: attempts which, he feared, would 'destroy the efficiency of the small army which Her Majesty's Government has at its disposal'. In 1847 the third Earl Grey proposed a far-sighted scheme to increase the garrison of the United Kingdom by withdrawing troops from the colonies, at the same time making service in the army more popular by reducing the term of service in the infantry to ten years. The duke accepted the first element in this scheme equably enough, since the defence of distant colonies appeared at this time to be less pressing than the defence of the homeland itself, but to the second he took strong exception.[48] His opposition was rooted in the difficulties the army faced in recruitment. Wellington believed a long training period was necessary to 'make' a soldier, and that it would be 'impossible' for the army to carry out its duties with men of less than ten years service. 'Short' service would only make recruiting still more difficult.[49] But there was another, more personal, objection, too. Wellington had won his victories with the old army, and he did not see why the system should be changed. The reason why the Whigs wanted to change it, he told Stanley in characteristic language, was that 'they have got a d----d good army, and they want to make it a d----d bad one'.[50]

Wellington was so upset with Grey that he offered the queen his resignation. This was not accepted: Wellington's prestige could not be lost to the ministry. In April 1847 he at last agreed to Grey's proposals, for reasons which are hard to explain, since he still felt its adoption would be highly damaging.[51] In fact, the measure had very little effect – ten years' service was still too long to attract many recruits – and it was to be another twenty-five years before Grey's 'liberal' system was adopted, when Cardwell introduced his short-service and linked-battalion schemes.

But the arguments over Grey's scheme did not help Wellington in his quest for trained soldiers to defend the country. The truth was, whether the duke liked it or not – and he did not – that in case of war the regular army would have to be supplemented by reserve forces of some description. The regular army did not have an effective reserve – 'pensioner' battalions were clearly not composed of very young or fit men – and Grey had hoped men discharged after ten years service could form the nucleus of a new one. Wellington saw clearly that reliance would therefore have to be placed on such reserves as were available, namely, the militia and yeomanry, and possibly also volunteers.

The duke did not think very highly of any of these forces. He told Fox Maule, the secretary at war, in 1847, when the latter was preparing a draft Bill to reorganise the militia, that:

> your army of reserve may be a good thing – nay – may be absolutely necessary by and by. . . . But happen what may and when it may, I say that the first and great object for this country is to have an army that can fight a battle. . . . Do not suppose that your 300,000 Local Militia and Volunteers will in three years do you half the service in a field of battle that 30,000 well trained soldiers would![52]

Wellington believed the yeomanry cavalry would only be useful in a peace-keeping role, not as a light cavalry force available for field service.[53] Still less did he think volunteer infantry would be useful in the event of war, at least in England. He certainly did not share the enthusiasm for volunteers that swept through the middle classes of British society in the 1850s. He told Grey that 'The services of these men must not be relied upon. [It would be] quite out of the question to use volunteers in the field.'[54]

Whatever Wellington's reservations, however, the problem of trained manpower remained acute. The duke was realistic enough to see that a reserve was necessary, and the militia force was the best available. As a result, he became a strong defender of it, and throughout his later career was anxious the militia should be maintained in a state of efficiency.

As early as 1820 Wellington was alarmed at the state of decay into which the militia had fallen: papers he was sent by Lord Sidmouth, the home secretary, only showed 'the absolute necessity of organising without loss of time the whole of the militia of the United Kingdom'. Seven years later he warned the secretary at war, Lord Palmerston, that, because steam power had speeded up naval operations, men would have to be ready for service as soon as war broke out. 'How this is to be done when our Peace Army is barely sufficient for the Police of the Country without the assistance of at least an organised militia & other local Corps I cannot devise.' He warned Palmerston that it was essential mobilisation arrangements for the militia be perfected in advance: 'I happened to be in Ireland when the Irish Militia was first raised; and certainly there never was confusion equal to that which attended the levy'.[55]

Wellington strongly opposed measures to cut down the force:

> as we have put down the Yeomanry, and knowing as I do that we have not the means of taking care of any of our dockyards if we should unfortunately be engaged in a war, I cannot consent to any measure which shall tend to diminish the efficiency of the militia.[56]

Nevertheless, reductions were carried out, and after 1831 the militia ceased to be enrolled for service. The whig governments of the 1830s even tried to disband the militia staff. The duke did not think this was 'safe': as he pointed out to Russell; 'the Militia is the only force in this country regularly organised by law and it is the first Corps de reserve'.[57]

Despite Wellington's efforts, the militia force in the United Kingdom effectively ceased to exist by the 1840s. When increased alarm at the state of the national defences became apparent in the middle of that decade, however, interest in the militia reappeared. Wellington was very keen to bring the militia to life again. In September 1845 he told Graham he would 'immediately' arrange for an inspection of the militia staff,[58] but Peel's government was overwhelmed by the corn law crisis long before anything could be done.

When the subject came up again for discussion in the cabinet in 1847, this time during Russell's premiership, Wellington once more urged vigorous measures; he told Anglesey the militia should be 150,00 strong.[59] The duke's hopes were disappointed on this occasion also: Russell's failure to carry an increase in income tax in the 1848 budget meant no money was available for the militia.

When the cabinet renewed discussion on the issue in the winter of 1850–1 Wellington was not pleased to discover that it was proposed to create a 'Local Militia', which could serve only in its own county, rather than a 'General Militia' which could serve anywhere in the United Kingdom.[60] His objections were shared by Palmerston, who Russell had just sacked from his post as foreign secretary, and who contrived to defeat the Bill and bring down the government. Wellington was happier with the new Derby ministry's bill, which was for a regular militia. He watched its passage anxiously, fearing the government might be defeated on the issue, but the measure eventually passed into law in June 1852.[61] Wellington did not live to see the only limited success of this act.

Wellington's response to the lack of trained regular troops in the United Kingdom and the perceived inadequacies of Britain's reserve troops was to advocate stationing an increasing number of men in permanent fortifications. The duke agreed with the view that less training was needed for garrison troops, and as time passed he steadily increased the number of men required for garrison duty in time of war. In October 1845 he calculated that some 40,000 men were needed for this duty: 10,000 each in Portsmouth, Plymouth, Milford Haven and the Channel Islands. This would leave some 25,000 to 30,000 to take the field. Two years later Wellington calculated garrison troops would number some 75,000 men: 12,000 each at Portsmouth, Plymouth, the Thames and Medway area, Cork and in the Channel Islands, 10,000 at Dover and 5,000 at Milford Haven. He believed 5,000 men were needed for the defence of Alderney alone.[62] If this estimate were correct the British army was, indeed, desperately short of manpower, and its effective strength for the field was in decline. Growing awareness of this bred greater reliance on fixed fortifications, but these, in turn, demanded yet more troops. Wellington encouraged this reasoning with his views on the difficulties of finding enough regular troops and of using partially trained reservists in the field.

Despite his doubts about the value of reservists, however, Wellington confessed to Anglesey in March 1847 that: 'I should be satisfied with the completion of the militia [to 150,000 men]. If this was done, 20,000 men added to the army and a few thousand to the artillery, I would engage for the defence of the country.'[63] This was not a very realistic pronouncement, given the duke's advancing age and infirmity. He told Russell's cabinet in April 1847 that he would be satisfied with a force in the country of 70,000 regular troops and 100,000 militia, 'but', he added, 'that force could not be got'.[64]

This pessimistic declaration sums up Wellington's feelings after some three years of trying to persuade successive governments to take steps to strengthen the national defences. As he saw, a well-trained militia would be a valuable addition to Britain's defensive forces, yet political considerations constantly delayed the re-establishment of the force.

As the years went by Wellington became increasingly alarmed at Britain's apparently 'defenceless' state. He also became increasingly outspoken in his efforts to convince the political authorities of the seriousness of the danger facing the country, and he increasingly felt himself isolated and ignored by them. In truth, he was not an easy colleague. He got on reasonably well with Peel and Russell, but he was not friendly with Grey, nor with Palmerston, who was usually a valuable ally of those calling for increased defence expenditure. Wellington objected to being 'ignored'. He told Peel in January 1845 that he only gave his opinion – 'it may be a very foolish opinon' – but he would like it given some consideration by the cabinet. The prime minister was forced to soothe the duke's ruffled feelings. His opinions, Peel told him, 'are entitled to greater deference than the observations and opinions of any man or body of men in this country'.[65] This exchange sums up how difficult it was to deal with Wellington at this time, but even so his views of defence planning remained very sensible. Unfortunately this tended to be overlooked because of the increasingly extreme language he used to enunciate them. This, coupled with the duke's feeling that politicians were not paying him any attention, resulted in a long letter to Sir John Burgoyne in January 1847. In it, Wellington argued that political considerations meant no real action had been taken on the vital issue of national defence, yet the country was in a position of great weakness. He went on to outline exactly what should be done: the naval arsenals and Channel Islands should be provided with garrisons totalling 65,000 regular troops and militia, whilst the militia force should be expanded to 155,000 men, which would cost only some £400,000. The duke stressed the vulnerability of the south coast of England, as well as for a field army able to move to any threatened point, and he urged that reserve supplies of military equipment be built up.

But these ideas, sensible in themselves, were presented in extravagant terms, and it was these rather wild expressions that caught the imagination of the public when the letter was published in the newspapers in January 1848. The result was that the duke was made to look ridiculous. In the privacy of his diary Richard Cobden, who saw a copy of the letter three months before it was published, remarked that: 'The letter is evidently written under strong conviction of the importance of the subject – but it is as obviously the production of a mind enfeebled with age'.[66]

At first Wellington thought the publication of the letter would be beneficial, hoping public pressure would force the government to act on the defence question. *The Times*, too, at first thought the letter only suggested 'prudent precaution'. Both *The Times* and the duke later changed their minds.[67]

Wellington declared to Russell that: 'My opinion has invariably been that the effectual and indeed only safe way of bringing the important object of that letter to the cognisance of the public was by the Gov't itself'. He was furious with the unfortunate Burgoyne: 'I am not surprised that Sir John Burgoyne should be annoyed, I say nothing of the personal trouble and annoyance to myself from this breach of confidence'.[68] The truth was that Wellington's feelings were hurt by the indifference and even ridicule occasioned by the publication of his letter.

The reception of the Burgoyne letter was final proof to Wellington that his views on national defence were not listened to, either by the public or by 'government'. It is understandable that he should think so. Of all the schemes he had proposed to help make Britain secure, none had really been adopted. The harbours of refuge had not been completed; very few fortifications had been built along the south coast of England; no force had been enrolled for the defence of Ireland; above all, the size of the regular army had not been increased. The duke had to contend with an increasingly strong anti-militarist feeling in the country, from middle-class 'Cobdenite' radicals and more traditional lower-class hostility to the army. At the same time, he was not getting any younger. He often repeated himself; his language, always exaggerated, became even more extreme; he found it more and more difficult to carry out his duties, but with no thought of giving up any, or allowing any deputy or assistant to do the work. Clearly he should have retired, but that was unthinkable; he was, after all, the duke of Wellington.

If any measure for ensuring the security of the British Isles were in contemplation, Wellington's advice was always sought, and his support was always necessary, before any steps were taken. He did not approve of major administrative changes in the army, and none were made: he was prevailed upon to support Grey's short-service plan, and it was adopted. He exerted considerable influence over all soldiers and those politicians interested in the defence question. Unfortunately, his views were not always fully understood, and in later years, when he was not there to refer to, some of the more damaging elements in his thinking came to prominence in British defence planning. Where the duke wanted fortifications to defend the whole coast as well as the naval arsenals, the latter began to receive protection on a gigantic scale – far greater than Wellington ever believed was necessary – and diverted resources away from other vital points. Where Wellington wanted a militia force, enthusiasts preferred a rifle volunteer force, which the duke would never have approved of.

It is probably easier for the historian to study Wellington's ideas on the defence question than it was for contemporaries. The repetitions, the hyperbole, can be seen in perspective; the danger is no longer imminent. His views were not so ridiculous as they appeared to Cobden; nor were they so perfect as they appeared to his legions of admirers. But whatever their merit, one thing is clear; despite the limits on Wellington's influence; despite the laughter occasioned by the publication of the Burgoyne letter; despite his increasing age and infirmity, the Iron Duke played a major role in formulating British defence policy in a period of unprecedented change. It was not the least challenging duty of his career.

Notes

1   *National Defences: Letters of Lord Ellesmere and the Duke of Wellington with the Speech of R. Cobden, Esq.* . . . (London, 1848), p. 17.
2   Wellington to the Knight of Kerry, 13 May 1846, WP 2/146/16.
3   Wellington to Haddington, 29 February 1845, Haddington Papers, Scottish Record Office, TD 79/54/A10.
4   Wellington to Russell, 12 August 1846, Russell papers, Public Record Office, PRO 30/22/5B ff. 354–5; Wellington to Prince Albert, 3 June 1848, copy, Queen

Victoria Papers, Windsor Castle, RA E1/3. I wish to acknowledge the gracious permission of Her Majesty the Queen to use and quote from these papers.

5   Wellington to Hill, 17, 21 October 1840, Hill Papers, British Library Add. MSS. 35060, ff. 543, 544.

6   Wellington to Russell, 12 August 1846, G. P. Gooch, ed., *The Later Correspondence of Lord John Russell*, i (1925), pp. 238–9; Wellington to the Queen, 12 December 1846, WP 2/134/121–2.

7   *Parliamentary Papers*, House of Commons series, 1837 (78), xxxiv, pp. 35, 40; Wellington to Melbourne, 4 January 1838, enclosing 'Observations on the draft Order in Council', Melbourne papers, BL Microfilm 589, reel 8; memorandum, 30 November 1849, copy, WP 2/164/30–1.

8   Memorandum (? April 1850), RA E 1/44.

9   Wellington to General Sir George Murray, 20 September 1845, Murray papers, PRO, WO 80/8; Wellington to Peel, 22 September 1845, C. S. Parker, *Sir Robert Peel from his Private Papers*, iii (1899), 405, 407. A fuller version of this letter survives in the Peel papers, BL, Add. Mss. 40461, ff. 237–44.

10   Wellington to Lord Stanley, 1 August 1845, WP 2/131/132.

11   Memorandum, 18 August 1824, WO 46/28, ff. 177–80; Wellington to Liverpool, 17 February 1824, Liverpool Papers, BL, Add. MSS. 38196, f. 125.

12   Wellington to Peel, 16 October 1830, Add. MSS. 40309, f. 188; Wellington to Dalhousie, 11 September 1844, WP 2/123/65.

13   Wellington to Peel, 15 October 1845, Add. MSS. 40461, f. 293; Wellington to Murray, 17 October 1845, Murray papers, WO 80/8.

14   Wellington to Peel, 7 January 1845, Parker, *Peel*, iii, p. 397.

15   Wellington to Peel, 17, 23 August 1844, Add. MSS. 40460, ff. 256–7, 260–1. See also Wellington's memorandum of 24 November 1844, *ibid.*, ff. 292–9.

16   Wellington to Peel, 16 October 1830, *ibid.*, Add. MSS. 40309, f. 188.

17   Wellington to Anglesey, 8 October 1847, Anglesey papers, Plas Newydd, Box liv. I am grateful to the marquess of Anglesey for permission to consult these papers.

18   Wellington to Peel, 12 August 1844; memorandum, 24 November 1844, Add. MSS. 40460, ff. 248–9, 292–9.

19   Memorandum, 18 August 1844, WO 46/28, ff. 177–80.

20   Wellington to Liverpool, 17 February 1825, Add. MSS. 38196, f. 125.

21   Wellington to Sir Herbert Taylor, 27 December 1824, WND, ii, 382; 'Memorandum on the defences of naval arsenals and dockyards and additions required', 20 December 1844, WP 2/126/8.

22   *Ibid.*, and see Wellington to Anglesey, 11 September 1844, copy, WP 2/148/18.

23   Wellington to Peel, 17 September 1845 and 'Memorandum on the means of defence of the country, 10 September 1845', Add. MSS. 40461, ff. 219–22, 210.

24   Wellington to Sir William Symonds, 2 March 1831, WP 2/56/56; 'Notes of the duke of Wellington's conversation with Mr Walker, 27 August 1847', Broadlands Papers, Southampton University, ND/A/5/1–2.

25   See correspondence in the Graham Papers, Bodleian Library Microfilm MSS. 120, 121.

26   Wellington to Symonds, 2 March 1831, WP 2/56/56.

27   'Notes of the duke of Wellington's conversation with Mr Walker, 27 August 1847', Broadlands papers, ND/A/5/1–4.

28 Sir Arthur Wellesley to Lord Hawkesbury, 7 May 1807; memorandum of December 1807, and Wellesley to Hawkesbury, 11 January 1808, WSD, v, 28–36, 202–10, 298–303.

29 Wellington to Graham, 5 October 1844, C. S. Parker, *The Life and Letters of Sir James Graham*, i (1907), p. 411.

30 Wellington to Russell, 12 December 1847, copy, WO 30/113; memorandum on the defence of Dublin (1850), WP 2/194/35.

31 L. J. Jennings, *The Croker Papers*, iii (1884), p. 189.

32 Wellington to Sir Herbert Taylor, 27 December 1824, WND, ii, 382.

33 Earl Stanhope, *Notes of Conversations with the Duke of Wellington* (1888), p. 84, 27 September 1836.

34 *National Defences*, p. 13.

35 See Wellington to Murray, 13 October, 17 November, 23 October, 13 October 1845, Murray papers, WO 80/8.

36 Stanhope, *Notes of Conversation*, p. 84.

37 'Memorandum on the defences of the North Foreland, Beachy Head, and Seaford', 5 October 1845, Murray Papers, WO 80/8.

38 See, for example, Add. MSS. 40460 and 40461, and Wellington to Anglesey, 11 September 1846, and other documents in the Plas Newydd papers, boxes liii and liv.

39 'Memorandum on the defences of the Naval Arsenals and Dockyards and Additions required', 20 December 1844, copy, WP 2/126/11. See also 'Memorandum on the means of defence of the country, 10 September 1845', Add. MSS. 40461, ff. 215–16.

40 Memorandum, 17 November 1847; Wellington to Prince Albert, 22 November, 6 December 1847, RA E42/13, /15, /19.

41 See Arbuthnot to J. C. Herries, 11 July, 2 August 1827, Herries Papers, BL, Add. MSS. 53730, ff. 48, 49.

42 *Parliamentary Papers*, House of Commons series, 1859, Sess. 1 (213), 15.

43 See third Earl Grey to Wellington, draft, n.d. (1847), WO 1/599; Wellington to Grey, 2 December 1851, WO 1/601.

44 Wellington to Stanley, 21 January 1843, copy, WP 2/96/115.

45 Memorandum (undated but August 1845), Parker, *Peel*, iii, pp. 202–6; Wellington to Stanley, 1 August 1845, WP 2/131/131–6; Stanley to Wellington, 13 February 1846, WO 1/597.

46 Memorandum, 8 November 1847, RA E42/6; Wellington to Russell, 8 December 1848, copy, Russell Papers, PRO 30/22/7D, ff. 279, 282.

47 Wellington to Grey, 8 December 1847; 18 December 1848; 11 December 1849 and 2 December 1851, WO 1/599, 600, 601. The letter for 1850 has not come to light; *Parl. Deb.*, third series, cxxii, p. 729, 15 June 1852.

48 Wellington to Russell, 25 January 1847, WP 2/151/88.

49 Wellington to Russell, 9 April 1847, copy, *ibid.*, 2/190/81.

50 L. Strachey and R. Fulford, eds., *The Greville Memoirs*, v (1938), p. 441.

51 Wellington to Russell, 25 September 1846, copy; Wellington to the Queen (January 1847), WP 2/149/3, 2/151/110–2; Wellington to Anglesey, 7 March 1847, Anglesey Papers, Box liv.

52 Wellington to Fox Maule, n.d. (December 1847), copy, WP 2/156/76.

53   See his brief statements in the House of Lords on the Irish and Scottish Yeomanry, *Parl. Deb.*, third series, xiv, pp. 165–6; xlii, pp. 349–50, 9 July 1832, 3 April 1838.

54   Third Earl Grey: 'Memorandum: Wellington on Russell's letter of 3 September 1847 respecting the National Defences', Grey Papers, Durham University.

55   Wellington to Sidmouth, 23 April 1820, Sidmouth Papers, Devon Record Office, Exeter, C1820/OM; Wellington to Palmerston, 17 December 1827, copy, and 19 April 1828, Broadlands Papers, GC/WE/42, 45.

56   Wellington to Peel, 1 May 1828, WND, iv, 416.

57   Wellington to Russell, 1 October 1835, WP 2/35/118–9.

58   Wellington to Graham, 6 September 1845, *ibid.*, 2/132/50.

59   Wellington to Anglesey, 9 March 1847, *ibid.*, 2/125/55.

60   Wellington to Russell, 15 February 1852, copy, RA E43/30.

61   Wellington to Lady Salisbury, 21, 24 and 27 April 1852, Lady Burghclere, ed., *A Great Man's Friendship. Letters of the Duke of Wellington to Mary, Marchioness of Salisbury, 1850–1852* (1927), pp. 262, 266–7.

62   Wellington to Murray, 13 October 1845, Murray Papers, WO 80/8; memorandum on national defences, 27 December 1847, WP 2/156/72–7; Wellington to Auckland, 18 September 1847, copy, PRO 30/22/6F, f. 98.

63   Wellington to Anglesey, 9 March 1847, WP 2/125/55.

64   Hobhouse, diary, 24 April 1847, Broughton Papers, BL, Add. MSS. 43750, f. 23b.

65   Wellington to Peel, 7 January 1845; Peel to Wellington 10 January 1845, Parker, *Peel*, iii, pp. 397, 398.

66   Cobden, diary, 8 October 1847, Cobden papers, BL Add. MSS. 43674E, f. 916.

67   Anglesey to Burgoyne, 11 February 1848, G. Wrottesley, *The Life and Opinions of Field Marshal Sir John Burgoyne*, i (1872), pp. 480–1; *The Times*, 5, 7 January 1848; Wellington to Lady Shelley, 23 January 1848, Wrottesley, *Burgoyne*, i, pp. 479–80.

68   Wellington to Russell, 7 January 1848, copy, RA E42/28; Wellington to Fitzroy Somerset, 21 January 1848, Raglan papers, Cefntilla House, 3/177. I am grateful to Lord Raglan for permission to use and quote from these papers.